CLOUDS OVER
THE GOALPOST

CLOUDS OVER
THE GOALPOST

Gambling, Assassination, and the NFL in 1963

LEW FREEDMAN

SPORTS
PUBLISHING

Sports Publishing books may be purchased in bulk at special discounts for sales promotion, corporate gifts, fund-raising, or educational purposes. Special editions can also be created to specifications. For details, contact the Special Sales Department, Sports Publishing, 307 West 36th Street, 11th Floor, New York, NY 10018 or sportspubbooks@skyhorsepublishing.com.

Sports Publishing® is a registered trademark of Skyhorse Publishing, Inc.®, a Delaware corporation.

Visit our website at www.sportspubbooks.com

10 9 8 7 6 5 4 3 2 1

Library of Congress Cataloging-in-Publication Data

Clouds over the goalpost : gambling, assassination, and the NFL in 1963 / Lew Freedman.

    pages cm

  ISBN 978-1-61321-398-8 (hardcover : alk. paper) 1. Football--United States--History--20th century. 2. American Football League--History. 3. National Football League--History. I. Title.

  GV954.C58 2013

  796.332'6409046--dc23

                                    2013019397

ISBN: 978-1-61321-398-8

Printed in the United States of America

CONTENTS

INTRODUCTION

THE YEAR 1963 was an extraordinary one for pro football. To reference the great Clint Eastwood film, it included the good, the bad, and the ugly. Great football was played, with the three most prominent achievers in the National Football League that season of fifty years ago being the three most famed, revered and pretty much longstanding teams, the Chicago Bears, Green Bay Packers, and New York Giants.

With all the positives that happened that season, specific events unfolded on and off the field that affected the league, both directly and indirectly.

Pro football in 1963 was only five years removed from the most heralded and important game in the sport's history: the sudden death championship game played between the New York Giants and Baltimore Colts. The result itself—the Colts victorious—was not of significant note to the sport. With that being true, however, the way it was accomplished, with it being the first title game determined in overtime and the audience that attracted, helped propel football into a new, more modern era.

It had been a long time coming. For decades, pro football ranked lower in popularity on the American sports scene than baseball, horse racing, boxing, and college football. Colts–Giants raised the status of the sport to a new level, and made it abundantly clear what had previously been theorized: That pro football was a gift to television programmers, who in turn had the keys to the vault to make owners in the NFL rich.

The game was growing and television helped it along. Cities that did not have their own team now wanted one, and the demand for expansion led to the creation of the American Football League in 1960; a league that, within a decade, was absorbed in its entirety as part of the National Football League. In 1963, the AFL existed more or less in a parallel universe, playing its own schedule (mostly in cities that did not have NFL teams). But the AFL played the role of irritant in a high-stakes competition for talent.

A merger lay in the future, but a savvy young NFL commissioner, who had served his apprenticeship in the league as the Los Angeles Rams' public relations director and general manager, was a man for his times. Pete Rozelle understood the importance of national television, equal distribution of TV revenue to the biggest and smallest cities in the league, and parity in the sport. In 1963, Rozelle was still learning on the job, but he played a huge role in several of the year's most important events; especially those that took place off the field.

Not long afterwards, in a black eye for the league, an incident that surprised and shocked innocent-minded fans, required Rozelle's attention. In a dramatic decision, Rozelle suspended Green Bay Packer star running back Paul Hornung, one of the league's most visible players and its points record-holder, and Detroit Lions star defensive tackle Alex Karras. They were accused of gambling, and specifically betting on NFL games. They would not be allowed to play in 1963.

This was the year when one of the NFL's marquee defensive players, the famed and colorful Gene "Big Daddy" Lipscomb, was found dead less than six months before the start of the '63 season, apparently of a heroin overdose with a needle stuck in his arm.

In September, in a development that clearly came under the heading of the good—if not the beautiful—the Pro Football Hall of Fame opened its doors in Canton, Ohio, and inducted its first class. As Canton was the city where the NFL was founded, it was a logical place to enshrine and honor the greats of the game.

If Rozelle acted as an impartial district attorney of sorts in his willingness to prosecute Hornung and Karras in April, his stewardship and statesmanship took a hit in November. On November 22, 1963, a day that shocked the nation, President John F. Kennedy was assassinated in Dallas, Texas. It was a Friday, and although other sports leagues—including the American Football League—all cancelled their scheduled games for the weekend, Rozelle made the ill-advised choice for the NFL to play on that Sunday.

For all of the difficult issues to chew on—perhaps a foreshadowing of America's sports future when the games became ever-more-interwoven with the issues and politics of the day—pro football was at its best when its young men of strength, speed, and talent roamed the playing field.

While the American Football League was fighting for its own existence, it was growing stronger by the season and offering better entertainment by sewing up fresher players. The AFL championship game pitted the San Diego Chargers against the Boston Patriots. The game was no classic, but it served as part of the increasing body of evidence that the AFL was here to stay, and it showcased a wide variety of talented football players.

The NFL could badmouth the AFL all it wanted, but fans were flocking to games and sat in front of their television sets, enjoying the wild brand of offensive football on display.

On the field, the NFL offered a great show in 1963. A gap-toothed, loud-voiced émigré from the East Coast had arrived in frigid Green Bay, and restored the glory of the past for the smallest town in the league. The Packers, whose fans own stock in the club, were (and still are) the only team to be owned this way, unlike those that are owned by a solo rich man (or corporation). With Vince Lombardi's arrival, he established a budding and continuing dynasty overnight.

By 1963, the Packers had played in the previous three NFL title games and were two-time defending champions. Even without Hornung, they figured to be the class of the league . . . though not if the Chicago Bears had a say in the matter. The Bears and Packers—in the same Western Division—featured the oldest rivalry in the sport. Their team founders were there at the founding of the league in the tight quarters in Canton. Lombardi may have been the second coming in Green Bay, but George Halas, the man who founded the Bears and had been involved in every major decision that the NFL made since 1921, was still coaching his team.

The Bears were a veteran squad, and did not hold the Packers in awe. Many of the stalwart Bears were also in the lineup in 1956, which was the last time Chicago reached the championship game. They lost that one to the New York Giants, which were another veteran team and the class of the NFL's Eastern Division in 1963.

In the era of the early '60s, only one team from each division advanced to the "playoffs." There were no playoffs as such, but rather a single championship game to determine the league's best team. Between the Bears and the Packers, only one could move on. The way the Bears viewed things as they gathered for training camp in 1963 was that they owed the Packers, as the Packers had swept past them in the regular season the last few seasons. And once they got by the Packers, they felt like they owed the Giants, as the Giants had bested them the last time they duked it out in a title game—and several of those same Giants were still playing, if aging.

"Papa Bear" Halas was also getting old, as were his key players. For the Bears, they didn't couch it that way publicly, but they saw the upcoming season as a last stand of sorts. They couldn't let the Packers whip them again and run the table for a third title in a row, and they wanted a last shot at the Giants before the veterans of each team retired.

That would be gravy; to polish off the Giants in the championship game. But the Bears knew that it would take all that they could coax from their bodies and will to first topple the Packers. That was the biggest story line of all during the 1963 season: The Bears vs. the Packers; in pursuit of greatness and in pursuit of a championship.

—Lew Freedman

1

HALAS AIMS AT THE PACKERS

GEORGE HALAS COULD always be charming, but years in the trenches had taught him how to win political battles, get his way, advance the interests of his Chicago Bears, and that growling and the tone of intimidation could be a useful weapon.

That's why when people often speak about him, they mention the staring power in his eyes and how his chin would prominently jut out in defiance for what seemed to be a half-mile. What a chin it was, seemingly almost square and a facial feature that appeared to enter a room about ten seconds ahead of the rest of him.

Many who came across Halas in his role as protector of the Chicago Bears and the NFL likely left the encounter thinking that the man should take a course in manners. It has long been a cliché about gruff football coaches—that it was their way or the highway—but the saying was probably invented for Halas.

Halas had little governor on his tongue so he was viewed as a blunt-speaking man. And saying the first thing that popped into his head while he prowled the sidelines during games was very much his habit. Nowadays, officials would slap Halas with a million yards a game in penalties for his foul mouth and aggressive gesticulations on the sideline, including slamming his fedora to the ground. The only reason Halas didn't get whacked with penalties during his coaching days was that he was pretty much the godfather of the league. A referee who wanted to continue officiating NFL games on Sundays did not want to raise Halas' ire too much. It was entirely possible that a confrontation which escalated too far could result in a termination letter. Halas had that kind of power, and you didn't want to get on his bad side.

When things didn't go right for his team on the field—even if officials had nothing to do with it—he could be equally explosive. Paul Hornung, the star Green Bay halfback, said he actually enjoyed listening to Halas rant as he violated the rules unchecked by storming down the sidelines almost to the end zone rather than staying at midfield near the team bench. "Coaches weren't supposed to be down there," Hornung said, "and he would cuss like a sailor. I loved it. It was an absolute honor to have him cuss me out during a ball game." To Hornung, it was a big laugh. If you viewed the situation with a certain attitude, Halas' behavior was a howl. In the modern era, such a performance would go viral on the Internet before the end of the game.

As for officials who didn't see the humor in Halas' tirades the way Hornung did, they were better off being anonymous rather than arguing right from wrong on the field, as Halas always thought he was right. He came by that opinion honestly. He was one of the league visionaries who had been there since its creation, and throughout the decades between the '20s and the '60s, he was a major player in every NFL decision; from team expansion and contraction to rule changes.

George Halas was born on February 2, 1895, in Chicago, Illinois. He attended the University of Illinois, and very briefly played right field for the New York Yankees. He couldn't hit his weight, going 2–22 with 8 strikeouts and recording a .091 batting average in 1919, and soon enough a newcomer named Babe Ruth took over the position and drove Halas back into football.

As an end, Halas played a season for the Hammond Pros, and then convinced the A. E. Staley Company—starch manufacturers in Decatur, located a couple of hours south of Chicago—to allow him to fund a football team. The Decatur Staleys were the forerunners to the Bears.

The meeting which founded the first organized professional football league took place in a Hupmobile dealership showroom in Canton, Ohio, on August 17, 1920. When the American Professional Football Association (APFA) began play on September 17, there were eleven teams, including the Staleys. The league's president was Jim Thorpe, who while still an active player, was the most famous name in the room. By 1922, the league was renamed the National Football League, but the starch company was experiencing financial difficulties. As a favor to Halas, the boss provided $5,000 in temporary support for one more season, as long as the Staleys in Chicago advertised starch for one final year.

Afterwards, Halas renamed the Staleys to the Bears because of help from the management of the Chicago Cubs baseball team. He was also going to call the football club the Cubs, but decided on the Bears, since football players were bigger than baseball players. Uniform colors were already orange and blue, selected for the Staleys because they were the colors of the University of

Illinois, Halas' alma mater. The Bears played their home games at the Cubs' Wrigley Field; an arrangement still in place when the 1963 season began.

The Chicago Bears were like family to Halas, but the NFL was his baby. And he was protective of every single aspect of the franchise. This even included the team he loved to hate the most: the Green Bay Packers. Actually, when Halas wrote his autobiography decades later, he called the rivalry "the happiest series of games."

Happiest, huh? That would be straining the definition of the word. Intense, competitive, hard-fought, grudge matches— all of those words might percolate to the top of the list before happiest. Players on both teams fed on the attitudes that Halas and Curly Lambeau, Packers founder and coach, brought to the two meetings each autumn.

George Musso, one of the Bears' early Hall of Fame players, said he could tell that Halas and Lambeau were coaching friends, but when they played each other, friendship was not involved. "Hell, you're not friends," Musso said. "You're out to win. And you win any damn way you can."

A Packer lineman from the late '30s named John Biolo said that Lambeau matched Halas' sideline shenanigans. "During a game, nobody would want to talk to him," Biolo said of his coach. An unnamed player in a biography of Lambeau, who died in 1965, said that in the week of practice leading up to a Bears game, players thought the coach might blow a gasket. ". . . oh God, he hated 'em so bad."

Another thing the two coaches had in common was penury. They headed two of the three (the third being the New York Giants) biggest-name teams in the NFL and by most assessments of their hired help were cheapskates when it came to forking over player raises. It was Mike Ditka, one of the stars of the '63 Bears team, who uttered perhaps the most vivid description applied to any sports team negotiator ever when he said of the owner, "Halas throws nickels around like manhole covers." Similar to Halas, Lambeau was no more generous with his payroll.

There was irony in the Bears–Packers symbiotic relationship. Not only were they two of the founding franchises and played each other twice a season, but they were the two most successful teams, winning the most championships, with the most number of great players on each squad.

Like Halas, Curly Lambeau was a team organizer and was the team's coach for decades. While they had so many similarities, they had two distinct personalities. Halas was a strong family man, married to the same woman from the 1920s until he died sixty years later, while Lambeau was an acknowledged womanizer. He flirted with the Hollywood show business lifestyle during the off-season and flirted with the actresses he met there. Too-public relationships with women not his wife caused him much grief during his Packers tenure.

Whatever it truly meant, Halas and Lambeau did not engage in the traditional gesture of sportsmanship involving a handshake between coaches at the conclusion of a game. There was some tension between the two egotistical men, but Halas understood that the Packers were almost always going to be a major obstacle between his Bears and a championship season.

Regardless of how Halas and Lambeau felt about one another personally, aside from respect for football acumen, Halas was probably the strongest owner-supporter of Green Bay's existence in the league. This related to Halas' strongest personality trait—

loyalty. If you helped him, he never forgot. If you were with him when times were tough, you were always with him. If you did him a favor, no matter how long ago, as the Packers had when the Bears had financial troubles during the depression of the 1930s, he remembered.

As the old guard changed, all of the teams from smaller towns started to fade away. Green Bay began to lose money. The Packers were playing before smaller crowds and some owners wanted to push them out in favor of a team that would provide them a larger road gate. The other owners sought to pressure Green Bay management to move the team to Milwaukee full-time, first at State Fair Park, and then in County Stadium, where they played twice a season. Halas wouldn't have it. He did everything he could to defend the Packers. To the astonishment of many in Chicago—and in Green Bay—in 1956, Halas was a guest speaker at a Green Bay sports banquet, where he waxed eloquent about the importance of the Packer franchise and helped raise money for a new stadium. "He was a real friend," said Art Daley, a *Green Bay Press-Gazette* sportswriter of the time.

Halas told everyone on his visit that the Bears–Packers rivalry was one of the most important aspects of the NFL's success and continuity.

That was the good side of Halas. But no matter how much he did for the Packers franchise, none of that graciousness ever spilled over to game day. When it was time to play the Packers, there was not a single thing more important going on. Longevity, and Halas, played a large part in making Chicago–Green Bay the most intense rivalry in professional football.

It wasn't really the same in the '50s, when Lambeau, who presided over six league championships, left for the Chicago

Cardinals, and the Packers fell into the bottom ranks of the league's teams, posting such horrible records as 2–9–1 in '53 and 1–10–1 in '58.

The arrival of Vince Lombardi in 1959 rejuvenated the Packers. By 1960, Lombardi had the Packers back in the title game, though they lost to the Philadelphia Eagles, 17–13. In '61 and '62, Green Bay won back-to-back crowns and looked just as strong as the '63 season approached. Add Lombardi's wins in those two seasons to the Lambeau total of six, and the Packers had eight titles on their resume as a franchise—at that moment one more than the Bears.

Lombardi had paid his dues. He played for Fordham as one of the school's famous "Seven Blocks of Granite" in the early 1930s, had been a high profile assistant coach for Earl Blaik at Army, and an even higher profile offensive coordinator for the New York Giants' powerful offense in the late '50s. By the time someone entrusted him to lead an NFL team, Lombardi was forty-six. He brought his East Coast accent and gap-toothed smile to Northern Wisconsin and within three seasons had not only become an icon in Green Bay, but was being acclaimed as one of the greatest coaches of all time.

Sometimes people left out the words "one of," and that began to get on Halas' nerves. Lombardi was at least as much a dictator to his players as Halas was, but Lombardi had savvy political instincts and did not want to make an enemy out of one of the league's most powerful individuals. A former *Chicago Tribune* sports editor has recounted a story that he heard about a special dinner between Lombardi and Halas—at Lombardi's invitation—where the two men bonded, exchanged stories, shared drinks, and walked out friends. That was in no small part to

Lombardi's political instincts, where he apparently repeatedly called Halas the greatest football coach of all time. Not "one of" the greatest, either. This was a man whom Halas respected; who was the talk of the football world. And it probably felt mighty good for Halas to have his ego stroked by Lombardi. It didn't matter in the least if Lombardi was sincere, and it made no difference whatsoever to how either man prepared for those twice-annual gridiron collisions, Lombardi had paid tribute to the older man, and that solidified their relationship in a way that Halas and Lambeau never shared.

Whether or not he believed he was a better coach than Halas, even in front of his own team, Lombardi sometimes praised the rival coach.

"Vince Lombardi loved George Halas because he had been one of the founders of the league," said former Green Bay center Bill Currie. "He'd say, 'I love that old man and every single thing he represents.'" The Packers couldn't believe it when words like that flowed from Lombardi's mouth, but it was Lombardi taking note of Halas being the personification of the history and tradition of the league. "We couldn't believe he was expressing love for an opponent," Currie said. "That just wasn't his shtick."

In comparison to Lombardi's praise for Halas, Halas had great respect for Lombardi. He was impressed with what Lombardi had been able to do in such a short time for the Packers. What that really meant, though, was the rivalry was back to its old level of intensity and that Halas burned to beat Lombardi and Green Bay.

By the 1960s, the Bears had won seven championships on Halas' watch. Chicago was an early league power, winning titles in '21, and again in '32, '33, '40, '41, '43, and '46. But Halas and the Bears had not won a title since. That was seventeen long years without a crown, and a month into the 1963 season Halas would turn sixty-eight years old. It was not clear how long he could continue to handle the demands of being the owner and the coach. Worse, though, his drought, coupled with Lombardi's ascension, meant that the Packers owned one more NFL title than the Bears and Halas. That was unacceptable.

As early as March of '63, six months before kickoff of the next season, Halas was on record with his optimism about how well the Bears could do. His forum did not get wide circulation because his quotes were only recorded in the team newsletter, "Bear News."

Halas had a lot to say about how the '62 season had gone wrong, although 9–5 wasn't really that bad.

Halas is noted as saying:

> *Actually, the 1962 season was a nightmare of improvisation. We had so many injuries to key backs and receivers that our offensive platoon didn't really settle down till the last month of the season. We have some rookies who figure to help us, but the real improvement should come from smoother execution.*

In 1962, the NFL draft consisted of 20 rounds. This was the height of the war with the American Football League, though, so the selection of a player did not guarantee his signing. The choice players who made the Bears from that draft were first round pick Ronnie Bull (7th overall), a running back from Baylor who was also picked in the AFL draft by the Dallas Texans, second round pick Bennie McRae (21st overall) from Michigan, fourth round pick Jim Cadile (49th overall) out of San Jose State, and seventh round pick Ed O'Bradovich (91st overall) from Illinois. They gained experience in a season pockmarked by injuries to many regulars.

Due to the competition for talent with the AFL, the NFL held its draft earlier and earlier, just as the college and pro seasons were ending, so they could jump in and negotiate quickly. Halas was already talking about rookies in March of '63 because that year's draft had taken place on December 4, 1962. In that session, he swung and missed more than connected in terms of plucking immediately employable players. The only memorable name was defensive back Larry Glueck, who was chosen out of Villanova in the third. Halas was wrong about his new draft class, but he was lucky that the '62 class made up for it.

In December of '62, Halas attended a Lombardi football-related party in Green Bay, and whether he was irritated by fawning over Lombardi, the comments of sportswriters about the burgeoning Packer dynasty, or something else entirely, he displayed a very determined outlook. Chuck Mather, a Bears assistant coach, said Halas returned from Wisconsin and said, "We're going to beat that son of a bitch." It didn't matter that he and Lombardi were friendly, but it would not be untypical for Halas to refer to a football rival in such words.

It might even be said that Halas began obsessing over Green Bay long before training camp began. Mather told a Halas biographer that the boss ordered him to study up on Packer plays and tendencies and dissect them thoroughly—and that was in January, a month after the '62 season ended and nine months before the '63 season started.

Obviously, Halas thought his team could finish better than 9–5, which had only earned it third place in the West, but he had come to understand that by focusing on Green Bay he might be able to beat everyone else as a by-product on the way to overtaking the Packers.

There was something about the '63 Bears that titillated Halas' mind even before the season started. The Packers were loaded with talent and had been dominating the league and appeared to have the makings of a long dynasty in the works. But that's not how Halas saw it.

"We entered 1963 feeling the touch of destiny," Halas said.

Probably the most interesting word in that sentence was "we." If the rest of the known football world had been polled, the tabulation of the results surely would have resulted in a consensus that the Packers, not the Bears, were a team of destiny in '63.

2

THE GOLDEN BOY AND MONGO
SENT TO THE WOODSHED

FROM THE MOMENT television sets clicked off following the Baltimore Colts' sudden-death victory over the New York Giants in the 1958 NFL championship game, pro football began riding the jet stream full bore to new levels of popularity. The upward curve of growth was moving faster than NASA's early rockets sent skyward as the space program began to take shape.

Throughout the twentieth century, Major League Baseball was referred to as the National Pastime. It was indisputably the most popular team sport on the American landscape, with college football as a distant runner-up. For much of the first half of the century, the only other sports that could push baseball off the front page of a newspaper sports section were a Triple Crown horse race or a major boxing title fight.

By the early '60s, if one tried to describe the increasing popularity of pro football, it could be explained in the context of those other sports. Football was moving up on the outside and pretty soon it would score a technical knockout over baseball to claim bragging rights as the biggest sport in the country.

Presiding over this era of growth was a young, vigorous commissioner named Pete Rozelle. On October 11, 1959, Bert Bell, one of the founders of the Philadelphia Eagles, who had become the long-time NFL commissioner, suffered a heart attack and died while attending an Eagles game against the Pittsburgh Steelers. In a secret owners meeting to replace Bell, the candidates had been reduced to two major candidates, but the votes were split. These sessions took on the drawn-out proceedings of the selection of the next pope, except there was no white smoke to signal a choice. Finally, after twenty-three ballots, Rozelle emerged as a compromised candidate.

Rozelle's first job in pro football was as the public relations director of the Los Angeles Rams from 1952–55, and then he left the team to do public relations work for the 1956 Summer Olympics in Melbourne, Australia. In 1957, he rejoined the Rams and became the team's general manager and initiated operating changes that were sound business practices and helped the team make a profit. He was not widely known outside of the back corridors of the game, so he was not viewed as a candidate for commissioner when the meetings began.

The effective date of Rozelle's appointment was January 26, 1960, and was two months shy of his thirty-fourth birthday. He was vibrant, handsome in a wholesome sort of way, and well-spoken. He took command of the NFL at almost precisely the same moment that the American Football League was created and immediately initiated a war against the establishment. It was also the same time that network television, ripe to embrace more football programming following the Colts–Giants draw, was primed to offer sweet deals to the league.

As the new General in charge of the NFL army, Rozelle dove into enriching the league through a savvy television arrangement. He was the figurehead empowered to verbally spar with the upstart AFL, and was entrusted with shaping the sport's image that would permit pro football to overtake baseball in the public's mind. Football was colorful, fast-moving, and the trendy sport of the changing sixties. Baseball was rooted in the past, slow-moving, and considered your grandfather's sport. At least that's the way some saw the battle lines drawn. Baseball had deep roots in family relationships, though, with fathers and sons, whole families going out to the park. It was one thing to be seen as hip for a young generation, but football wanted to make friends with the older generation, too.

So the last thing Pete Rozelle needed in the spring of '63 was a scandal that could tarnish the spreading image of the NFL as the "it" sport. Rozelle was quietly leading an investigation into the behavior of some of the league's prominent players. The accusations were simple: players bet on football games. That type of gambling was a no-no. What was to be done about it? How should Rozelle handle the matter, publicly or quietly? Should there be punishments for the players?

Paul Hornung of the Green Bay Packers was one of the biggest stars in the league, owning the single-season point-scoring record. Alex Karras, who later gained more fame for acting in film and television, was a three-time All-Star defensive tackle for the Detroit Lions.

Hornung's nickname was "The Golden Boy," and it seemed perfect for several reasons. Not only did he have a thick mane of blond hair, but he seemed to possess a golden touch on the gridiron. Hornung was born in Louisville, Kentucky, attended high school there, and went to Notre Dame. He won the 1956 Heisman Trophy for the Fighting Irish and is still the only player to win college football's most prestigious award while competing for a losing team.

The No. 1 pick in the 1957 NFL draft by the Packers, Hornung had the perfect dimensions for the fast and powerful back that he was at 6' 2" and 215 pounds. Hornung could run, kick, catch, and throw, as he did as a college quarterback. In 1960, he set the league's all-time record for scoring in a single season with 176 points. He held that record until 2006, when San Diego Chargers running back LaDainian Tomlinson scored 186 points, with Hornung's total still second all-time. It should be noted that Hornung collected all of those points in the NFL's last 12-game season.

Enhancing Hornung's stature was that he was the highest scorer on the league's best team. As coach Vince Lombardi shaped the beginnings of the Green Bay dynasty in the early '60s, Hornung was a cornerstone of their offense. He had twice been selected for the Pro Bowl and was voted the league's Most Valuable Player in 1961.

Although defensive players almost never gain equal notoriety to offensive stars, Karras was the other-side-of-the-ball equivalent to Hornung, minus the scoring record. In college at Iowa, Karras won the Outland Trophy as the nation's best college lineman. At 6' 2" and 250 pounds, Karras was also a No. 1 draft pick in 1958. Like Hornung, he was chosen for the Pro Bowl in '59 and '60.

Hornung was friendly with reporters, and was known to sports reporters as "a good quote." Karras was a witty man, and the country began to discover just how funny he could be when he played himself in the movie *Paper Lion*. The film was about magazine writer George Plimpton's fling as a training camp quarterback with the Lions and was just the beginning for Karras in show business. After he retired from football, he went on to be a broadcaster on ABC's *Monday Night Football*, worked in television, and filled the classic movie role of Mongo in the Mel Brooks comedy *Blazing Saddles*. Part of Mongo's shtick was that he was a behemoth of a man, whose size and strength allowed him to do just about anything—including punch out a horse. This was not so different from Karras' daily tasks of disposing of offensive linemen and sacking quarterbacks.

While Rozelle was still consolidating his power as the new, young commissioner, Hornung and Karras would end up taking the lead as villains in the drama that was about to unfold. Rozelle was trying to put the brightest public face on the NFL while also quelling inroads made by the AFL and continuing the growth of the league, and this was the last thing he needed.

On April 17, 1963, Rozelle conducted a press conference in his New York office—the NFL's headquarters—announcing indefinite suspensions—without pay—for Hornung and Karras. Less frequently remembered is that five other Lions players, plus the Detroit club, were also fined by Rozelle. Among the Detroit five were several top players, including lineman John Gordy and four defensive players: Joe Schmidt, Sam Williams, Wayne Walker, and Gordy Lowe. Their punishments were $2,000 each, and the team fine was $4,000.

The crime they were accused of was betting $50 each on the result of the 1962 NFL title game between the Packers and the New York Giants which Green Bay won, 16–7.

Rozelle had spearheaded the ten-month investigation, which he said included fifty-two interviews, and revealed that Hornung was accused of betting up to $500 on numerous college and pro football games between '59 and '61. Rozelle accused Karras of betting between $50 and $100 at least six times on NFL games within the previous few years. Karras said he did bet, but that the stakes were cigars and cigarettes in friendly wagers. Rozelle suggested Karras' real problem was associating with "known hoodlums," as described by the Detroit Police Department.

Karras' five teammates were blamed for making the one-time bets while being with Karras as they visited a friend's house in Florida the preceding winter. The $4,000 fine slapped on the Lions was because Detroit police had sent a report about Karras hanging out with undesirables to coach George Wilson, who it was said did not forward it to the proper team authorities.

In his autobiography, written fourteen years later, Karras, who died in 2012 after a long illness, called 1963 "the blackest year of my professional life." Karras said he knew people who liked to gamble his whole life. He said it felt as if gambling was part of his Greek heritage, and he liked to gamble. "It's been part of our ethnic character for thousands of years," he wrote. "I never thought it was sinful. I never attempted to hide it or felt a need to do so." In the midst of the NFL investigation, Karras agreed to go on a televised news show and, when he was asked if he ever bet on a game in which he was playing, he said "Yes, I have."

Karras took a lie detector test for Rozelle during which he was asked if he had ever shaved points or thrown games and stated that he had not. While not accused of doing anything drastic like that, Karras admitted that he had bet on five NFL games during his career. The combination of that, plus his TV appearance, is what most likely sealed his fate for the suspension.

Rozelle emphasized that no criminal laws were broken that he was aware of; the players did not bet against their own teams at any time and did not sell insider information to gamblers or bookies. Hornung had already ceased making bets the preceding season.

Knowledge of the 1919 Black Sox Scandal, when the Chicago White Sox were accused of fixing the World Series against the Cincinnati Reds, and various point shaving scandals in college basketball may have been in the back of Rozelle's mind. Whether they were or not, he did not mention them during his press conference. Nor did he cite a previous NFL problem involving gambling. In 1946, on the eve of the championship game, an accusation surfaced that Giants players Merle Mapes and Frank Filchock were offered bribes to throw the game against the Chicago Bears. In a hurry-up, last-minute investigation, Mapes admitted it was true that he had been approached and was suspended for the game. Filchock denied it and was allowed to play, but later testified in a court case that he had been offered the bribe.

The circumstances in 1963 appeared less nefarious, but Rozelle took the situation seriously.

There is clear evidence that some NFL players knowingly carried on undesirable associations which in some instances led to their betting on their own team to win NFL games. There is clear evidence that contrary to league policy many players have been free in giving information concerning their team. There is evidence that not all member clubs of the league have been as diligent as league policy requires in taking precautions against undesirable associations by players and in following through on league directives concerning safeguards.

No specific length of the suspension for Hornung or Karras was mentioned by Rozelle, but he said the earliest the players could appeal for reinstatement would be in 1964, the following year.

Rozelle chain-smoked steadily throughout his news conference and said he had felt under tremendous stress in attempting to come to a fair decision. Handing down the suspensions reflected a determination that was "the most difficult I've ever had to make in my life."

Rozelle said he informed each player by telephone of the suspensions and that Hornung was contrite while Karras was angry.

Although the AFL was in a cut-throat fight for talent with the NFL and the Canadian Football League (CFL) also frequently went head-to-head for skilled players with the NFL, both leagues instantly announced that neither Hornung nor Karras would be eligible to play in their leagues while they were under suspension from the NFL. Each player could have been of very valuable assistance to a team in either of those leagues, but apparently the respective commissioners felt their hire would have represented a poor public relations choice.

Hornung was playing golf in Kentucky when Rozelle made his announcement, but was conciliatory in his comments when reporters found him. "I did wrong," Hornung said. "I should be penalized. I just have to stay with it."

It was very important for Hornung to stress that his gambling was only social and that he had always given his best in the games he played. "They [the bets] were made with friends," he said. "They were strictly sporting."

If that was a gracious response along the lines of what Rozelle may have wanted to hear, Karras did not respond in the same fashion. It sounded as if given half a chance he wouldn't mind sacking Rozelle as he sat right at his desk.

"It comes as a big shock to me," Karras said of the Rozelle suspension. "I haven't done anything I am ashamed of and I am not guilty of anything."

Karras believed that the suspension was going to lead into a lifetime ban from the sport, and he intended to go ahead with plans to open a bar with friends in Detroit, some of whom he worried were considered undesirables.

Lombardi was restrained in his reaction. Hornung was one of the best players on the two-time defending NFL champion Packers and the coach and player had a good relationship. Lombardi defended Hornung by saying there was no time he felt that the halfback was not giving his best and or not trying to win. "However," Lombardi said, "there was a definite violation of the player contract and constitution and bylaws of this league in regard to gambling which is punishable by suspension. The commissioner had no other alternative..." As *New York Times* columnist Dave Anderson put it, in reference to Rozelle's suspension of Karras, "His first real test came when he had to suspend Hornung and Karras. 'You gotta do what you gotta do,' said Lombardi to Rozelle. That showed he was the commissioner."

Although at no time during the Rozelle news conference had there been a hint that Hornung, Karras, or the other Lions players had not tried to win, that was the undercurrent question surrounding the matter. Rozelle, Lombardi, the players, all addressed it. That was what NFL higher-ups most feared. They might have all agreed that a $100 bet here or there on a game was not that major a sin. But throwing a game, fixing a game, not playing your hardest in a game in an attempt to lose, was the great, dreaded, mortal sin that would be catastrophic for the league and the sport. That's why there was such a rush to clarify that no such terrible action took place by any of the accused players.

In complete contrast, in fact, Gordy, the Lions' prominent offensive lineman nailed with a fine, said the setting where he and the others were watching televised football was benign. They were sitting around shooting the breeze as the title game played out when someone suggested making bets on the outcome. They were in a private home socializing. It didn't seem as if they were doing anything wrong. They definitely didn't think they were violating any language in their contracts.

From Gordy's perspective, and the summary he offered of the scene of his so-called crime, it just sounded like a bunch of guys hanging out, just as fans would in their basement den.

One veteran newspaper columnist of the time, the *Washington Post*'s legendary Shirley Povich, astutely grasped how the average fan might not think what Hornung and Karras did was a big deal. Those fans, especially of the teams affected, he wrote, might well be thinking, "Boys will be boys and all that sort of thing and anyway no harm was done and where was the sin?"

Povich said Rozelle was looking deeper.

> *What Rozelle knows is that it is no good for a football player to bet on football games in which he is playing, regardless of the fact he may be wagering on his own team. This is not merely because he is violating the virtual oath he took when he signed his contract, but because there are other important reasons, all of them designed to keep the game clean.*

In Green Bay, also known as Titletown, where the Packers are veritable gods and Hornung was as close to Zeus among those gods as it was possible to be, the players frowned over the news that he would be sidelined for the foreseeable future.

"This makes me sick," said Green Bay guard Jerry Kramer. "We all thought the world of Paul. He was such a great pro. You can't tell how much this will hurt us. I hate to see a good guy like him get fouled up."

Quarterback Bart Starr and receiver Boyd Dowler both used the word "shock" in their reactions. Shock was a fair response across the board; from players, coaches, and fans, if for no other reason than no one saw a suspension coming. This was a quiet investigation without the dribs and drabs of evidence leaking out, although there had been some rumors addressed by Rozelle that other players' actions were being reviewed. He said other individuals talked about were exonerated and he named them.

Packer legend Don Hutson was not as diplomatic in his reaction to Hornung being suspended as contemporary teammates were, and sounded as if he was on the side of the morality police. "This is terrible," Hutson said. "It's hard to understand why a fellow like Hornung, who certainly made plenty of money as a player, would do something like that. It sure was a dumb thing to do, to put it mildly."

It is important to note the context; both for Hutson and for Hornung's teammates. They did not know if he would ever play again. Hutson may well have been thinking that Hornung had squandered the rest of his career over a couple of bets.

At that moment, it was possible that the Green Bay Packers and Detroit Lions and that Paul Hornung and Alex Karras could look at the situation and Rozelle's penalty and be forced to consider them similar to career-ending injuries. In 1989, Major League Baseball commissioner Bart Giamatti suspended Pete Rose for life when it came out that he had bet on baseball with the possibility of later appeal for reinstatement. Rose was retired as a player and was managing the Cincinnati Reds at that time. However, in Rose's case, twenty-four years later, the suspension remains in effect. Likewise, the eight players suspended from the Chicago White Sox for life after the Black Sox Scandal remain officially suspended decades after their deaths.

No one equated Hornung's and Karras' violations to be anything on par with those who threw the World Series, but that situation was a chief precedent among major sports that was on the books. As was the lifetime suspensions due to gambling-related reasons of such NBA players as Alex Groza and Ralph Beard, as well as Sherman White, who was a senior in college when he was indicted, and was prohibited from ever playing in the NBA.

In 1963, the NFL was divided into two halves: the Eastern Division and the Western Division. As the Super Bowl was still years away—as was a playoff system—the ultimate goal was to reach the championship game. The only path to the title game was finishing first in one of the divisions. The league had 14 teams, with seven in each division. The division breakdown was as follows:

EASTERN DIVISION	WESTERN DIVISION
New York Giants	Chicago Bears
Cleveland Browns	Green Bay Packers
St. Louis Cardinals	Baltimore Colts
Pittsburgh Steelers	Minnesota Vikings
Dallas Cowboys	Detroit Lions
Washington Redskins	Los Angeles Rams
Philadelphia Eagles	San Francisco 49ers

There was no particular discussion about it at the time, five months before the regular season was due to start, but one of the chief beneficiaries of Rozelle's decision to bench Hornung and Karras were the Chicago Bears. Each of the players' rival teams would be weakened by the loss of a star player for the entire year.

For a man as in love and involved with the NFL as George Halas was, he was not about to shout "Yippee!" about the situation given that his league—his favorite entity in the whole wide world outside of his family—was taking such a public relations hit. But he knew, he recognized (and how could he not) that his Bears stood to gain if those players were not available to their teams. In a Halas biography written many years after his death, it was noted that "the Packers were nearer to the world of mere mortals than they had been since Lombardi arrived from New York."

While the '63 season was going on, Karras made appearances on the pro wrestling circuit; just one area where the multi-talented big man was able to express his personality. He later starred in network sports broadcasting, as well as in movies and the hit TV show *Webster*.

Hornung, who said Karras never should have been suspended, though he knew he was going to be, said, "During that strange year of my suspension, I was received like a hero rather than someone who had done wrong."

That statement meant two things; the fans did not seem to hold any grudge against him, and the suspension lasted just one year.

In March of 1964, Rozelle made another announcement: Hornung and Karras were being reinstated to play football again. "That's wonderful news," Hornung said. "I'm very, very happy," said Lombardi.

Even though he was reinstated, Karras never forgave Rozelle. Almost a decade and a half after his suspension, Karras told the *Des Moines Register*, "I don't like Pete Rozelle. I don't talk to him."

Once, after Karras returned to active duty for the Lions, he was at midfield with the officials for the pregame coin toss. The referee asked him to call heads or tails with the coin in the air and he said, "I'm sorry sir, I'm not permitted to gamble."

Both Hornung and Karras returned to the NFL full-time in 1964, and in 1965, Hornung collaborated on a *Look Magazine* story with well-known sportswriter Al Silverman, carrying the headline "Why I Gambled . . . And What It Cost Me." In that story Hornung said that he met with Rozelle in New York in January of 1963 to discuss the gambling issue. He had already denied gambling on the telephone and Rozelle wanted him to take a lie-detector test. After thinking about his situation for a short time, Hornung telephoned Rozelle back, said he was willing to come in and take the lie-detector test, and would give a full confession. Despite his approach, Hornung said in that *Look* article, "I probably could have lied out of it."

Hornung said he had been gambling his whole life in one form or another; from playing poker with friends when he was a youth, to pitching nickels and dimes, to playing pinball and following the horses—the last a pastime easy to take up given that Churchill Downs was not far away and the Kentucky Derby was the biggest event in the state. In fact, in 2013, Hornung owned a three-year-old colt that he thought was good enough to compete for the Triple Crown. He turned its care over to Racing Hall of Fame trainer D. Wayne Lukas' barn in Louisville.

It was fair to say that Hornung was still a gambling man in the horse racing discipline. It was also obvious that his days with the Packers, when the team won five championships in the 1960s, were still dear to his heart. Hornung named his young thoroughbred "Titletown Five."

Hornung said he began betting on football games in 1959, once the Packers began to improve. He worked with a friend who bet the games. "I simply forgot that a player has an obligation to the sport and to the public," Hornung said.

Some fifty years later, Hornung said that he held no grudge against Rozelle. "No, I didn't," Hornung said. "He had to do something."

He also reiterated all those years later that neither Karras nor his teammates should have been punished by the league. "Karras opened his big mouth and said, 'I bet $50,'" Hornung said. "It was criminal what they did to the Lions."

During his year away from the game, Hornung returned to his hometown of Louisville and worked in the real estate business and made speeches. "I made more money than I had playing football."

Rozelle took a stand and brought the issue of gambling out from the shadows into the glare of media attention. It cost two star players a season of their careers, whether the punishment was justified or not. Before 1963, it was improper for NFL players to bet on pro football games. After 1963, attention on gambling was magnified a hundred-fold.

Per order of the league, just before summer training camps opened for the '63 season, a new sign went up designed to attract players' attention in each team's home locker room. The signs read NO GAMBLING.

3

"BIG DADDY" LIPSCOMB

GENE "BIG DADDY" Lipscomb had a heart as big as a mountain, and compared to the football players of his day, he was as large as a Himalayan peak. He made his friends laugh and opponents cry. And in a much tamer era of professional football, the big man flaunted as colorful a personality as any show business figure. It may have been his outgoing ways or his flamboyant wardrobe, but long before a time period of instant communication, Lipscomb was a sports figure who transcended cities.

A defensive tackle 10 seasons with the Los Angeles Rams, Baltimore Colts, and Pittsburgh Steelers, Lipscomb weighed in at between 280 and 300 pounds at a time when the opposition blocking him might weigh 240. Big Daddy was big compared to other football-playing humans, and he was bigger than life to those who knew him well. A caring man who loved kids, meanness did not come naturally to Lipscomb on the field. He had to practice it.

Given his hard upbringing battling out of poverty, overcoming the murder of his mother at the age of eleven (he never knew his father), and being African American, too, Lipscomb learned early in life that it could be a hard world beyond his front door. It would have been natural to be bitter, but instead Lipscomb became someone who conquered and enjoyed; someone who may have been gigantic physically, but who never used his size as a bully, and always embraced those less fortunate than he. He identified with them; those lost souls who had bad luck.

When it came to storytelling, Lipscomb knew how to entertain the sportswriters. When it came to his teammates he was like a brother to the other black players on the team, as few as they were in the '50s and early '60s. He loved to party, drink, stay out late, and always drove the fanciest Cadillac in the neighborhood. They said when Big Daddy parked his yellow Caddy in the ghetto, no one ever touched it. No one vandalized it. Big Daddy didn't have to mingle with poor people in a dangerous neighborhood, but Big Daddy never put himself above anyone else. Because if you knew him, you knew that it wasn't as if he was going to go buy a house with a white picket fence in the suburbs.

Lipscomb was a famous football player, all right, but he was still a guy who drank at the corner tavern downtown, whose ego never grew so big that he was spoiled or thought he was more important than anyone else. The thing about Big Daddy was that he was a different man outside the limelight. Those who knew him best, those closest to him, thought in some ways he was still a scared little boy inside; insecure about his past. They knew things about him that team owners, NFL administrators, and even the fans that adored him would never know. There was definitely more to Big Daddy than his expansive public image embraced.

From a distance, the nightmare of May 10, 1963, might have seemed logical. On that day, Eugene Allen Lipscomb was found dead at the age of thirty-one in a strange apartment in Baltimore. Police said he had died of a self-administered heroin overdose. There was shock in the football world, but Lipscomb had a reputation of someone who partied hard. Men like Commissioner Pete Rozelle despised the news that one of his players had died in such an unseemly way. The National Football League was supposed to be family entertainment, and having a star player's death be associated with drug-taking was unseemly.

The permissive age of the '60s drug culture had not yet arrived. Heroin belonged in a horrifying world that few understood or could relate to. If you were involved with heroin, you were a bad guy and got what you deserved—that was, at the time, the pervasive thinking.

Once again, just like the gambling scandal resulting in the suspension of Paul Hornung and Alex Karras, this was a headline that NFL honchos did not want to see in print. They wanted the story to fade away, and fast. They pretty much got their wish at the time, given how the police analyzed the death scene. But half a century later, old football teammates and friends of Big Daddy still don't believe the public reports. They never for a minute accepted that Lipscomb had died from a self-administered heroin overdose. They always believed that he was murdered.

Karras played the same position as Lipscomb, but was much smaller at 6' 2" and 250 pounds. Karras was nearsighted and played without glasses, but he could still see the gigantic Lipscomb fine. "He had to be the most intimidating figure in pro football history," Karras said. "I never could see too well without my glasses, but, on or off, the mere sight of him quickened my heartbeat, set the adrenalin flowing, and made me take off in the

opposite direction. I'd take an oath on it—the man stood 7' 9",
weighed 8,217 pounds, breathed fire..."

Lipscomb's life was a remarkable story. It was marked by trag-
edies and dreams achieved, a rollercoaster of ups and downs, and
the more you read and the more you heard, the more there was
a feeling that what was summed up in newspapers of the time
was oversimplified.

Lipscomb was born on August 9, 1931, in the small community of Uniontown, Alabama. At the depths of the Depression his father took a job in the Civilian Conservation Corps
and passed away from an illness. His mother, Carrie, became
part of the Great Migration, when African Americans forsook
their native South for better opportunities in the North in
the years before World War II. Lipscomb was three when his
mother moved him to Detroit. She went looking for hope
and found despair. She was murdered when Lipscomb was
eleven—stabbed forty-seven times while she was standing at
a bus stop.

After that, Lipscomb was raised by his paternal grandfather,
Charles Hoskins, who disciplined him harshly. Not that living
with him in any way was an idyllic existence. Especially since he
was big for his age, Lipscomb took on odd jobs as a kid because
his grandfather charged him room and board. Lipscomb had
almost no true childhood.

Lenny Moore, Lipscomb's best friend on the Colts, wrote in a
book years later that he sometimes heard Lipscomb cry himself
to sleep, and that despite a smiling and generous exterior he
was always sensitive about his lack of education and haunted
by some of the terrible things he endured growing up. Other
former teammates said Lipscomb would sometimes burst into

tears unexpectedly. Some said he even carried pictures around of his mother's dead body.

Then, as now, pro football teams follow a format when listing players on their roster. Next to a player's name was their height (Lipscomb stood 6' 6"), their weight (depending on the day, maybe 300 pounds), and a reference to the college they attended. Next to Lipscomb's name for college, it said "None." Lipscomb did not go to college; to play football, or for any other reason. Later, that perpetual appearance of the word "none" grew to bother him, almost haunt him. It followed him around, a label he couldn't shed, whether it was in the game program or on the tongue of the announcers broadcasting his games.

After high school, Lipscomb joined the Marines and was stationed at Camp Pendleton in California. Someone tipped off the nearby Los Angeles Rams that they might take a look at this guy who was not only huge but could run fast. The Rams liked what they saw and they signed Lipscomb to their team in '53. That was the beginning of the gradual transformation from Gene Lipscomb to "Big Daddy" Lipscomb. It wasn't a bad thing at all. Discovering he was good at something was great for his self-esteem. Adopting a persona that allowed him to shift from the image of a killer on the field who could intimidate all of those smaller, weaker opponents helped his game. It also gave Lipscomb cover to act as an outgoing night owl, which attracted people to him away from the field.

Certainly in the beginning with the Rams, Lipscomb was a pretty raw specimen. He didn't have much football experience, and learning on the job in the pros was not an easy task. But the more Lipscomb played, the better he got. Before his career ended, he had been a three-time Pro Bowler.

One thing Lipscomb learned quickly, though, was that he was stronger than just about everyone else out on the field. Over the years, the comment has been used by other humongous linemen, such as Bubba Smith, but Lipscomb uttered the original pass-rusher summary of the job. Appearing stern-faced as he said it, and only breaking into a grin at the end of his little speech, Lipscomb described for sportswriters his approach to tackling ball carriers and disrupting offenses. "I just wrap my arms around the whole backfield and peel 'em one by one until I get to the ball carrier," he said. "Him I keep."

End of play.

"I won't actually say I'm the best," Lipscomb said once, "but on my really good days, I can't think of anybody any better," which he followed with a wink.

So did he mean it or not? How could you not love a guy like that?

When you are the biggest guy on the block and you tackle people for a living, it's not difficult to make people fear you. Lipscomb had a large head, somewhat bullet-shaped, wore a thick mustache, and possessed a frown that could wilt a spring flower. He made some opponents want to tiptoe around him, but he was a different person off the field. "I don't want anybody to think that Big Daddy is a mean man," he once said.

While most might think that it was self-evident why football people dubbed Lipscomb Big Daddy, his size alone was not the reason. Lipscomb was one of those guys who, for the life of him, couldn't remember names. So he addressed numerous people as "Little Daddy." Turnabout certainly made sense.

It was such a cool nickname that when Lipscomb entered the world of professional wrestling as an off-season career move, he could use the same appellation. During Lipscomb's football era, the pros didn't make much more money than most other workers in American society, and they had to work part-time jobs during the off-season. One thing about Big Daddy and pro wrestling, though, was that he refused to play the role of a heel, or villain. He only wanted to play the part of a good guy.

Lipscomb was not the only big-guy football player who indulged in pro wrestling; the choreographed show that was half-sport, half-entertainment product. Among others were Bronko Nagurski, Leo Nomenelli, Vern Gagne, Dick The Bruiser, Ernie Ladd, Ed "Wahoo" McDaniel, Alex Karras, and Steve "Mongo" McMichael (a little confusing, since Karras played the movie part of Mongo in *Blazing Saddles*). For a big, strong guy, it was an acceptable way to make a few bucks. It also added to the flavorful image.

"I am in wrestling because I think it is good for football players," Lipscomb said in 1961. "If I wrestle three or four nights a week during the off-season, I will not have much trouble getting down to my proper weight for the new season because by wrestling I have kept an edge on my physical condition." The phrasing sounds a little bit stilted, but the point came across.

Lipscomb was always looking for love and was married and divorced three times. Most professional athletes attract groupies' attention whether they want to or not, and Lipscomb was a chick magnet. After Lipscomb's death, one former teammate, Brady Keys of the Steelers, said, "Big Daddy Lipscomb drank, screwed, and dominated football games."

Big Daddy was still absorbing the football trade while with the Rams, and they gave up on him too soon. Lipscomb had never had any money before, and once he got some, was attracted to the area's night life. He also had limited discipline and liked fooling around with his teammates. Los Angeles ran out of patience, and Lipscomb was picked up by the Baltimore Colts on waivers for $100 for the 1956 season. Coach Weeb Ewbank loved Lipscomb and recognized his potential. Ewbank, a Hall of Fame coach, took over the Colts when they were atrocious and acquired all of the talent that won NFL titles in '58 and '59, including Lipscomb.

Big Daddy could overpower most of the men that other coaches assigned to block him. So, to avoid embarrassment, they had to resort to underhanded tricks to equal the playing field. In the trenches where the officials' vision was sometimes blocked by colliding large bodies, that often led to illegal tactics, such as holding. If they couldn't stop Lipscomb from stomping their quarterback legally, they'd rely on illegal tactics. It came with the territory, but Lipscomb had to devise counterattacks. "If a player starts holding," he said, "I smack the ear hole of his helmet. That's what I call working out a problem."

By the early sixties, Lipscomb developed a new area of interest. The United States was setting off rockets to compete with the Soviet Union for outer space supremacy. And with that, Lipscomb decided he wanted to become an astronaut. He guessed he could trim down to around 260 pounds and maybe that wasn't too much weight for NASA to handle on a flight to the moon. He was very specific about wanting to fly to the moon—something America was working towards—but alas, Lipscomb never lived to see a lunar landing, which first occurred six years after his death, on July 20, 1969.

Ironically, it was almost seven years to the day before the actual man on the moon landing that Lipscomb had broached

the topic with well-known *Baltimore News-Post* sports columnist John Steadman, and the story was accompanied by a small
photograph of Lipscomb with a space helmet added.

"I'm serious, my man," Lipscomb said. "I want to be one of
them astronauts. I'd like to get up on the moon, look around,
wave the American flag, and then get a little glory for Big Daddy,
too."

After being an All-Pro, Lipscomb wanted to be All-World, or
perhaps Ambassador to the Moon would better suit him. As he
continued:

> *Suppose I got to the moon first. Do you think the moon people
> would start throwing things at Big Daddy? If they did, I'd
> just lay a bear hug on them and cut off their breathing. But
> mainly we need a public relations man to go to the moon.
> And who can make friends faster than Big Daddy?*

By that point in his life Lipscomb was a three-time divorcee, so
he was on the prowl for romance.

> *The first thing I'd do is look out the window of my spaceship
> and see what the happenings were all about. If they got any
> good-looking chicks up there I might get engaged. Wouldn't
> that be something if Big Daddy came back from the moon
> with a moon girl?*

If anyone thought there was a fuss about rocks being retrieved
from the moon, Big Daddy was primed to initiate an interga-
lactic incident.

That was Lipscomb at his charming best with reporters. He
could not know he was less than a year away from his own
death.

Lipscomb was traded from the Colts to the Steelers as part of a five-player deal and played for Pittsburgh for two seasons. However, he kept his home in Baltimore and was still enormously popular in the city.

The fact that Major League Baseball was the national pastime throughout the first half of the twentieth century and beyond also made that sport the focal point for equal rights more so than pro football. Football was not hospitable to African Americans between the early '20s and immediately after World War II, but far more publicity attended the desegregation of baseball than football.

By the late '50s and early '60s—with the Civil Rights Movement poised to explode across the United States—there were usually a handful or so of black players on each team, except for the Washington Redskins, whose owner George Preston Marshall was an abashed racist. (Pressure applied directly by President John F. Kennedy in 1962 made the Redskins integrate.) However, when football teams traveled to southern cities for exhibition games, they still faced discrimination. Black players were separated into other hotels, not allowed to stay with the rest of their team.

The African American players on the Colts were a tight group. They included Lipscomb, Lenny Moore, the future Hall of Fame running back who was his best friend on the team, lineman Sherman Plunkett, Jim Parker, another Hall of Famer, defensive back Johnny Sample, and defensive back Milt Davis. At one point the black players demanded a meeting with owner Carroll Rosenbloom to say that they would not put up with on-the-road discrimination. Rosenbloom said that he sympathized with their complaints because he felt discrimination as a result of being Jewish.

Nonetheless, to Moore and others, it was a shock when Lipscomb was traded to Pittsburgh in 1960. "There was really no reason given," Moore wrote in his memoirs. "I think it was because the management was afraid they couldn't control Big Daddy anymore, who wouldn't tolerate any more mistreatment of the blacks on the team. I was devastated to see my best friend leave the team."

Moore believed that Lipscomb had matured and was thriving in a Colts environment of close-knit fellow black players who understood him. Even after Lipscomb was traded to the Steelers, he and Moore remained friends, living in the same area of Baltimore. While admitting that Lipscomb wanted to settle down and raise a family—unlike the one he had in his youth—Moore understood why it never quite worked out. "Big Daddy just wasn't the marrying type. He continued to date other women, drink a lot of liquor and live the good life. He also continued to carouse."

It was not just the other black teammates who provided a support system for Lipscomb. Buddy Young, formerly a running back for the Colts, worked in the team front office. He liked Lipscomb and sought to help him in different ways.

"He was just a big feller who needed schooling," Young said. "He had the potential, but his talents needed brushing up and he had to be given confidence in himself."

Young was one of the smallest players in NFL history, but he was an older African American to whom Lipscomb listened and looked up to when he offered advice.

"This little guy is a godsend," Lipscomb said. "He made me really recognize how big I am."

In Lipscomb's last week alive, he spent a lot of time with Moore. Lipscomb told Moore that he planned to play softball on Thursday night, two days later. He said he was going to go to New York for a jazz concert Friday. They agreed to get together on Thursday after softball, but the meeting never took place.

Lipscomb did play softball, but then went to the Uptown Bar, and, as was his custom, consumed large amounts of VO whiskey, his favorite. Lipscomb had the capacity to ingest VO the way a more average-sized man might throw down lemonade. At some point, Lipscomb disappeared from the bar.

It was what occurred after that, in the hours through the night and into the next morning, that still remains murky. The story emerged from police investigations this way:

On the night of May 9, Lipscomb left the Uptown Bar and joined a man named Timothy Black, then twenty-six, at his tiny apartment at 434 North Brice Street, a narrow flight of stairs up on the second floor, and he partied deep into the night with Black and two women. Black told police that in the morning he left the apartment to go out and grab breakfast, and that when he returned home about 4 a.m., Lipscomb was slumped over the kitchen table with a needle in his arm. After an emergency phone call, Lipscomb was rushed by ambulance to nearby Lutheran Hospital, but was pronounced dead before he reached medical care at 8 a.m.

On May 10, authorities announced that the famous football star had died from a heroin overdose.

Then Black changed his story. He said that after the two women left the apartment in the middle of the night after drinking Country Club malt liquor, he and Lipscomb went out on the street to score a $12 bag of heroin that they cooked in a wine cup. Black said Lipscomb injected the heroin on his own, but immediately fell onto his arm, then slipped to the floor and began drooling. Black said he employed cold packs, seeking to revive Lipscomb, but failed. Another man, Robert Douglas Waters, who had once dated Lipscomb's sister, saw the yellow Cadillac on the street and showed up at Black's apartment. He told Black they should prepare a solution of salt and water and inject that into Lipscomb. That did not rouse him either and they then called an ambulance. While waiting for the ambulance Black said he slapped Lipscomb across the face trying to bring him back to consciousness, but that only sent him to the floor. Black claimed that he took half of the same bag of heroin, but had no such dramatic reaction.

Police did find a syringe and other drug paraphernalia in the apartment. Black gave the police Lipscomb's wallet with $73 in it and car keys. That was another thing that bothered some of Lipscomb's friends. Moore thought Lipscomb had $700 with him and Young thought he probably had about $500. He was leaving town for a weekend in New York and going onto Pittsburgh to sign his new contract. Where did all the money go?

Black was arrested and charged with involuntary homicide and given $10,000 bail. Then the charge was reduced to possession of drug equipment and bail was lowered to $3,500.

NFL reaction was immediate and forceful. Other players, coaches, and team officials were stunned and depressed to hear of Lipscomb's death. They also had difficulty assimilating the cause of death. Lipscomb had not been known to take drugs. It was trying enough to digest the news that the biggest and strongest player in the league was deceased; it was something more to accept the method of his demise.

"It's impossible for anybody to convince me of this," said Steelers coach Buddy Parker. "We were too close to him, the doctor, the trainer, the coaches. We would have known."

Rosenbloom said, "I'm extremely shocked and saddened by the news of his death."

Praise came from many quarters about Lipscomb's football talent, but those who were teammates, who got to spend time with him up close, talked of his winning personality.

"He was a colorful player and character," said former Colt John Sandusky. "Locker rooms throughout the NFL will miss the laughter he produced."

Only two days after his death, a memorial service was conducted in Baltimore to honor Eugene "Big Daddy" Lipscomb. Thousands of people visited the funeral home, lined up for blocks outside; sometimes four wide over a period of twelve hours. They paraded past an open casket at the Charlie Law funeral parlor. Lipscomb was attired in a dark blue suit accessorized with a white, silk tie. Lipscomb's body was subsequently shipped to Detroit for burial and among the pall bearers were Moore, Jim Parker, Johnny Sample, and Sherman Plunkett.

From the moment Lipscomb's cause of death was announced, friends disputed it strongly and loudly. It became promptly known to the police and the public that the massive, powerful Big Daddy was a sissy when it came to needles, as he had a phobia about them. One after another, anecdotal stories came out about Lipscomb's aversion to needles, and friends said it was inconceivable that he would voluntarily inject a needle into his arm.

Dr. Raymond Sweeney, who was the Steelers' trainer for the two years when Lipscomb played for the team, witnessed the player's reaction to needles and discussed it with him after he was injured in the first half of a game against the New York Giants. "We wanted to shoot him with Novocain," Sweeney said. "But he said he never had a needle in him in his life and would rather play hurt."

Steve Rosenbloom, son of the former Colts owner, said that as part of their annual team physicals players were required to receive inoculations. "They had to sneak up on him as part of the incoming annual physical," Rosenbloom said.

Moore was adamant on that point as well, saying that when the Colts wanted the players to get flu shots, Lipscomb hid in the locker room. Moore added another revelatory point that illustrated his skepticism.

> *Big Daddy was right-handed, yet the heroin was administered to his right arm. Now, how can a man shoot himself up using his weak hand if he was terrified by needles and had had no practice [that I knew of] in shooting heroin?*

Moore immediately dismissed as "absurd" that Lipscomb was a heroin user. Lipscomb always wore short sleeves that showed off his muscles and none of his friends ever saw needle tracks, and he displayed no behavioral changes. Moore said he spoke personally to the coroner who said there were only three fresh needle marks and no old ones.

Buddy Young saw Lipscomb two days before his death—his arms bare in a short-sleeved shirt. No needle marks. Lipscomb sometimes bragged, "I'm a B and B man; booze and broads." Nobody doubted that, but drugs? Never.

A few months after Lipscomb's death, Black was put on trial in Baltimore, accused of possession of narcotics equipment. However, the presiding judge delivered a not guilty verdict because a recent change in the law by the Maryland state legislature created what was termed "a gap" in the law. So Black walked away and there was never any other prosecution related to Big Daddy Lipscomb's death.

Several months later, Ed Linn, a well-known sports magazine writer and author, interviewed Black who told him that for a six-month period he regularly procured heroin for Lipscomb. Black said they were not friends, but conducted business. Linn met with Lipscomb's third and last wife, who still lived in the same neighborhood he did and she added her voice to the chorus about needles. "He could never have put a needle in himself," she said. "He would never even let a dentist pull a tooth without me sitting in his lap."

The autopsy indicated that Lipscomb had five times the lethal amount of heroin in his system, and for conspiracy theorists who suggested he had to have been otherwise drugged for that amount of heroin to be forced into his body, the city assistant medical examiner Dr. Rudiger Breitenecker said that there was no evidence of any such substance in Lipscomb's bloodstream.

For the most part, except amongst his most loyal friends, Lipscomb disappeared off pro football's radar screen. To them, his death remained perhaps the greatest mystery to ever infect the sports world. In 1999, *Sports Illustrated* writer Bill Nack—like others haunted by the lack of satisfying explanation as to what happened during Lipscomb's final hours—pursued the topic. He mounted a massive search for Timothy Black. Accompanied by Moore, Nack went to the address he obtained, only to learn the man had died from cancer a week earlier.

Fifty years after Lipscomb's death, many of his close friends have passed away. The Baltimore police files have regarded his situation as a closed case for decades. If Black was guilty of more than negligence, unfortunately there's no way to prove it at this point. However, one of Lipscomb's friends is still around and was willing to share his beliefs about what happened on the fateful night the famous football player perished.

In early January of 2013, George Taliaferro turned eighty-six. In the late 1940s, he was an All-American football player at Indiana University in Bloomington, where he still resides with his wife. As an undergraduate, working quietly with the President of the University, Taliaferro helped integrate the IU swimming pool and on-campus restaurants at a time when there was still great hostility for blacks at the school. In recent years, he has been honored by the NAACP and other organizations for his efforts.

After college, Taliaferro was drafted by the Chicago Bears, but chose to play for the Los Angeles Dons of the All-America Football Conference. Taliaferro played for four other teams (including the Baltimore Colts) and retired in 1955. In 1956 and 1957 Taliaferro worked as the recreation director for a church and Lipscomb and Colts owner Carroll Rosenbloom gave him money to fund the program.

In the early '60s he was still living in Baltimore, in the same neighborhood as Lipscomb, and the men were close friends. Before Taliaferro spent years working at predominantly black Morgan State University, he worked for the Baltimore prisoners' aid society, a private organization that provided prerelease counseling to inmates within thirty days of their departure from prison.

Living in the same neighborhood, Taliaferro chatted with Lipscomb on a regular basis. They both got involved in community activities to help young people, with Lipscomb purchasing Little League equipment for the youngsters in the area. The young teens were the ones who protected Lipscomb's Cadillac, said Taliaferro.

> *If that car had a speck of dirt on it, there were thirteen or fourteen kids out there cleaning it. Never asking him, never saying anything to him, this was their payback for the way he treated them. I don't know of all the cash donations he made to each child. He became a Pied Piper for the kids.*

Taliaferro mostly knew the daytime Lipscomb, but said he knew the nighttime Lipscomb as well, not because he once came to his home for dinner, but because Big Daddy would talk about his nocturnal actions, like drinking and smoking, going out to bars, and hanging out with the wrong people. Taliaferro didn't do any of those things. "I would tell him, 'You may not want to be there. You may not want to do that. This is a decision that you have to make.' I was not dictating to him."

On the morning that Big Daddy Lipscomb was found with a needle in his arm, Taliaferro was in his car listening to the radio on his way to the Maryland State Penitentiary to see clients. There was a news bulletin that Big Daddy was dead and that drugs were probably involved. That was all that was known at the time.

It didn't really surprise me. I was saddened beyond belief. I was saddened to know that Big Daddy had come to this end. It didn't surprise me because he was dealing with people in the underworld. The circumstances knocked me off my feet and I said, 'Big Daddy was murdered.' I said that to myself because of the information that had come over the radio—the fact that it was drug-related. It was stated it was an overdose. I didn't believe that. I simply couldn't believe it.

I knew he drank. He would not have voluntarily taken drugs on top of drinking because he enjoyed drinking, because he enjoyed the high of drinking. It took a huge amount of alcohol to make him inebriated to the point that he couldn't function. When he got drunk he was more of a comedian than at any time in his life. He would tell you stories ad infinitum about everything, football, life, women, everything. He never mentioned children, though. Not in an inebriated state. Children were sacred to Big Daddy and he was going to influence the life of every child that he could. But it was, 'Don't be like me. I love you, but don't be like me.'

What happened next inside the Maryland State Penitentiary is what influenced Taliaferro's opinion that Lipscomb was murdered, more than his own intuition. When Taliaferro entered the detention area of the prison, there were trustees walking around, and within minutes, four of them said to him, "Did you hear what happened to Big Daddy?"

Each one of those men said roughly the same thing: "They got Big Daddy." Taliaferro responded, "What do you mean?" There was no explanation for who "they" were. Troubled by the hints being dropped, Taliaferro returned to his office a few blocks away and telephoned someone he knew who worked in the bar business and probed for information.

This is the story that Taliaferro heard:

This was at a bar where all of the guys went who played softball. Good and bad guys, not just hoodlums. There were upstanding citizens. I pieced this thing together through Big Daddy's friend, who was part-owner of the bar. He said, 'They had a softball game and the winner gets to order the drinks. The loser pays for the drinks.' There were 12 or 13 guys on a team. Big Daddy was drunk at that bar the last time anybody saw him alive.

Working backwards, Taliaferro said he discovered a day earlier that there had been discussion at the bar. "What had transpired was that Big Daddy had been convinced by a drug dealer to lend him $500. Now that's a lot of money back in the early sixties, unlike today. The guy, as I understand it, promised Big Daddy, 'I can give you back $1,000 tomorrow.' Big Daddy always kept a large amount of money on his person. Who is going to try to rob Big Daddy? Heroin and crack and all of that stuff weren't as common then as they are today, and you really had to be stoned out of your mind to pull a gun on Big Daddy Lipscomb. I know the name of that guy [who was the drug dealer]. It was Timothy Black.

Taliaferro said he was told that Big Daddy got into his car with another man and went to collect his $1,000. Lipscomb was next seen on the verge of death with a needle in his arm. The motive in Taliaferro's mind was to avoid paying back the $1,000.

How much is an overdose? You have to have some idea as to the dosage. Big Daddy did not have that information and would not have injected himself with his left hand when his right hand was dominant. I don't believe this guy wanted to kill Big Daddy. He wanted to block out the activities of that evening. I don't have a criminal mind.

The true answer to what happened that night died with Big Daddy Lipscomb. The tragedy—less than a month after the gambling scandal—combined to make 1963 the worst off-season the National Football League had ever experienced.

4

FOOTBALL AT LAST

COMMISSIONER PETE ROZELLE was lucky he didn't end up with a lifetime case of heartburn stemming from the spring of '63. The gambling scandal was bad enough publicity, but the unseemly death of one of the league's star players was a shock that no one saw coming. They would both put stains on the NFL.

Pro football had never been rocked by two such notorious off-season incidents in NFL history, and nothing since has ever matched that monthlong stretch of high-profile disaster for the league. It takes a lot to shake a fan's faith, as sports administrators have learned in recent decades. Neither labor strife nor drug scandals have squashed the enthusiasm of resilient sports fans despite interrupted seasons or the ruination of star players' reputations. As long as the teams play, they root. And at no time is a fan more engaged and more optimistic than when his team is 0-0, the new roster is taking shape, and he can dream of a championship.

The Chicago Bears gathered for summer training camp workouts in the blistering heat of July at St. Joseph's College in Rensselaer, Indiana, the same site the team had used since 1944. St. Joseph's was a tiny Catholic college in an out-of-the-way town located about 85 miles from Chicago.

Bears owner and coach George Halas was a creature of habit, and the team ended up using St. Joseph's to prepare for its regular season for several weeks each summer for the next thirty years.

One thing that distinguished the Bears' training camp from other teams' was the organization's connection to the annual Chicago Charities College All-Star Game; an exhibition match that pitted a team of former college all-stars on their way to the pros against the defending NFL champs. The game was begun by Arch Ward—the sports editor of the *Chicago Tribune*—who also spearheaded creation of the Major League Baseball All-Star Game.

The first of these matches took place in 1934, and was played annually (except in 1974, due to the NFL strike) until 1976. In '63, the defending NFL champs were the Green Bay Packers. However, the all-stars always scrimmaged against the Bears (in years in which the Bears weren't the opponent), so Halas constantly reminded his players that they had to report to camp in shape. While arriving at training camp in good condition may be automatically assumed in the twenty-first century, in the 1960s, players held off-season jobs, so they didn't spend their off-seasons working out, as they do today. And this wasn't just in the NFL. In Dan Shaughnessy's book, *Spring Training: Baseball's Early Season*, Hall of Fame third baseman George Brett spoke about the difference of how players arrive to spring training now, compared with when he played. (Brett played professionally from 1973–93, all with the Kansas City Royals.)

What's changed the most is the shape players are in when they report. We used to come to spring training to get in shape. . . . These guys today come here in shape. They're practically football players. They're on winter workout programs, then they come here and there are workout rooms and strength and conditioning coaches. There's just a lot more individual work than there used to be . . .

As a motivator for the Bears to show up in some kind of condition, one of the first things Halas demanded of his troops was that they run the mile in less than seven minutes. The ritual became known as the Halas Mile, and it was a despised task, particularly for the big guys. For linemen weighing 240 pounds, the mile might as well have been a marathon. It was a foreign concept to bodies better designed for arm wrestling, power lifting, or tangoing with similarly sized opposing linemen. They were not cross-country runners.

"I hated running that mile," said Chicago offensive lineman Roger Davis. "Everybody did. If you were not prepared for it, it was a killer."

Bears assistant coach Chuck Mather came up with the idea for the dreaded mile. Mather learned that there was a requirement that the Boy Scouts of America had to run a mile for credit in under seven minutes, so pro football players should be able to hit the same threshold. If the Bears were aware of the mile's origins, they probably would have pinned a merit badge on Mather's butt.

While this is most likely lost on today's players, a similar scenario played out before the 2010 NFL season during the Washington Redskins' training camp. Albert Haynesworth, who had just signed a seven-year, $100 million contract with the team (including $41 million guaranteed), arrived to camp in poor physical condition. He was immediately put through a conditioning test by new coach Mike Shanahan, in which he would have to complete two 300-yard shuttles (which was broken into six 25-yard "out and back" sprints), and would not be allowed to practice with the team until he passed. While players in today's game have much higher salaries and sometimes are regarded to have more job security then their coaches, it was the complete opposite in Halas' day.

In addition to the mandatory mile, Halas was also a great one for weight clauses in dealing with his players. This was the dictator in him. If Papa Bear thought your best playing weight was 225 pounds and you thought your best weight was 230 pounds, the boss was going to win the argument. Halas' policy was to fine a player $5 a pound for being overweight (*his* definition of overweight) for the first three pounds and then $25 a pound after that. Given that players were making roughly $10,000 a year, that was not chicken feed the way it would be to present-day players.

The Bears were coming off a 1962 season in which they finished 9–5. It was not a bad season overall, but in their two head-to-head games against the world champion Packers, the Bears looked like a Division III college team, falling 49–0 and 38–7. Those kind of defeats gnawed at Halas no matter who the opponent was, but it was always more galling if humiliation was dished out by the Packers.

The Bears and the Packers rivalry is the oldest and most intense in pro football history, and it would not be far-fetched to term it a sibling rivalry. Going back to the beginnings of the league in 1921, the Bears and Packers were like brothers; only the sons of different fathers. There was nothing Halas relished more than beating Curly Lambeau and his Packers. Now the arrival of Vince Lombardi in Green Bay after a fallow 1950s (with the Bears going 14–5–1 from 1950–59) had juiced up the rivalry anew.

Green Bay and Chicago were both situated in the Western Division. In 1960, the Packers represented the West in the NFL title game against the Philadelphia Eagles, although they lost 17–13. The Packers would win the crown in '61 and '62 and, although Paul Hornung was sidelined for the 1963 season, the rest of the deep and talented Packers were back and seeking a third consecutive title.

Eventually, besides Hornung, ten players (Jim Taylor, Ray Nitschke, Herb Adderley, Forrest Gregg, Bart Starr, Jim Ringo, Willie Wood, Dave Robinson, Henry Jordan, and Willie Davis) from that time period (and all from the '63 team) would be inducted into the Pro Football Hall of Fame; as was their coach, Lombardi. So yes, Hornung was benched for the year because of the gambling scandal, but only the most naïve judge of talent would think that the Packers shaped up as significantly less formidable than the preceding season.

For that reason Halas began preaching his gospel for '63 early and often in training camp; or rather, just as soon as his men had completed that blasted mile. The challenge for the season, he said, was to beat Green Bay. The Bears had two chances to beat the Packers, and they had to beat them both times in order to win the Western Division and reach the championship game.

"Right away, Halas started talking about the Packers," recalled defensive back Richie Petitbon, fifty years later. "There was no question about it: the Packers were the team. He said, 'If you want to win the championship, you've got to beat the Packers.'"

Halas knew what he was talking about, but outside the training camp grounds few doubters of the Packers' ability to sweep to a third straight title could be found. From the long view of history it is no stretch to proclaim that the Packers of the 1960s were the best team of the decade, if not of all-time. Many consider Lombardi to be the best coach of all time. They were coming off a 13–1 regular season in 1962, and a second straight conquering of the New York Giants, the best of the East. In all, 14 players on the 1962 team earned All-Pro recognition from some source.

"The Packers had a solid ballplayer at every position," said Bears defensive back Roosevelt Taylor.

Green Bay really was a team without a weakness. The only community-owned franchise in American professional sports, the Packers were about as beloved as any team in any major sport could be by their hometown fans. Green Bay was unique because of that peculiar stock-affiliation and for being the smallest city in any league, with approximately 63,000 residents in Green Bay during the early 1960s. It would not be very many years until City Stadium (before it became Lambeau Field upon the death of Curly Lambeau in '65) had a capacity which exceeded that number.

Lombardi was a god in Green Bay after resurrecting the team from the extreme doldrums of the 1950s, and adding championship trophies to the pile collected by Lambeau. The players were revered as well. Typically, Lombardi's face featured a smile in nationally distributed photographs, but up close, his players might see a face of rage ranting and railing at them to live up to his exacting standards.

Although the words got somewhat twisted over the years, the phrase "Winning isn't everything, it's the only thing" is what stuck. Lombardi drilled his men as if that's what he said and thought, and there was just something about the determination and chasing the big prize inherent in that sentence that everyone in sports loved.

It wasn't just what Lombardi was famous for (or noted for) saying. The reason why people listened to him was because he had built a best-in-the-sport dominating football team that could steamroll everyone else virtually overnight. Winning was the key. If you won you could say anything, and the Packers were quickly transformed from losers to winners under Lombardi. In 1958, the Packers finished 1–10–1. The next season—Lombardi's first—the Packers finished 7–5. There was no long-term building plan. Two seasons into his tenure, Green Bay was already playing for the title. In his third season, the Packers won it all.

"He set standards to create a winner," said Packers tackle Norm Masters, "and he knew what the end result would be. From day one, you knew from how he presented himself that he had a strong grasp. And as we started to win, we all became believers."

The Packers executed on both sides of the ball, with stars on both offense and defense. In 1962, Green Bay scored 415 points and allowed just 148. Many years later, Starr singled out that team as the finest among all of the Packer champions.

That probably was the best year we had during the glory years. Everything just kind of aligned right that season. We avoided injuries that season. It was our fourth year with Vince, so we all knew what he wanted. And a lot of our core guys were in their prime. It was an incredible season.

Starr threw to Max McGee, Boyd Dowler, and Ron Kramer. Jim Taylor (who set the franchise single-season rushing record of 1,474 yards; a record that lasted for forty-one years) and Paul Hornung ran. Hornung kicked. Forrest Gregg, Ringo, and Jerry Kramer blocked. Ray Nitschke organized the tacklers—and the Packers forced 59 turnovers that year.

"That was a great football team," Willie Wood said. "Probably the best of any we had there."

After two straight championships and three straight championship game appearances, the Packers thought of themselves as invincible, too. If the Packers had assumed an attitude tinged by a bit of arrogance, then, well, they had come by it honestly.

Nitschke, the 6' 3" 235-pound middle linebacker who was the heart and soul of the Packer defense, was a seven-time selection as either first- or second-team All-Pro. He embraced the image of being a mean player, but he also stressed that the only way to play and succeed in the NFL was to be supremely confident. "I've always thought I was the best middle linebacker in professional football . . . if the time comes when you don't believe you're the best, you'd better find another way to make a living."

Each September brought a fresh start, but the Packers looked in no way diminished, despite losing Hornung. They were the closest thing to perfection. I mean, how could you beat them? And that was the other thing; this was not like the NCAA basketball tournament, where you prepared to beat the Packers once, won the game and went on, or lost it and went home. Beating the Packers meant beating them over the long run; beating them out for the division crown. Beating the Packers meant playing better than the Packers from September to December, so that you were the last team standing in the West and were the one that advanced to the championship game.

As intimidating as the Packers' record was, as dominating as they were in '62, and as overpowering as they looked gazing back at their three most recent seasons headed into '63, the Bears were not short on confidence either. Halas growled his message across training camp every day, but the Bears were also a talented bunch. As a group, many of them had worn the Chicago colors for several years.

Among those who suited up for the '63 Bears, tight end Mike Ditka, lineman Stan Jones, defensive end Doug Atkins, linebacker Bill George, and coach Halas were elected to the Hall of Fame. The Bears also had good, reliable talent at all other positions, even if they were not as explosive on offense. Their defense was scary good, and the trio of linebackers—Bill George, Joe Fortunato, and Larry Morris—constituted about as good an all-around unit as there was in the sport.

There was also another thing, an intangible that was possessed by the '63 Bears: They knew they were good. They knew they had been good, but many of them were aging, and if retirement encroached with any kind of extra speed they would move onto civilian life without a championship on their resume. Some of the best of the Bears—several on that impressive defensive unit—had been together for years. They had been around so long that they had played in the '56 championship game, the last time Chicago went that far, though they lost to the Giants, 47–7.

Halas had been attached at the hip to the NFL since the league was founded in the early twenties and was at the helm when the Bears had won their seven championships (1921, 1932, 1933 1940, 1941, 1943, and 1946). It had been seventeen years since the Bears had last won a title on his watch. That was a long time, and the clock was ticking for Halas, who was sixty-eight and had an aging squad.

"We had a veteran team," said Roosevelt Taylor, who at the time was only two years into his pro career. "A lot of those guys had been together for like nine years. We had a handful of guys who suffered through losses. It was definitely time."

Players think differently than fans talk. Just about anything will pop out of the mouth of a fan; from a disparaging comment spoken in frustration that evaporates a minute later to praise for a player who made a great play immediately anointing him a star of the future.

The players live and practice with one another: they spend hours a day dissecting an opponent's strengths and weaknesses. To most of the known football world it appeared to be a hopeless assignment for any football team with designs of dethroning the Packers. Still, for the Bears, it was not just Papa Bear's relentlessly pounding the idea of greatness into them, but a feeling welling up inside of themselves. They could not control what the Packers did during the '63 season—or at least not more than twice a year—but looking around at the material on the roster, the Bears sensed their own potential.

"I thought in training camp in '63 that we had the capability of being a championship team," said quarterback Bill Wade.

The season started on September 15, with the opener against the Packers in Green Bay. The Bears would find out soon enough whether they were dreamers or realists.

5

BEARS–PACKERS I

FIRST GAME OF the season.

Right there, staring the Bears in the face, were the Packers. No wonder George Halas blabbed more than ever about beating the team he loved to hate.

Mathematically and logically it was difficult to claim that the entire season rode on a September game when both teams' records were 0–0, but Halas knew that for the season of '63 to turn out differently from the previous two Chicago had to make an immediate statement. In his mind, the September 15, 1963, NFL opener in Green Bay took on the stature of a 60-minute goal-line stand.

This was the one game that Halas wanted to jut his big, square jaw right in Vince Lombardi's face, and leave it there for four quarters; at least metaphorically. During that era the schedule-makers frequently sent the Bears to Green Bay to open the season. They did so from 1957–60, but hadn't done so for the two preceding years.

"We always opened in Green Bay," is the way Bears center Mike Pyle remembered it. "Halas always stressed its importance in the last two or three weeks of training camp. 'You win this game, you got a chance to win it all.'"

Training camp at St. Joseph's was a little bit like being sentenced to a minimum security prison with Halas as the warden: your time monitored through all waking hours, your bed-time set, and practically nothing to do for free time. After two months of hanging out in Rensselaer, Indiana, Green Bay seemed like a major metropolis to the Bears players. One player who perpetuated the image of St. Joseph's as "a penitentiary" was lineman Stan Jones. Jones said he hated the place, and that at times when he was with the Bears Halas actually had the door to the dormitory chained shut. The boss also had hired a security guard to patrol the grounds, and his job was most assuredly to squeal on player movements rather than keeping intruders out. The players evidently nicknamed the guy Dick Tracy.

When training camp opened Halas announced to his assembled candidates that only tight end Mike Ditka and quarterback Billy Wade were assured of starting jobs. Clearly, this was a ploy to motivate the Bears to work hard and sweat a lot under the July sun, but it was fairly transparent, too, because nobody was going to beat out linebackers Bill George and Joe Fortunato, or for that matter defensive end Doug Atkins. Halas was playing a kind of psych game. He opened camp with the following speech:

A new, impersonal era is at hand. A veteran has to earn his job. No special consideration will be given for his past accomplishments. Pampering is out. There will be no pussy-foot playing, no more pussy-foot coaching, no more pussy-foot conduct. I've simply decided I've been at this business too long to play the role of nice guy anymore.

Bears players who had been around for a while likely swallowed their bubble-gum when they heard that soliloquy; initially because it sounded so funny and secondly because they probably blinked and thought, *Did he just refer to himself as a nice guy?*

The opening game was always important; but an opener against the Packers ratcheted up the importance. But this time, in '63, the way Halas was thinking, it could be one of the most significant games of the season.

"Any game against Green Bay was big," said Bears fullback Rick Casares. "When you arrived to play with the Bears as a rookie, you were immediately preparing to play the Packers."

Casares was a burly back who grew up in Tampa, Florida, and attended the University of Florida. He stood 6' 2", weighed 225 pounds, and he was the Bears' second-round draft pick in 1954. Given that scouting was not as sophisticated then as it is now, it's not known for sure that the Bears were aware of Casares' teen-aged success as a Golden Gloves boxer. But whether they knew that or not, he had toughness written all over him.

Casares made his debut for Chicago in 1955. The after-college gap was due to him being in the Army, which was the only outfit Casares ever thought he would be drafted by. But he gave credit to playing football in the service for toughening him up for the pros.

It didn't take long for Casares to convince the Bears that they'd made the right choice. On his first play as a rookie in the back-field against the Baltimore Colts, Casares took a handoff and ran

81 yards for a touchdown. Casares believes that single play gave him more status in Halas' eyes and helped make his career.

By '63, Casares was two-thirds of the way through his NFL career, so he was familiar with Halas' rails about the Packers. "That was Halas, strictly Halas" is how Casares recalls the source of the pumping up of the team to play Green Bay.

Yes, the fans talked about the Green Bay games, and certainly so did the assistant coaches. But Halas was the one who instigated the discussions, the pep talks, and not just when the Packers loomed ahead on the schedule. It was as if there was always a low burning ember inside him aware of the Packers, and he would periodically throw lighter fluid on it to get it to flare up.

"It was the strongest rival we had, that was the Packers," Casares said, "but he absolutely kept thinking about them."

As an all-around football figure Halas' nature included characteristics of a player, coach, and team owner. To the Bears of the 1960s Halas the player no longer existed. They now dealt with Halas, the general manager who negotiated their contracts and annoyed them in those sessions, off the field. But mostly they dealt with him day-to-day on the field as a coach. Halas was gruff and demanding, and his people skills were lacking when it came to doling out pats on the back and making a guy feel good for contributing. The one thing his players never questioned about Halas was his desire to win.

"He was competitive," Casares said. "He was fiercely competitive, even in practice. Forever in my mind is the picture of him running up and down the sidelines yelling at the refs. They tried to restrain him. I always liked that about him. He wasn't the easiest guy to get along with, but he instilled a fieriness in you."

It was in the 1940s when the Bears were collecting championships—before, during, and after World War II—that they were first nicknamed "The Monsters of the Midway." It was a description that related to the defense. In the early 1960s the Bears believed they also had a superb defense that could contain any opponent.

The defense did good work in '56 when the Bears had reached the championship game. In '57, their defense again outshined their offense. In '59, their defense allowed just 196 points all season. Then things got shaky. It wasn't clear if the D, with many of the same players, was getting too old and slow, or if assistant Coach Clark Shaughnessy was the one slowing down.

By 1962 Shaughnessy was turning seventy. His No. 1 claim to fame as a coach was his brilliance in implementing the "T" formation, an offense that was deemed unstoppable for the teams that adopted it. In 1951, Halas made Shaughnessy an irresistible offer. He hired him for a combination of duties and bestowed multiple titles upon him; from technical advisor to vice president of the franchise to defensive coordinator. The T formation had been good to Halas, as his championship teams employed it with gusto in the 1940s. But in the 1950s, he gave Shaughnessy the assignment of coming up with the defensive antidote to his poisonous offensive weaponry. It was as if Shaughnessy was a mad scientist turned loose in a lab, almost being told to undo his life's work.

Once unleashed, no one had been able to come up with a counter effect to a nuclear bomb, either. Shaughnessy was only so successful. In 1962, impressed by the agile mind and energetic work habits of another assistant on his staff, Halas promoted George Allen to defensive coordinator. Shaughnessy was on his way to the College Football Hall of Fame, Halas to the Pro Football Hall of Fame, and eventually, Allen would join him there.

Allen was probably the original sleep-in-his-office coach. He inhaled the game and was always tinkering; imagining new schemes and itchy to implement them. For the Bears' veteran defense it was like walking into a hailstorm. They were bombarded by so many new ideas that they didn't know which way to turn. Yet Allen took the same personnel and molded it into the most terrifying defensive unit in the league.

That was the season that Stan Jones, who had been an all-star guard for a decade, was giving a lot of thought to retirement. Jones had attended the University of Maryland, and was a fifth-round draft pick in the 1953 draft. He stood 6' 1" and weighed 250 pounds. That would be puny for an interior lineman today, but was ample enough in the 1950s. Jones became a seven-time Pro Bowl pick, but like most players—even the stars of his era—he didn't make enough money from pro football to relax during the off-season. Throughout most of his career he was a school teacher in the non-football months and as his playing days were winding down he thought about making that his full-time career.

In 1962 the Bears were a bit shorthanded on the defensive line, and Allen asked Jones to try playing defensive tackle as well as guard. In other words, play both ways. Rather than shy away from making the change as an established star on borrowed time, Jones was intrigued by the challenge. By 1963 he was committed to playing defense full-time and found it refreshing. Jones' first scheduled start as a defensive player was the season opener at Green Bay.

On the eve of the season opener a prominent Chicago sports columnist, Bill Gleason, wrote a story suggesting the defense looked pretty good, except for two question-marks: Jones, the defensive tackle, and Bob Kilcullen, the defensive end. The two big guys were eating breakfast in a Green Bay restaurant called The Spot, and it just so happened that Gleason was there too. Jones said he wasn't particularly bothered by the story, but Kilcullen yelled across the restaurant to Gleason that they were going to show up for the game regardless of what the writer thought.

While he was coaching Halas conducted a weekly press conference for the Chicago sportswriters who covered the team. At his regular session leading up to the Green Bay game, he said, "The Packers are stronger than last year, except for the loss of Paul Hornung's kicking. We're playing the champions and we know it. What else needs to be said?"

During his own pregame session, Packers coach Vince Lombardi did nothing to antagonize the Bears either, dropping compliments like rose petals in their path. "They are a much better football team," Lombardi said. "Their whole system is much simpler than it was a year ago. Consciously, or unconsciously, we've been looking forward to the Bears for two weeks."

Halas had made his thinking as clear as possible to his men in Rensselaer. "The one thing explained to us by Halas from the beginning," said running back Ronnie Bull, "was that for us to win the championship, we had to beat Green Bay twice. We were working on Green Bay from the beginning. That was our goal."

Consciously, Halas had been looking forward to playing this game against the Packers since almost the end of the previous season. He was ready to rumble. But it wasn't as if the defending champion Packers weren't going to be prepared for the Bears. Not only was it their season opener as well, but the rivalry definitely was a two-way street.

Quarterback Bart Starr was an unheralded 17th-round pick out of Alabama in 1956, mainly because he'd hardly played his senior year because of injury. He endured the lousy Green Bay stretch of the late 1950s, before Lombardi showed up and had time for the Bears–Packers rivalry to ooze into his bloodstream. "Huge," Starr said.

So the feeling was always there, but when the Packers improved the importance of those games increased exponentially. "The Bears fit in very strongly to the whole thing," Starr said. "You recognize how important it is. They're playing in your division and you're going to play them twice a year."

The weather on September 15 at City Stadium was mild. The game-time temperature was 54 degrees and the wind was gauged at just 7 mph. This was going to be a test for the new-look Bears defense under Allen.

"We wanted to lose the coin flip and let the defense set the tone for us," said Bull.

This day was also going to be a test for the Packers' new-look offense without Hornung, who had been suspended for the season for gambling by Commissioner Rozelle.

Replacing Hornung in the starting lineup was halfback Tom Moore. Moore had been with the club since 1960, when he was the No. 1 draft pick out of Vanderbilt, so he wasn't going to have any rookie jitters. In fact, Hornung had been injured for a chunk of the previous season, and Moore had been selected for his only Pro Bowl appearance that year after filling in. He was the secondary choice to tote the ball behind fullback Jim Taylor.

It didn't really matter much who was running or throwing the ball this day. The stars of the game on both sides were the defensive squads. "We stayed with the game plan and everything went our way," said Bull.

The game was low scoring and yardage was harder to come by than a six-pack of beer on a blue-law Sunday. It was as if the offenses were operating in quicksand.

Total Packers running yards: 77
Total Packers passing yards: 83
Total Bears running yards: 107
Total Bears passing yards: 129

Final score: Bears 10, Packers 3

It was a slugfest of a game, and the result was very satisfying for George Halas.

Chicago scored first in the first quarter on a 32-yard field goal by Bob Jencks. Before the first quarter was over, Green Bay had tied it on a 41-yard field goal by Jerry Kramer . . . and that was all of the scoring for the first half. As time ran out in the half, there began some murmuring among the crowd of 42,237 fans.

Only they didn't. Chicago notched the only scoring drive of the third quarter when fullback Joe Marconi scored a touchdown on a one-yard run with Jencks kicking the extra point. That made the score 10–3, which led to a scoreless fourth quarter. Jim Taylor was held to only 53 yards rushing and future Hall of Fame quarterback Bart Starr threw for four interceptions. On the other end of the field Bears quarterback Bill Wade called a masterful game, completing 18 of his 24 passes.

The Bears had not beaten the Packers since the opening game of the 1960 season, and had been outscored 87–7 in their two losses against them the year before. The triumph was a hard-nosed one, but by any measure for the Bears it was most assuredly progress.

"They beat us," said Green Bay center Jim Ringo.

In every way. It broke the Packers' 13-game home winning streak, which started after losing to the Lions to start the 1961 season. Quite simply the Bears' defense overwhelmed the Packers' offense, which was not something that could be said very often under the Lombardi regime.

"We had nothing going," Lombardi said. "We were lucky to get away 10–3."

The Bears had possession of the ball as the clock ran out, and Halas ordered Wade to fall on it for the last play. Wade followed orders, but wasn't keen on doing it again in similar circumstances. After the hike, as the final seconds ticked off, half the Green Bay defense jumped onto the prone Wade trying to get him to drop the ball.

"Coach, don't ever ask me to do that again," Wade informed Halas afterwards as he wiped blood from a fresh cut over his right eye collected in the pileup. "From now on when we want to kill time, I'm gonna sneak that ball right into the line. At least that way I can protect myself."

Years later, in retirement following an 11-season pro playing career and another 27 years as an assistant coach in the NFL,

Stan Jones picked the Bears' victory over Green Bay that day as the most memorable game of his career.

"It was a big game because Green Bay was the world champion and it was the opening game."

Jones laughed because it was as if the Packers had read that critical Chicago newspaper column and incorporated it into their game plan. From the first possession Green Bay sent Taylor at Jones and Kilcullen on the left side, counting on Forrest Gregg and Kramer to open holes. Only there were no holes. Jones and Kilcullen were stone walls that could not be penetrated.

"They came after us pretty good," Jones said. "We didn't have to go chasing around looking for them because they came right at us."

Beating the Packers meant something. It was too early in the season to know if the victory was going to make a big difference in the final standings or not, but just in the moment it was tremendous as a self-contained win. Throughout the 1950s the Packers had been one of the weakest teams in the league and Jones got used to beating them. Then Lombardi showed up and changed the dynamic of the rivalry overnight.

"When Lombardi came in," Jones said, "they had a good team. You wanted to beat the best and of course they were the best. We didn't allow them to score a touchdown. It was a great moment. I want to tell you the satisfaction of that. We were on the train going back to Chicago and we kind of celebrated a little bit."

A day later, Jones said, Gleason wrote a poem about how he and Kilcullen played, in essence a mea culpa—a confession— that the left side of the Bears' defensive line might just be okay. Although it wasn't exactly the level of literary fame that accrued from another Chicago newspaper poem about guys named

Tinkers, Evers, and Chance, Jones could still chuckle about that nod decades later. "It was very satisfying."

Again, it was too soon to tell whether the performance was a one-time thing or just foreshadowing, but no other team's defense had humiliated the Packers that thoroughly in years. Was it an omen? Call it a definite maybe.

In the locker room after the victory, Halas practically vibrated from excitement and pleasure. "Gentlemen," he said, "this is the greatest team effort in the history of the Chicago Bears."

At first mention that sounds like hyperbole, off-the-cuff comparing a regular-season opener to so many games over so many years of play. Yet the fact was that Halas (except for his World War II service) had been present for every one of those games.

In the privacy of their locker room, the Bears voted to give a game ball to Halas. Jones lobbied for another game ball to be given to linebacker Joe Fortunato, who was in his first season as team captain and getting better every year he played.

"That was a great defensive game," Fortunato said. "We just knocked the crap out of them."

As telling as the first win was, an entire season stretched out ahead of the Bears, and Fortunato knew that a couple of months down the road, the Packers would be waiting for them again. He also understood that a second win over Green Bay might be as imperative as the first one.

6

A PRO FOOTBALL HALL OF FAME

GEORGE HALAS WAS a single-minded man. If the matter related to pro football it was on the front burner. If the issue had nothing to do with pro football, and especially if it occurred during the football season, it could wait.

The arrival of September on the calendar always meant the start of football season. That's the way it had been for Halas' whole life. Only in September of 1963 there was an interruption as Halas drilled his team in preparation for its upcoming war with Green Bay.

Someone called a time out, but Halas didn't mind so much this one time. A week before the regular season kicked off Halas was summoned to Canton, Ohio, the city where the NFL was born. Just about everyone else who had been gathered in the Hupmobile showroom in Canton more than forty years earlier for the founding of the league had since passed on. Halas, present at the conception in 1920, was not only still above ground, but was still coaching and running his team.

On September 7, 1963, the doors to the new showcase of professional football swung open with a special ceremony, inducting the first 17 members of the Pro Football Hall of Fame; what had long been acknowledged in conversation was formalized in public. George Stanley Halas, born in 1895, became one of the charter members of the inaugural Hall of Fame class.

While some of those years still stretched ahead, Halas was the only person who was involved with the NFL over its first fifty years of existence. He was a founder, player, coach, owner, and an ambassador for the game, with the best interests of the league and sport always first in his thoughts; Halas' touch could be seen in the comings and goings of franchises, rule changes, implementation of policies, and selection of commissioners.

Halas was the godfather of the NFL. He out-lived his fellow founders, out-worked his fellow coaches, out-lasted numerous franchises, and eventually won 324 games and eight championships. When Halas spoke at league meetings everyone listened. He had been there, done that, seen it all, and sometimes even saw the future.

He had been in the room when Jim Thorpe was named as the first commissioner. He was pals with the late commissioner, Bert Bell. He even helped broker the backroom compromise that made Pete Rozelle commissioner.

"We all respected Halas because he ran the NFL," said Bears defensive back Roosevelt Taylor. "He was tough. Whatever he said was the law."

There was an about-time feel to the creation of the Pro Football Hall of Fame, as the National Baseball Hall of Fame had opened its doors in 1939. If baseball was known as the National Pastime and ranked as the most popular team sport in the country, by

1963 the gains of pro football in society and among sports fans certainly demanded the opening of the sport's own Hall of Fame.

Baseball's Hall of Fame was situated in the tiny town of Cooperstown in upstate New York, based on the fanciful myth that a Civil War–era general named Abner Doubleday invented the game while romping through the farm fields of the community during a period when he was stationed there. Later, just about all aspects of the origin story attached to Doubleday were debunked, but the baseball hall wasn't moving.

Riding its fresh wave of popularity stemming from the 1958 Colts–Giants sudden-death championship game, nicknamed "The Greatest Game Ever Played," and growing interest from networks willing to throw money at the NFL for permission to televise their games, the timing for a Pro Football Hall of Fame seemed ripe. There was interest from a variety of communities when deciding on a location, but Canton had made the best case. It had actual, well-documented tradition on its side (unlike baseball), a solid history in the sport, and the desire to make the city football's true home.

An article in the *Canton Repository* first advanced the idea in print that there should be a pro football hall of fame, and that it should be in Canton. The December 6, 1959, article was headlined, "Pro Football Needs a Hall of Fame and the Logical Site is Here."

The community rallied. Members of the Chamber of Commerce and the Jaycees formed a supervisory committee to shepherd the plan into fruition. The Canton City Council and the local board of park commissioners worked together to make 14 acres of land available for the hall. The location was right next door to the venerable Fawcett Stadium, where football was and continued to be played. Local businesses spearheaded a fund-raising operation.

The Canton Bulldogs, one of the league's original franchises, had gotten away (folding in 1927), but the Canton fathers didn't want to lose their football connection. Before a decision was made to build a hall and where to put it, Pete Rozelle, on the job as commissioner for only a short while, spoke out in favor of Canton. Representatives of the city made a sales pitch to Rozelle at a meeting in Philadelphia, and he walked out of it sufficiently impressed to throw an endorsement their way. "I think Canton is the logical site. The owners of the teams in our league are definitely interested in a hall of fame. We discussed it at our league meeting last winter. I'll be glad to do all I can in lending you a helping hand."

Even during those very early discussions the idea of holding an annual exhibition game at the site of the hall of fame was definitely part of the plan. Detroit, Michigan, and Latrobe, Pennsylvania, were two other communities seeking a stamp of recommendation to host the hall. In fact, Latrobe's historical tie-in to pro football was older than Canton's. Research showed that the first pro football game was played in that town on September 3, 1895, between the Latrobe Athletic Association and the Jeannette Athletic Club.

However, despite some additional competition from Los Angeles, California, and Green Bay, Wisconsin, the owners made the decision to support Canton at a meeting on April 27, 1961. Canton had the best proposal, and as soon as the approval was set in concrete it seemed like the building was as well. People in Canton and surrounding Stark County raised $378,000 for construction in three months, though each NFL team donated $1,000 apiece. On August 11, 1962, ground was broken for the building. When the grand opening was scheduled, sure enough, an exhibition game was played as part of the festivities. The subtitle to the opening was "Football's Greatest Weekend," and the nickname has stuck over the decades.

The distinctive dome still serves as the roof, and while the original building has been expanded and modernized several times, when the Hall first opened, it featured only two rooms.

At least one sportswriter of the period compared Canton's gung-ho approach to the failure of interested parties to establish and build a college football hall of fame, which had been talked about for years. That well-known syndicated columnist, Harry Grayson, marveled at Canton's work ethic, saying, "The colleges have been dilly-dallying for fourteen years." A College Football Hall of Fame was founded in 1951, after two years of discussion, but still did not have a building at the time.

In the months leading up to the announcement of those selected for the first class of inductees, the excitement grew. In 1962, *Peterson's Pro Football Magazine* conducted its own narrow poll, asking a mixed group of sportswriters, former players, and coaches for a straw vote. They were asked to consider "What individual, whether player, coach, owner, official, or administrator has contributed most to the growth, stability, popularity, and general public acceptance of professional football since it first took on a semblance of organization forty years ago?"

The late commissioner Bert Bell and Halas were the top vote-getters, followed by Red Grange, Don Hutson, Jim Thorpe, Sammy Baugh, Frankie Albert, Paul Brown, Joe F. Carr, Dutch Clark, Bill Dudley, Otto Graham, and Ernie Nevers. That made for 13 individuals receiving support.

When the charter class was announced for induction the list featured 17 names and it was not an identical poll, plus four.

The Inaugural 17:

Sammy Baugh	Don Hutson
Bert Bell	Curly Lambeau
Joe Carr	Tim Mara
Dutch Clark	George Marshall
Red Grange	Johnny "Blood" McNally
George Halas	Bronko Nagurski
Mel Hein	Ernie Nevers
Pete Henry	Jim Thorpe
Cal Hubbard	

The four on the prospects list not elected were Frankie Albert, Paul Brown, Bill Dudley, and Otto Graham. Graham would get inducted in '65, Dudley in '66, and Brown in '67. Albert was never elected to the Pro Football Hall of Fame, but is a member of the College Football Hall of Fame.

When the first induction ceremony was held, it was a grand weekend. And for a change, Rozelle could be out in public to speak at a non-game function that represented good news. The gloomy spring of the gambling scandal and the death of Big Daddy Lipscomb were for once overshadowed by a feel-good event. A lengthy parade attracted about 45,000 people along the route, and an enthusiastic writer for the *Canton Repository* said it was "one of the most impressive and inspiring" of occasions for the city "since the days President William McKinley brought attention to Canton."

McKinley, whose father operated a foundry in the city, was assassinated in 1901 and is buried in Canton.

"It's beyond all expectations," Rozelle gushed. "Canton [which had a population of approximately 120,000 at the time] certainly could show the much larger cities how to conduct such a project. I am particularly impressed, considering that this is only the beginning and all this was accomplished in one year."

Rozelle was not just saying such things to make his hosts happy either. Rozelle spoke to the league's public relations director and ordered him to send the same message to every NFL owner. "Extremely impressed with Hall of Fame. . . . I urge all general managers and club owners to watch Sunday's Hall of Fame game on TV. Taped highlights of HOF building and dedication ceremonies will be shown during halftime."

At the time of the ceremony, five of the inductees had already passed away. That included the football figure of keenest interest to the local population, Jim Thorpe. Thorpe, who was born in 1888, died in 1953 at the age of sixty-four. Thorpe grew up as part of the Sac and Fox Indian nation in Oklahoma, and had been acclaimed as the world's greatest athlete. He won a gold medal in the Olympic decathlon in 1912, played both Major League baseball and professional football, and was the first commissioner of the National Football League, chosen for his name recognition.

Some of Thorpe's greatest efforts on the gridiron were recorded for the Canton Bulldogs. Thorpe was represented at the induction ceremony by a friend, Pete Calac, who told the gathering, "I know that Jim has that famous, big grin on his face today up there in the Happy Hunting Grounds."

When Halas was young and still playing defensive end for the Bears, he had his share of encounters with Thorpe on the field. Halas told enough stories to make it clear that Thorpe was the superior player of far greater speed. In his autobiography, Halas recounted a game when he was with the Hammond Pros in 1919, before the NFL was founded. They went up against Thorpe's Canton Bulldogs and on one play Halas caught a pass.

Thorpe knocked me to my knees. Today the referee would whistle the ball dead, but in those days a carrier could keep on crawling. There I was, on hands and knees, scrambling along like a crab, trying to get an extra yard or two. Jim threw a leg over me and sat down on me. 'All right, if you are a horse, I'll ride you,' he said. After the game I thanked him. He could have thrown both his knees into my ribs, practically ruining me.

As Halas remembered how close his career was to ending by way of Thorpe, the greatest single play made in his career involved Thorpe as well. In November of 1923, the Bears were facing the Oorang Indians at Wrigley Field. With the rain pelting down and the field covered in mud, the Indians drove down to Chicago's two-yard-line. Going for the touchdown, the Indians handed off to Thorpe, who was hit at the line of scrimmage and fumbled. The ball popped into the air and into Halas' arms, and he recalled what happened next.

We slipped and slid. I sidestepped and took off. I heard an angry roar. It was Thorpe, coming after me. I ran faster and faster, but I sensed he was gaining. I could hear the squishing of his shoes in the mud. When I could almost feel his breath I dug in a cleat and did a sharp zig. Thorpe's momentum carried him on and gave me a few feet of running room. He narrowed the gap. I zagged. Again he lost a stride. He turned and came on. I zigged. I zagged. Zig. Zag. Just short of the goal Thorpe threw himself at me and down I went, into a pool of water. But at the same time I slid over the goal.

Halas described the scene with the drama of a Hollywood car chase. He knew that in a flat-out race, he couldn't beat Thorpe on sheer speed, but he was just elusive enough to pull off the feat. It was a record-setting 98-yard touchdown return with a recovered fumble. The record lasted for forty-nine years.

It was not as if Halas did not appreciate the recognition of being named as part of the first Hall of Fame class, but the ceremony had come at a bad time. It would have been fun to arrive early and schmooze with the old-timers that included Nagurski, one of his best players, but Halas was still coaching. His mind was focused much more intently on the future—the season about to unfold—than the past. Even more inconvenient, his Bears had an exhibition game that night in New Orleans against the Baltimore Colts.

Halas did show up for his induction, but only barely. One comment Halas made in '63 that may have summarized up the entire year and not just being inducted into the new Hall was, "If you live long enough, lots of nice things happen."

The Bears founder certainly spent more time in Canton when the NFL was being created than he did on his induction day. Traveling with fellow inductee Red Grange, who was currently the Bears' radio broadcaster, the duo flew into Canton, which is about 50 miles south of Cleveland, on Saturday morning. Halas did deliver an acceptance speech that in Hall of Fame archives runs barely more than a typed half page single-spaced.

Even though his speech was short, Halas did bring a nice touch with his words. After the usual thank-you amenities, he told a story to the crowd, repeating what he had said to some of his grandchildren a few weeks earlier when chatting about this upcoming weekend.

Somehow the conversation got around to an earlier trip that I made to Canton some forty-three years ago when we met in Ralph Hay's showroom—automobile showroom—and founded the National Football League. I told them some of the informal aspects of that meeting and among them being that there was a lack of chairs and also that we had to sit on the running board of the car. That prompted my nine-year-old grandson to say, 'What is a running board, Grandpa?' I [was pondering] the problem of answering that difficult question when my fourteen-year-old grandson said, 'Running boards are those things that you see on those funny, old cars in that television series known as The Untouchables.' That little incident demonstrated to me how things can change or disappear until a chance remark or a question—a child's question—stirs your memory.

There was no question that Halas had many memories of the NFL's beginnings and the years since. Halas was gracious enough to praise some of the men who were sitting in that showroom with him, but who did not operate teams that lasted in the league.

On my trip down here, my memory was stirred back quite a few years when I think of the wonderful men who did so much to develop football in this area and throughout the country. [Joe Carr]of the Columbus Panhandles, who was president of the National Football League from 1921 to 1939, some eighteen years, and you can be sure that some of those years were pretty tough. They were the pioneers and this is the land where football set down its roots and here is the Hall of Fame where its history and traditions will be preserved and remembered.

Halas never touched on his own accomplishments in his speech and neither did he dwell on the Chicago Bears' role in the league's development. In fact, he didn't even mention his franchise until the final sentence of his speech. "Let me say for all the Chicago Bears, right from the original Staleys in 1920, down to 1963, just two heartfelt words, thank you!" It was not the Gettysburg Address in terms of indelible comments, but the occasion would not have been complete if Halas had not been able to attend and if he had not at least uttered a few words at the grand opening.

By 2 p.m. that afternoon, Halas and his traveling partner were back on a private plane flying to New Orleans for a Saturday night exhibition game. The Bears would win 14–7, but that was certainly incidental to the day's proceedings. Nobody was going to remember the result of that preseason game for more than ten minutes. Halas going into the Pro Football Hall of Fame and the building opening its doors had a much more lasting impact.

Although Halas' first trip to the Hall of Fame was a hasty one, in some ways he never left. Not only is there a plaque honoring his contributions to the game, but the address of the Pro Football Hall of Fame is 2121 George Halas Drive Northwest.

7

BEARS ON A ROLL

THE BEARS HAD one in the bank over the Packers after the opener but they still had to keep it up. It wouldn't do at all to have a letdown. Coach George Halas—and his players—recognized that the team's strength was in their defense. No one wins games, though, without moving the ball on offense and scoring points.

Halas was not one of those wide-eyed wild men willing to try anything on offense. He was more on the conservative side; a coach who believed that grinding out the yards meant you were grinding down your foe. Oh, he was not averse to seeing a little speed come out of the backfield, but he wasn't going to go all reckless with his play calling.

Still, Halas liked Willie Galimore as a halfback complement to Rick Casares at fullback. The only problem was that Galimore couldn't stay healthy. In 1962, at the very least as an insurance policy, Halas drafted an All-American back out of Baylor in the first round.

At 6 feet and 200 pounds, Ronnie Bull was solid. He earned all kinds of honors while at Bishop High School, in the Corpus Christi, Texas, area and played in several college All-Star games. During this time period, the NFL and the AFL had been bickering over talent and Bull had also been drafted by the Dallas Texans (before they moved to Kansas City and became the Chiefs). The contract offers from the Texans and Bears were similar, but there was one major difference in Dallas' plan.

"The Texans wanted to play me on defense," said Bull. "I looked at both sides. The money was pretty much the same."

Bull wanted to carry the ball, so he signed with the Bears. His introduction to Chicago fans, however, was a big fizzle. Chosen to participate in the annual Chicago Charities College All-Star Game at Soldier Field, Bull got a case of the flu so bad he ended up in the hospital.

That also meant that when he reported to training camp in Rensselaer, he was even further behind in learning the plays. "So they moved me to defense for the first two games," said Bull. For Bull, this was exactly what he thought he was avoiding by signing with the Bears. But then Galimore hurt his knee at the end of one practice and the coaches tossed Bull the offensive playbook and told him to learn it in a hurry.

"I was determined to make an impression because I didn't want to go back to defense."

The week following the opener in Green Bay, the Bears traveled to Minnesota to face the Vikings. Unlike the Packers game the Bears easily handled the Vikings and cruised to an easy 28–7 victory. Bull scored the game's first touchdown on a 24-yard pass from quarterback Bill Wade and Chicago never trailed. Tight end Mike Ditka also got into the end zone, catching two touchdown passes of 36 and 10 yards from Wade that day.

The bruising Ditka, who was 6' 3" and weighed 230 pounds, was in the process of reinventing the tight end spot—with Halas' cooperation. Growing up in Pennsylvania coal country, Ditka had innate throwback toughness to him; the kind the old-timers had who never wore helmets. When people hear that Ditka was a catcher during his youthful baseball days, they immediately nod their head. I mean, what other position would he have played?

Before Ditka came along those who played tight end were in the game to block, not grab as many balls as a wide receiver. Halas and Ditka were on the cusp of a revolution in the way the position was viewed. As a rookie in '61, Ditka caught 56 passes, with 12 of them going for touchdowns. While he caught 58 passes the next year with only 5 touchdowns, by the time the '63 season rolled around it was well-established what kind of target he could be. And on the sidelines Halas was his loudest cheerleader. "Ditka is going to be one of the greats of this league if he isn't there already. What desire and determination that young man has. Ditka is one of the finest No. 1 draft picks I ever made."

When the bruiser was first getting noticed for the way he plowed through defenders and less than gently knocked them over, Ditka said simply, "I like to play football and I only know one way to do it." Just what way that was got cleared up while talking to a different sportswriter. "I like contact," Ditka said. "I like to hit. And I don't mind getting hit myself. You can get hit and knocked down and go back and hit the other guy harder."

The third game of the season was a bit of an aberration for the Bears. They won 37–21 over the Detroit Lions—also on the road—but that was more points than they were used to scoring or allowing. What was becoming apparent was the significance of Billy Wade's play-calling, throwing, and hard-nosed quarterback sneaks when needed. In today's game, NFL teams are built from the quarterback position outward. Franchise quarterbacks are the hottest commodity in the game. While preferable to have such a stud to call upon, the mindset of the early sixties was not as focused on the passing game as it would become in later years.

For the Bears, over a period of more than a decade the hunt for the perfect quarterback to lead their team had been a frustrating and complex one. Sid Luckman—who was like a son to Halas—was one of the greatest quarterbacks of all time; leading the Bears through their glory years of the 1940s. Luckman retired in 1950 and was replaced by Notre Dame's Johnny Lujack.

Lujack became the man of the hour, stepping into the role seamlessly. There was only one problem—he despised Halas and they were unable to work together. In a shocking move, Lujack walked away from the sport after the '51 season. After that, Halas' seemingly reliable nose for talent failed him. He traded for and drafted a tremendously fine group of quarterbacks, and then mistakenly discarded them one by one for different reasons when any one of them could have helped.

At last, enter Billy Wade from the Los Angeles Rams where he led the league in passing percentage (1959) and yards gained (1958). Wade was from Nashville, Tennessee, where he stayed for college to play for Vanderbilt. He was 6' 2" and 200 pounds, very solid physically, and after breaking in with the Rams in 1954 after two years in the Navy, was picked up by the Bears in 1961 at the age of thirty-one.

Bears assistant coach George Allen, who had worked as an assistant with the Rams in '57, was responsible for obtaining Wade. He lobbied Halas to make a quarterback swap of Zeke

Bratkowski for Wade, and it paid off. The trade was actually between three teams, as the Rams sent Wade to the Bears for defensive back Erich Barnes and the Giants sent Linden Crow and a No. 1 draft pick to the Rams for Barnes, John Guzik, and a No. 5 draft pick.

Wade threw for 22 touchdowns with Chicago in '61, and was even better in '62, completing a league-leading 225 passes for 3,172 yards. Today's game has given fans the 5,000-yard passing season with some regularity, but in the early 1960s throwing for 3,000 yards meant you were a star, and Wade was named an All-Pro in '62.

Halas wasn't the only one in Chicago who kept waiting for Sid Luckman to be reincarnated. Wade found that out the moment he felt the first breeze off Lake Michigan in the Windy City and it carried some boos on the clouds.

> I'm not another Luckman. I'm not and never will be, so the fans can forget it. I'm just me. The No. 1 challenge to anybody playing quarterback in Chicago is the challenge of Luckman. The fans in Wrigley Field keep looking down there on the 50-yard-line and wishing they could see Sid there again.

There was irritation in Wade's voice when he made that proclamation, but just being Billy Wade proved to be satisfactory. He was mature enough to understand the tendencies and bad habits of fans and the ups and downs of a demanding sport. "Football stresses the great lessons of life," said Wade. "It makes a man humble. It unites people. It teaches value and self-discipline."

Quarterbacks make a lot of big decisions on the field, and in the Detroit victory Wade had to do a large amount of decision-making in that game. He ended up throwing touch-down passes to three different teammates; the first to Angelo Coia, the second to flanker Johnny Morris, and the third to Mike Ditka, with all three taking place in the first half. Wade also got into the end zone himself, with a one-yard run before the end of the half, making the score 35–0. With the 219 yards in the air, the Bears added 104 yards rushing for a little balance. It was probably a good way to keep the natural conservatism in Halas content, too. Even with all the comments about Luckman Wade still showed his understanding and knowledge of his teammates, especially when breaking down their strengths and weaknesses.

> *You take your offensive personnel and you try to figure out what a man like Mike Ditka can do best. Then you try and reason what Johnny Morris can do better than anyone else. The same goes for Angie Coia and John Farrington, the other receivers. And for your running backs—Ronnie Bull, Willie Galimore, Rick Casares, and Joe Marconi. I had to laugh when I read that my old rival on the Rams Norm Van Brocklin said the other day that Ditka wasn't very fast.*

Sitting on the bench most of the time in Los Angeles Wade felt his career wasting away. Being traded to the Bears represented a second chance and a chance to prove that there was more in his right arm than anyone was crediting him with. He was a good fit for Chicago and it was a big day in his life when Halas made him the starting quarterback in '62. That endorsement by the coach coming into training camp was also good for the ego and security. In Chicago, Wade didn't have to wonder about being yanked for a single mistake.

Too much time had passed Wade by for him to gather gaudy career stats, but there was one goal sitting right in front of him that seemed quite attainable. "I'll settle for the opportunity to quarterback a championship team," he said. Funny thing, that's exactly what the Bears wanted from Billy Wade.

The one thing that neither the Bears nor Wade could afford was the starting quarterback getting injured. That would disrupt the rhythm of an offense that was better than most opposing teams believed, but was still considered second-string to its own defense. Behind Wade on the depth chart was Rudy Bukich. Like Wade, Bukich had passed through the Rams system, but also made side stops with the Washington Redskins and Pittsburgh Steelers. Although Bukich had some good years for the Bears later in '63 he was virtually an untested, career backup.

But in the fourth game of the season, Chicago was to rely on that second stringer. It was unseasonably warm, in the low 70s, for an early October date with the Baltimore Colts at Wrigley. This was easily a game that might have gotten away. Although the Colts championship years of '58 and '59 were receding in the rearview mirror and coach Weeb Ewbank had been let go (now with the New York Jets), Baltimore had a young coach just starting out that looked as if he might amount to something. Don Shula was the rookie head man and a coach destined decades later to break George Halas' record for wins by an NFL coach.

At the time of the matchup, Shula only had one win on his resume. . . . He did not get his second win that day. The Bears eked out a 10–3 win by scoring 10 points in the fourth quarter and holding the Colts to 45 yards rushing. Jim Martin of Baltimore and Roger LeClerc of Chicago traded field goals, but the

Bears won on a 44-yard Bukich pass to Bull with an extra point thrown in from Bobby Jencks.

Bukich, a product of the University of Southern California, was on his second stint with the Bears. A '58 and '59 member of the squad, Bukich saw almost as little action as a spectator driving past Wrigley Field, throwing only one pass in parts of two seasons. Bukich was then shipped to the Steelers and re-acquired in '62. Chicago fans had no idea what to expect this time, but Bukich wasn't too worried about a steep learning curve. He took one look at the playbook and said, "No trouble at all. These are the same plays they had when I was here the last time."

Inactivity did provide free time for Bukich to continue working towards a doctorate, and he did own a nickname that hinted at some of his football prowess if ever exploited. He was called "The Rifle."

Maybe "The Bazooka" would have been more appropriate. "You won't believe this," Bukich said, "but when I was playing for Southern Cal, I threw a ball 92 yards in practice."

Bukich pulled out the Colts game as a relief pitcher by design, not happenstance. Wade was having an off-day (5–21–50–0–1) and Halas yanked him. Bukich was a change-of-pace replacement, and good things unfolded under his command. The solid performance didn't win Bukich the starting job, but it did win the Bears the game to move them to 4–0.

Besides that single touchdown pass, the Bears' other points came on a 16-yard field goal. Roger LeClerc had been the team's regular kicker since his rookie season in 1960. Field-goal kicking was a less precise art in the early '60s and LeClerc's accuracy percentage was around 50 percent. Early in the season, Halas decided to give rookie Jencks a chance to handle the three-point booting, but the move approved to be disastrous, with Jencks missing 10 tries in a row after hitting that 32-yarder in the first quarter of the opener against the Packers.

That put LeClerc, who was also a 6' 3" 235-pound backup linebacker, back on the front lines and his role would be supremely important later in the year. LeClerc played his college ball at Trinity in Connecticut, and thought he had the chance to play pro at linebacker. Of course he walked into a team that had Bill George, Joe Fortunato, and Larry Morris manning the three linebacker slots, so it was a good thing that he brought his foot along to fill a square-toed shoe. "I had no intention of kicking when I came to the Bears," said Leclerc. "In 1960, I didn't kick at all, outside of messing around during practice. Come to think of it, I might have kicked off once."

The Bears subsequently traded kicker John Aveni and gave the place-kicking job to LeClerc, while also using him as a fill-in at all three linebacker spots, both defensive end positions, and both defensive tackle slots. Although LeClerc's finest moments as a kicker probably came later in his career when he boomed five field goals in a game and hit 18 in a season, many of his kicks during the '63 campaign came at the most important times.

As an offense the Bears were still finding themselves. The defense was set—versatile and tough—but the Bears weren't as explosive at the skill positions as other NFL contenders like the Packers and Giants were.

"We've got a relatively young team and I think when you have a group of young players you improve," said Wade. "We're doing that. Our passing should improve as we go along."

Given the Bears' goals, it probably had to.

8

THE OTHER GUYS

BILLY WADE PROBABLY never would have been the Chicago Bears quarterback in 1963 if not for the stubbornness of George Halas. For some reason, Halas had developed a grudge against George Blanda, a worthwhile free agent signing out of Kentucky in 1949, but a player whom he refused to allow a full chance at the quarterback job for years.

Blanda ran the team in '53 and '54 with adequate results (7–11–1). After that, Halas let Blanda do some kicking, but otherwise kept him on the bench for seasons at a stretch during the '50s. Then in 1959, Halas ran Blanda out of the National Football League altogether.

Since Blanda wasted years on the Chicago bench, it was no surprise that he was bitter. "He was too cheap to even buy me a kicking shoe," Blanda once said.

But the quarterback coached in college by Bear Bryant got his revenge. When the American Football League started in 1960, Blanda became just about the biggest star in the upstart league. And that wasn't all. On and on Blanda played, becoming pro football's all-time leading scorer and setting a record by playing for 26 seasons. By 1981, Blanda was a member of the Pro Football Hall of Fame.

Halas spent years trying to find a star quarterback, yet ran off Johnny Lujack, traded away Bobby Layne, and treated Blanda like dirt. Blanda was well-liked by his teammates, appreciated for his talent, and the other Bears hated the way Halas had treated him.

"Loved him," said Chicago fullback Rick Casares. "We were all angry as hell that Halas let him go. I always said he should have been starting. We would go around saying, 'Poor Blanda. Poor George.' When he went to Houston he made more money in one year than he did in his whole career with Chicago."

That's because Blanda was a star with the Houston Oilers. Blanda was called "an NFL reject," like many of the players the fledgling AFL hired when it first kicked off. But the Oilers won the title after the 1960 season, the 1961 season, and reached the title game in 1962. In 1961, Blanda threw for 3,330 yards and 36 touchdowns and was the league's MVP. He was by no means a has-been, but rather on his way to becoming an all-time great.

But he always remembered the truly humble beginnings as the Oilers franchise took shape before winning the AFL's first two championships.

"My memory is of 102-degree heat, more than 150 football players," he said, "rainy, sticky days, and the job of putting something together from scratch."

The American Football League began play in September of 1960 with eight teams: the Houston Oilers, Boston Patriots, Buffalo Bills, New York Titans, Los Angeles Chargers, Oakland Raiders, Dallas Texans, and Denver Broncos. It was created through the initiative of multi-millionaire Lamar Hunt, based in Texas, and the majority of the owners were very well-heeled and able to absorb the large financial losses likely to be incurred. They were money men who had been shut out of the National Football League when they went shopping for expansion teams. NFL commissioner Pete Rozelle and coach Halas—who chaired the expansion committee—rebuffed the gentlemen who comprised what they later termed "The Foolish Club." Only after determining the seriousness of Hunt and the other millionaires did the NFL scramble to create new expansion teams.

The general belief was that sooner or later, the AFL owners would get tired of losing money and go away only that didn't happen. Hunt's timing was perfect. At the same time the television networks turned to the NFL for pleasing, time-filling programming, the nation's hunger for more football seemed voracious enough to embrace the AFL, too, and TV millions came the AFL's way.

A quick impression of the style of play offered by the AFL was that the new guys on the block played more of an air-it-out passing game, that the teams did not have the depth of their NFL counterparts, and they didn't play as tenacious a defense. The AFL had trouble competing in Los Angeles against the NFL's Rams and in New York against the NFL's Giants. The Dallas Texans couldn't overcome the Dallas Cowboys' NFL backing, even though the two teams got going at the same time. By 1963, the Chargers were in San Diego, the Texans were in Kansas City, and the Titans had become the Jets, bought out of bankruptcy for $1 million by Sonny Werblin.

Werblin made his money in the music and entertainment businesses and understood the significance of star power. A few years later he would pay Joe Namath an unheard-of $400,000 to play quarterback, and transformed the young man from Pennsylvania's coal mining country via the University of Alabama into "Broadway Joe."

Talent was where the battle lines were drawn in the war between the NFL and the AFL: acquiring talent, developing talent, and showcasing talent. In today's game, the annual pro football draft of college players takes place in April. In the early '60s, with the leagues fiercely battling to sign All-Americans and players with prominent names, both leagues kept moving their drafts earlier and earlier—as far back as the December immediately after a season concluded.

In 1963, one of the stars of the American Football League was San Diego Charger running back Keith Lincoln. Lincoln played for Washington State and was taken in the second round by the Chargers in '61 and in the fifth round by the Bears. Halas called Lincoln on the phone, but Lincoln said the Bear boss' approach turned him off. "He was saying, 'Why do you want to go there?' The Bears were negative."

The Chargers flew him to Los Angeles—they hadn't moved yet—"and they tried to wine you and dine you," said Lincoln.

While the Chargers talked up the idea of being part of something new and playing in the sunshine, everything Halas said was designed to badmouth the AFL. When the Chargers offered him $20,000, it sounded good to Lincoln, who had just gotten married. "I'm a poor guy getting out of school and I never had anything. It was a no-brainer for me. They [the Chargers] had deep pockets and their guys were believable."

There was good reason to believe that the Chargers had a vault to draw upon since the principle owner was Barron Hilton of the Hilton hotel chain. The Bears lost out on Lincoln, but recovered by drafting Ronnie Bull in '62, who became the NFL rookie of the year.

Roger LeClerc, who was drafted as a linebacker by the Bears but ended up making more significant contributions as a kicker, was also drafted by the Denver Broncos in 1960. The AFL hadn't played a down yet and LeClerc didn't pay much attention.

"That was a funny thing," LeClerc said. "I received a telegram from Denver that I was their No. 1 choice, but I never did hear anything more from them and wondered if it was legitimate." The Broncos never contacted him again and he didn't contact the Broncos. "Because of the newness of the AFL at the time," LeClerc said a few years later, "I felt a bird in the hand was worth two in the bush."

Bears defensive back Roosevelt Taylor was from New Orleans and attended Grambling State University. When he came out of school in '61, the AFL-NFL war was under way, but hadn't yet reached its full intensity. He was also not in as much demand as some of the top names in college ball. That included one of his Grambling teammates, the 6' 9" 320-pound defensive tackle, Ernie Ladd.

"I didn't know anything really," Taylor said of being savvy enough to check into both leagues. "All I knew was that the NFL was trying to shut 'em down and they were trying to stay alive." Oh, he heard one more thing, too: "The AFL scouted the little black colleges long before the NFL started."

The AFL's goal was to take a run at the absolute best talent coming out of the colleges each season and make rich enough offers to young players to sway them away from the NFL. The first really big test case for the AFL revolved around the future of Billy

Cannon. It is difficult to underestimate Cannon's importance to the American Football League, both as an individual who agreed to sign with the league when he did, but also as a name player.

A fabulous all-around athlete, Cannon stood 6' 1" and weighed 215 pounds. He ran the 100-yard dash in 9.4 seconds and the 40 in 4.12. In 1958 Cannon was the star when his hometown Louisiana State won its first national football championship. In 1959, Cannon won the Heisman Trophy.

At the very end of that calendar year—December 29—before the AFL had held tryouts or training camp, Bud Adams, the owner of the Houston Oilers, signed Cannon to a personal services contract. Adams said the deal called for Cannon to sell his petroleum products in Louisiana and it called for $100,000 spread over three years and presented Cannon's father with a Cadillac. It was misdirection. After Cannon and LSU played in the Sugar Bowl on January 1, 1960, Cannon apparently gave Adams his autograph again, updating the contract for him to play for the Oilers. Cannon signed that paper under the goal posts, in uniform, but years later said, "The bit under the goal posts was just for show." It was the original contract with Adams that counted, he said.

Meanwhile, however, between Houston commitments, the Los Angeles Rams—whose general manager at the time was Pete Rozelle—had also signed Cannon to a contract. No petroleum products were involved, but a $10,000 bonus check was, apparently prior to the Sugar Bowl, seemingly jeopardizing Cannon's eligibility for participation in an amateur game. Cannon, however, never cashed the check.

Eventually, the entire Cannon fiasco ended up in federal court. The Rams sued for an injunction, preventing Cannon from playing for the Oilers. Cannon announced through his attorney that he would never play for the Rams. By the time the matter reached the courtroom Rozelle was NFL commissioner and Cannon was having memory lapses as long as the 18 ½ minute gap on Richard Nixon's Watergate tape. Nixon, then vice president, ironically was one bystander at the Heisman Trophy dinner who overheard Cannon telling people he was glad to be going to play for the Rams. Cannon testified he didn't remember saying that.

The court ruled in favor of the Oilers, making the AFL the winner in its first major showdown with the established NFL.

"I felt in my heart I did what was best for me and my family," Cannon said much later.

Cannon became one of the early stars of the league, becoming an all-star performer at running back and tight end. Though he never matched his Heisman heights, Cannon scored 65 touchdowns and was a two-time AFL champion.

Although later in life Cannon served prison time for counterfeiting, he became a successful dentist and was elected to the College Football Hall of Fame in 2008.

That first year Cannon was a symbol, but the AFL shocked the NFL by signing 75 percent of the older league's first-round draft picks in 1960. Obviously, the Cannon lesson was that if there was going to be a war the AFL was going to fight tenaciously. Perhaps the need for such thinking was obvious in the beginning, and maybe that's why the league hired Joe Foss as its first commissioner. A World War II hero, the Marine captain aviator shot down twenty-six Japanese Zeros in the Pacific and won the Congressional Medal of Honor, then served as governor of South Dakota. It might be said that Foss fit in just so because he was used to taking flak from every direction when he signed on with the AFL.

Foss' record demonstrated that he had guts, a campaigner's gift of gab, and stamina. It was also felt that if he could sell himself to an electorate he should be able to sell the AFL to the masses.

> *I never stopped selling it. When we started, people didn't know whether the league had to do with basketball, baseball, hockey, or what. I traveled 250,000 air miles that first year, speaking to every sort of convention and meeting that would have me.*

Increasingly valuable TV contracts were inked by Foss as the staying power of the AFL became apparent, the nation's appetite for pro football expanded, and the product became more entertaining. That was one thing about the AFL from the start: it might as well have been called the American Fun League. Compared to the NFL, the AFL featured more wide-open passing games and higher scores. There were game-breaking stars easy for fans to attach themselves to who had admirable talent.

If you watched the Denver Broncos (and could get past the ugly striped socks that endure as a nightmare in memory), you saw old pro Frank Tripucka throw to Lionel Taylor and the euphoniously named Gene Mingo kick field goals (he made 27 of 39 in 1962). Mingo once had the family poodle at training camp on a leash because his wife was banned from taking it where she went. Taylor also had much success, with seasons where he caught 100 passes ('61), 92 ('60), 85 ('65), 78 ('63), 77 ('62), and 76 ('64). He looked as if he was about to run right out of those silly socks any minute.

When it came to wide receivers, Taylor was not particularly fast . . . he just caught everything that was thrown in his direction. "Taylor's got the greatest hands I've ever seen on a receiver," said Broncos coach Jack Faulkner. Taylor was another player who got away from the Chicago Bears, trying out but not making the team as a receiver, but rather a linebacker, in '59. A few years later, after improving, he became an All-Star in the AFL. Taylor was super reliable, holding onto the ball if he got his fingertips on it, and once beat himself up verbally for a drop that occurred because he smashed into the goal post so hard it left him dizzy. "There's no justification for dropping a pass, not even one. Once you get your hand on the ball it should be yours."

Houston featured Blanda throwing to Charlie Hennigan and handing off to Cannon. But they weren't the only teams with skill.

- The Dallas Texans halfback Abner Haynes, who came to training camp as an unknown, became just about the best runner in the league immediately.
- The Oakland Raiders swiftly developed a pirate-like identity and turned loose a top-caliber runner named Clem Daniels. They also acquired Art Powell, whose brother Charlie was a heavyweight boxer, from the New York Titans, after he once led the league in receiving yards and did so again en route to 479 career catches.
- The Boston Patriots were always hurting for money, but Gino Capelletti, out of Minnesota, became a fixture as a kicker and wide receiver and remained with the team as a broadcaster after retiring, being a part of the franchise for nearly fifty years.

- The New York Titans couldn't draw fans even with the famous Sammy Baugh as their coach, but begat the New York Jets, Joe Namath, and victory in Super Bowl III, which was a major moment for the AFL, though after the war was pretty much decided.
- It may have been chilly in Buffalo, but the Bills played good ball and featured the thundering Cookie Gilchrist at fullback. And the Chargers, even if Los Angeles didn't embrace them and they moved down the highway to San Diego, were one of the most exciting teams of all time. Coach Sid Gillman was a guru of the modern passing game and he tested his ideas in the Chargers' laboratory. He invented plays that buried other teams and he unleashed the misleadingly named wide receiver called Bambi on the football world. Lance Alworth was as electrifying running pass patterns as the lightning bolt on his helmet.

Jack Kemp, future Congressman and Republican vice-presidential candidate, got the Chargers going, but by 1963 he was the starting quarterback for the Bills where he had his best seasons on the way to seven All-Star games. Already reasonably famous Kemp became better known as a national leader later in life.

Kemp said that he did not plan a life in politics after football despite being president of the American Football League Players Association. Any sports fan had to love his answer in comparing football and politics, though. "They're both extremely competitive," Kemp said. "There are elements of individual initiative required in both, but at the same time a large degree of teamwork is required." That was just in case people thought all he did in the huddle was shout, "Go long!"

In Houston, Charley Hennigan was a pass-catching machine. In 1961, he grabbed 82 passes and gained 1,746 yards. In 1964, he caught 101 passes. His height and weight were listed as only 6' 1" and 187 pounds, but his play made him seem bigger.

When Joe Foss looked back on his tenure as commissioner of the AFL, he said that he was proudest of the league offering opportunities to players who might otherwise never have had them. Hennigan fit that description perfectly. He was a high school chemistry teacher when he showed up at the Oilers' training camp and his before-tax pay was $270 a month. Hennigan displayed some skills, but played poorly and was the last man to make the team. "I had good speed, quick feet, fine moves, loose elbows, and no hands. I was sleeping with a football each night, but fighting with it each day."

Despite a rough camp, the Oilers kept him anyway. Hennigan made a bit more money over his seven seasons with Houston while catching 410 passes. A knee injury eventually sent him back to teaching, though with a PhD that he'd picked up in his spare time.

Abner Haynes was another such find. He came out of North Texas State, where he dazzled, but it was a big jump from the North Texas State "Mean Green" to the pros, and Haynes started slowly in the Texans' training camp. He made the team, and when given a chance in the '60 season gained 875 yards rushing and caught 55 passes. He made the AFL All-Star team the first four years of the league's existence and was the AFL player of the year.

Haynes, who grew up in Denton, Texas, was not only one of the biggest-name stars in the new league, but was one of its most enduring stars.

It's like a dream and I keep thinking I'm going to wake up and find out that none of this stuff really exists. I suppose every kid thinks about the day he'll do something big right out there in front of the folks from his home town.

In 1960, Haynes and Clemon Daniels, who came out of Prairie View A&M—one of those less publicized black colleges that Roosevelt Taylor was talking about—were both with the Texans. Haynes beat out Daniels for the starting job and Daniels moved on to Oakland where he became the Raiders' No. 1 guy. Daniels rushed for between 766 and 1,099 yards five times while playing in the Bay Area.

Compared to Daniels' early life, getting regularly tackled by 250-pound men with malicious intent seemed to be a minimal obstacle. His father left home when he was a youth and he had to go to work construction as a teenager alongside men. No predominantly white college recruited him and after finding it hard to get a chance to start in the league, he was the top rusher by the '63 season. "I haven't made it big. But I'm very definitely on my way to reaching my goal. I want to be the best running back anywhere—and a useful citizen."

After retiring, Daniels was a schoolteacher and then became a businessman, investing in the Oakland community and creating a college scholarship fund for Bay Area students.

One of the AFL's most dynamic stars and unusual ones, too, was Buffalo running back Cookie Gilchrist. He had already gained notoriety in the Canadian Football League and playing in the AFL just added to his legend. At 6' 3" and 250 pounds, Gilchrist was a battering ram in cleats; an outsized running back that carried tacklers downfield on his back. He carried the ball well over 200 times a season and rushed for 1,096 yards in 1962 and averaged over 1,000 yards a season from '62 to '65. You could almost hear the thundering hooves of a buffalo when Gilchrist ran for the Bills.

Gilchrist never attended college, and before he was old enough to drink legally or vote, took his powerful body to Canada. As large as many of the linemen who sought to tackle him, Gilchrist was the first AFL runner to crack 1,000 yards and was chosen as the AFL Most Valuable Player in '62.

Al Davis, who was then coaching the Raiders before becoming the team owner, called Gilchrist "the most dominant player in our league." Gilchrist lived up to the billing, rushing for 243 yards in a Week 13 game against the Jets in '63; then the record for any pro league. He also rushed for five touchdowns in that same game.

At a time when a good contract for most pros was $20,000 a year, Gilchrist was making $28,000 and wanted more. He irritated fans by portraying himself more as a mercenary than a loyalist, but that was then before sports fans got used to it. "I'm a businessman," Gilchrist said. "I look at life as the securing of my future."

In the early 1960s, the entirety of the AFL hadn't quite reached that point, though it was working on it.

"People think I'm an oddball because I'm a Negro who speaks up," Gilchrist said. "But I have a lot on my mind. It's an internal disease, and it will eat me alive if I don't get out of my system what I think about things."

In 1963, there was plenty on the minds of many African Americans. The Civil Rights Movement that would update American society from the days of Reconstruction to a more equitable landscape was moving forward, and there would be no rest until justice turned the corner in the United States.

The American Football League was more color blind than the NFL. The competition for talent, the need for stars, and the willingness to do anything to weaken the enemy meant that the AFL was ready to fork over bigger checks to more black football players than the NFL was in the habit of doing. Very soon there would be African American athletes speaking out in many forums, in many sports, letting those internal feelings out. But for the moment, just as he was doing on the football field, Gilchrist was running a yard or so ahead of everyone else.

Whenever AFL teams played an exciting, high-scoring game with some of these stars lighting it up, the NFL used to retort that they did so because there was no defense and the league didn't have any worthy linemen. But in fact there *were* linemen who played nearly their entire careers during the 10 seasons of the AFL who made it to the Hall of Fame. Oakland center Jim Otto was one of football's great iron men. Otto, who fittingly wore 00 as his number, played in 210 straight games, 14 a season every year from '60 through '74. That didn't include preseason exhibitions and playoff games, which added to the regular season put Otto on the field for 308 consecutive games.

Selected All-AFL nine times, Otto was also chosen for three Pro Bowls after the AFL-NFL merger. A 25th-round draft choice, Otto built his body from 205 pounds to 255 to become a star center.

Otto's body paid for his commitment by undergoing forty surgeries. A first-year-eligible Hall of Famer, Otto was elected in 1980. He said he was "so choked up" when he heard of his selection that he couldn't even tell his wife at first.

When the rich men who gathered to found the AFL met, they were believers . . . but there was no guarantee of success. The track record of sports leagues challenging other established leagues and surviving was not good. Even now, more than a half century after its startup, the AFL is the biggest success story of its kind (probably with the American Basketball Association [ABA] running a close second).

Faith was critical. Bud Adams, the Oilers' owner who did eventually move his team to Tennessee, said he sought other investors, but he couldn't tap the wallets of wealthy friends. "To the guys on the street, it was a big gamble," said Adams, who turned ninety in January of 2013. "I was going to sell some interest in the team, but I couldn't get anybody to take it."

Ralph Wilson, who turned ninety-four in October of 2012, was the founder of the Buffalo Bills, and his name now adorns the stadium the club plays in, even though he is no longer involved in daily management.

"My friends thought I was a real chump," Wilson once said. "They all laughed at me."

Those who played in the early days of the AFL never gave much credence to NFL insults about them putting an inferior product on the field. The Chargers' Keith Lincoln played in postseason All-Star games like the Hula Bowl and the East-West game with the best collegians and also scrimmaged against the Bears. He was not intimidated by anyone he played with or against then, and their going into the NFL didn't suddenly make them any better.

"I got to know a lot of those guys," said Lincoln. "We had two good scrimmages with the Bears and I realized, 'Hey, these guys put their pants on the same way I do.' We [the AFL] were growing twice as fast as they were. It was two-to-one."

Dick Westmoreland, one of Lincoln's San Diego teammates who also played with the Miami Dolphins later in the sixties, never bought into that NFL argument. "The NFL was supposed to be the best. I didn't think so. We were featuring a wide-open game. You know, we were the best thing that happened to the NFL."

In 1960, Al Davis was hired as an assistant coach for the Chargers, a job he held through the '62 season. He became the Raiders' coach in '63 at age thirty-three, and Oakland went from 1–13 to 10–4 in one season under Davis. That earned him AFL Coach of the Year honors.

Davis' motto which later became famous was, "Just win, baby." When he was chosen as AFL commissioner in 1966, he brought a killer attitude to the job. He wasn't interested in the AFL being granted parity by the NFL. If it was up to him it would have been a fight to the death with Davis certain of the NFL's annihilation. As its base grew more stable, the AFL had begun going hard after the NFL's biggest stars, with a targeted effort on stealing quarterbacks. This was Davis' go-for-the-throat style. Davis was a hawk.

When Davis was chosen as AFL commissioner he immediately announced that he had no interest in a common draft with the NFL and just as little interest in a merger. Davis' bold statements were a counterpoint to a recent declaration from Pete Rozelle over on the other side saying that all NFL teams were making money and were hardly in trouble. Davis had previously sat in on some merger discussions and dismissed the other side's position because "the NFL demands were ridiculous."

But other AFL owners wanted peace and believed that the NFL would listen to fresh merger talks, so they met behind

Davis' back with NFL counterparts. The deal was struck to create an inter-league championship game and a complete merger in 1970. Davis quit and returned to the Raiders, eventually becoming the franchise's sole owner, a property he held until his death in 2011.

It can be argued that the AFL's secret deal, pushing Davis aside, helped shape his testy relationship with the NFL for the rest of his life. He was the proud leader of the silver and black and fought the league on big issues such as moving his team to Los Angeles against the other owners' wishes.

"Don't let the culture tell you what to do," Davis said in a 2010 ESPN *30 for 30* documentary, titled "Straight Outta L.A." "That's being a Raider." He said he was perfectly happy with some of the descriptions of his actions. "Maverick is fine, 'cause I am."

In 1963, when Davis was just beginning his head coaching career that would lead to ownership, he demonstrated his football acumen with that superb leadership job, but came up shy of leading his Raiders to the championship game. At the time, Davis was Oakland's fourth coach in four years.

"Come on, when you go out there, remember you're the Raiders of Oakland," Davis said to his players in '63 without being able to imagine he would spend the rest of his life with the team. "We've got to start building a tradition." He did that all right. Davis was thirty-four at the time and an early magazine story about him noted that he teased visitors by saying, "Come in, sit down, and let me tell you some lies." For those who don't remember, Davis (who college-hopped as an undergraduate before earning a degree from Syracuse) began coaching at twenty-one at Adelphi College.

While the Chicago Bears were looking over their shoulders for the Green Bay Packers, over in that other league, the San Diego Chargers and Boston Patriots were on a collision course in an AFL championship contest. This was the fourth season for the league that was supposed to be doomed from the outset. Some of its players were among the most famous in the sport. Football fans knew their teams and coaches. The hopeless case league was thriving.

In fact, Blanda, who had every reason to be bitter about the Bears and the NFL, and didn't take kindly to insults about the AFL's caliber of play, was a stand-up defender of his league.

I know a lot of National Football League players and they'll say anything to defame or degrade our league. They overestimate their own abilities. We have overall finer and faster ends and better backs. We're more like the NFL every year. I definitely think we're as good.

9

BEARS ON FIRE

THE DAY THE Bears really shook up the rest of the National
Football League during the '63 season came a month after
the dig-it-out victory over the Packers. They were 4–0 on
their way to the Los Angeles Coliseum in a match-up with the
slumping Rams.

Over the years, it usually didn't matter if the Bears were good
or bad; anytime they made the trip to the West Coast, they
crumbled. The Bears in the warm sun were like Samson with his
hair trimmed. They took one peek at the Pacific Ocean and lost
all their strength.

The Rams were usually pretty good, too, but not this year.
They were 0–4 when the Bears alighted on the far shore and it
didn't hurt any that Bill Wade still held a little bit of a grudge.
How could he not? Wade spent seven years with the Rams
pining to get off the pine, and during that time, he mostly sat
and watched other quarterbacks with that yellow ram curl on
their helmets lead the way.

Now Wade was at the helm of a first-place team, back in the town that rejected him. This was a time to show off; to prove definitively that his old team made a mistake . . . and boy did he. Wade was thirty-three years old, but no one would have blamed him for acting as gleeful as a high schooler.

On that mild, 66-degree day at the Coliseum the Bears hung 52 points on the Rams and Wade threw three touchdown passes while barely playing in the second half. The final score was 52–14 after Chicago added 21 points worth of insult in the fourth quarter. If Wade was smart, he should have penned a thank-you note to tight end Mike Ditka, who had the greatest game of his Hall of Fame career, catching four touchdowns for 110 yards.

Up until mid-October the Bears' defense was the talk of the league . . . but nobody saw their scoring explosion coming. *You mean they have an offense, too?* Now that was scary. Most NFL guys thought it would take three weeks for the Bears to score 52 points. And some touchdowns came from guys who weren't even starters. Rudy Bukich, Wade's backup, had already thrown three TD passes.

Ditka, though, pretty much single-handedly overpowered the Rams. They could have had a herd of Rams on him that day and it wouldn't have mattered. Ditka out-muscled, out-ran, out-thought, and out-performed their entire defense. He scored on touchdown passes of 13, 25, and 2 yards from Wade and from 14 yards out from Bukich.

"The game when I caught four touchdowns against the Rams was my best," Ditka said years later, though stressing that was as an individual, not team, accomplishment went. "We were a better defensive team than offensive team that year. Only that game, we really crushed them. We never really scored that many points. The game against the Rams was one of those games where everything went right."

Ditka scored the first touchdown of the game in the first quarter and the Bears led 7–0 after one. But Ditka had two more TDs in the second and Chicago led 28–7 at halftime. Mixed in there was an interception runback to the house by defensive back Bennie McRae so that the defense wouldn't feel left out.

"Bill Wade kept throwing to me and I kept running for touchdowns," said Ditka. "Tight ends didn't score four touchdowns in a game."

They didn't until Ditka came along, anyway. He began rewriting the job description for tight ends as soon as he hit the NFL in '61 out of the University of Pittsburgh. At 6' 3" and 230 pounds, he had the typical size of a tight end, but the moves of a split end with the speed to match. Defenses didn't know what to do about him because he was the square peg in the round hole that blew up their schemes.

One of the funniest anecdotes buried in the scrapbook of life goes back six decades to how Ditka's mother feared for his health when he first went out for the high school football team in Aliquippa, Pennsylvania, as he was such a small boy. "I attended practice to make sure he didn't get hurt," said Charlotte Ditka.

She didn't make clear how she would have prevented such an occurrence—maybe by stepping in on a linebacker. Mrs. Ditka's guess was that Mike weighed around 120 pounds at the time. Once she thought the coach was picking on him by making him run and she spouted off. The man just smiled back at her and said he was going to make him into a man. That wise coach, Carl

Aschman, spent decades coaching high school ball and it was no surprise to hear that he considered Ditka his best pupil. "I never coached anybody who had greater desire," said Aschman.

It would have been easy for coach George Halas to tout his own genius and say how he recognized all along when he was sitting with a list of college players arrayed in front of him in his draft room that Ditka was going to be this special. Instead, about halfway through Ditka's rookie season, Halas said to reporters, "Gentlemen, I think we have the finest rookie in the league playing for us." A couple of weeks later Halas added, "Ditka has exceeded our expectations."

Ditka eased seamlessly into NFL play and maintained a high standard. He won the NFL's rookie of the year award, prompting Halas to predict his star's improvement. "He will be an even greater player in years to come because of his drive, competitive leadership, and desire." When it came to identifying Ditka's football personality, Halas definitely hit it on the head.

A combination of raw talent, grit, and hard work produced results rarely seen in a rookie turned Ditka's teammates into fans as well. "He's the greatest rookie I've ever seen," said Chicago's All-Pro linebacker, Bill George. "He could play guard, any place you wanted to put him, and be great."

While the AFL was making its name for "airing it out," the NFL really wasn't a throwing league in the early '60s. The glory belonged to freight-train runners like Cleveland Browns fullback Jim Brown, who led the league in rushing all but one season during his short Hall of Fame career. Tight ends were like the children who were supposed to be seen but not heard. Yet in 1961, his first season, Ditka finished fifth in the league in receptions (56, tied with Dallas' Billy Howton) and second in touchdown catches (12, tied with Pittsburgh's Buddy Dial). He averaged 19.2 yards per catch, which was particularly unusual, as he was not a downfield receiver.

Listening to Ditka's gruff response to questions about how he handled defenses' increasing attentions probably had Halas beaming.

> *Football isn't a game in which I'm trying to be a glamour boy. I probably made enemies my first year in the league. On the field I believe that everybody is equal. I didn't take any lip from anybody. I hear them say, 'Let's knock his can off.' I don't think they can.*

No one has yet. Even Ditka's Army-style haircut exuded his no-nonsense attitude. And from his rookie year to his time as a head coach, that part of him never changed. Nor, as it turned out with the Bears' winning streak, did Ditka change his clothes. His Sunday ritual consisted of waking up, putting on a suit, going to church, and then heading to the game. Being undefeated meant that the superstitious Ditka had to wear the same suit to church and the game every Sunday until a loss intruded. But the way the Bears were playing a wardrobe change was not on the horizon.

Of course, that wasn't all. He also wore the same tie, put his shoes on the same way, and ate the same food each Sunday. No one was going to blame him for blowing the winning streak.

"Sounds silly, I know," he said, "but when things are going good, who am I to change things?"

A week later, on October 20, everything did change. After their one-sided win over the Rams Halas said, "We're playing over our heads."

Halas appeared to sense something. Only a few days later, the San Francisco 49ers ended the Bears' winning streak, with a 20–14 victory.

"It was one of those days where we could do nothing right," said Bears running back Ronnie Bull. "It was a tough one."

Chicago's offense was the talk of the league the previous week, but after falling behind 17–0 and failing to come back against the 49ers, the Bears did not look quite as invincible.

The game was a serious letdown. San Francisco was winless, 0–5, heading into the contest at Kezar Stadium. Only a few years earlier the 49ers fielded a backfield of Y. A. Tittle, Joe Perry, Hugh McElhenny, and John Henry Johnson. It was nicknamed "The Million Dollar Backfield" and "The Fabulous Foursome," with all four players ending up in the Hall of Fame. By comparison, the '63 49ers started in the nickel and dime backfield, and the way they handled the Bears that day, there would have been change left over.

Trailing 17–7 at halftime, Halas made the locker room decision to yank Wade for the second half in favor of Bukich. While Bukich did steer the Bears to a late touchdown, he also threw two interceptions. Controversy in the newspapers followed. Even then, when a quarterback got the hook someone was going to comment on it, perhaps not so loudly or insistently as an avalanche of Twitter blather would descend, but Halas' move did not go unremarked upon. Ed Stone of the *Chicago American* wrote that Halas "choked" by pulling Wade in favor of Bukich.

Strong words. And Stone probably didn't help his already shaky status with Halas, as he had previously taken apart the coach's statement about the team playing over its head. Stone wrote that Halas knew it was not true when he uttered it and that it was an insult to his assistant coaches. Oops. A few days later, the Bears proved the veracity of Halas' comment.

So Stone was oh-for-two. Still, he did not (and could not) expect what happened next. One day in his office he was informed by his sports editor that he was no longer the Chicago Bears beat reporter and that he was being moved into the office as a copy editor. Stone said he was never told why the change was made, but he knew it was the result of muscle applied by Halas to the ultimate superior—the editor of the paper—who was one of his pals. Halas was not above such a petty response since he believed everyone in Chicago should be a cheerleader for his team, and newspapers are certainly not above bullying an employee to appease a powerful local figure.

This was the Bears' stub-their-toe game; the inexplicable loss. No matter how it was sliced and diced, the Bears should not have lost to the 49ers. Meanwhile, the Packers had won every single game since their opening-day loss to Chicago. With Green Bay thumping the St. Louis Cardinals on the same day Chicago lost to San Francisco, both teams arrived at matching 5–1 records, tied for the Western Division lead.

The loss was a potential tipping point for the Bears. They could roll with it, regroup, get angry and take their frustration out on the next opponent, or they could mope and moan and reel from a crack in their confidence and blow the whole season with a mental letdown. Fortunately for Chicago, their next foe was a get-well team. The Philadelphia Eagles, NFL champions as recently as 1960, were in the midst of a several-year rebuilding stage. They were on their way to a 2–10–2 record in '63, but then the 49ers had been calculated to be the worst team in the league when they pulled off the upset the week before.

After a two-week sojourn in California, the Bears were the home team against the Eagles at Wrigley Field. The Bears were victorious, edging out the Eagles, 16–7. While the final outcome may have been closer than many had anticipated, in actuality it was not as close as the score. The Bears collected a 45-yard field goal from Roger LeClerc and a 23-yard touchdown pass from Billy Wade to Joe Marconi in the first quarter. The last score came in the third quarter, when Willie Galimore scored on a seven-yard run (the extra point on Galimore's touchdown was missed).

Before the Eagles game Wade reflected on his change of status, going from a spare part in Los Angeles to the main signal caller in Chicago.

> *Things have worked out real well. The main thing is a matter of respect. I think Halas has respect for me and my football ability. I've made a lot of errors and he hasn't made public comments about it. I'm glad I'm playing for him.*

Still, the win over the Eagles was more a triumph of the defense. Philadelphia could not move the ball. When the Eagles tried to run, the Bears line stopped it, and they finished with 88 total rushing yards for the game. When they tried to pass, the Bears hounded Eagles quarterback King Hill into making major mistakes. Final Philly passing stats: 10 for 25, 134 yards, four interceptions. (One pass was made by halfback Timmy Brown, which resulted in an interception.) J. C. Caroline, Richie Petitbon, Roosevelt Taylor, and Dave Whitsell—the entire defensive backfield—shared equally, with one pick apiece. The best part of the day for Hill was his 46.0 punting average on four kicks.

The win soothed Halas a bit. He had not been a happy camper after the 49ers loss, and the one thing the Bears didn't enjoy was being around Halas when he was mad. There were times when Halas could be almost irrational when blowing his stack, but the worst was listening to him going off when he was justified. Petitbon said he thought Halas delivered pronouncements sometimes with such a deep-voiced authority that "he sounded like the pope." The only exception being that he employed a vocabulary the pope would never dream of using in public. "He was the cursingest guy in the history of the world," Petitbon said of Halas. "He was something else. He was tough."

The image of toughness always permeated Petitbon's mind when his thoughts turned to Halas. Whether the story was apocryphal or not, Petitbon remembered hearing that Halas' mother ran a laundromat during Al Capone's Chicago mobster days, and that she refused to contribute payola for protection. It was said that Halas drove around the neighborhood with a shotgun across his lap and the bad guys left him alone. At least, that's how Petitbon recalls the tale.

"How the hell could I negotiate a contract with a guy who beat Al Capone?" Petitbon said.

There were no contract negotiations going on in the middle of the '63 season, but in a sense you were fighting for your job with your performance every week. Even though Wade said Halas didn't hassle him when he made mistakes Halas was prone to turn to Bukich if the offense was bogged.

"Wade was efficient as heck," said fullback Rick Casares. "Billy knew his stuff. He just directed the team. He was a cool customer."

Wade was never cooler than against the Colts in a rematch in Baltimore following up the Eagles victory. Chicago had bested the Colts, 10–3, early in the season, so the second game shaped up as a close one and it was.

This was not a perfect game for the Bears, but rather excellently executed. Wade ran the team with dispatch, a picture of that efficiency Casares raved about. The Bears went for ball control and churned out 164 yards over land. Wade threw just 12 times, but completed nine passes for 126 yards, including a 17-yard TD pass to Casares. Wade also ran for a touchdown from a yard out, providing a 7–0 first-quarter lead in a game where the Bears never trailed.

The Bears' defense recorded four sacks and one interception while holding the Colts to 229 net yards. This was becoming a regular day at the office for the defense. After the mini-slump in California, they were getting sharper by the week. While their offense wouldn't see 52 points again, with their defense they didn't need to.

"Our defense was so good," Casares said. And that's coming from a guy on the offensive side of the ball.

It was a testament to George Allen's creativity and adaptability that the defense was that tough because the Bears kept losing players to injury. Young second-year man Ed O'Bradovich got hurt and played just six games. Veteran defensive tackle Fred Williams, a four-time Pro Bowler, got hurt and played just five games. Maury Youmans, a defensive end like O'Bradovich, got hurt and missed the entire season. That's a lot of beef missing in an unexpected weight-loss plan.

On the offensive end halfback Ronnie Bull wasn't feeling his best. He had gotten kicked in the head during the Eagles game and had to spend a night in the hospital. Bull came back, but those defensive players were out for the rest of the regular season. Yet somehow, the defense was able to get better each game.

"That was a special defense," said defensive tackle Stan Jones. "It had good people on it. We had a good group. We set all kinds of records. George Allen deservedly got credit for it. But we were very good at it."

They were going to have to be. After the blowout game over the Rams the offense never approached those heights again. Halas was right about them playing over their heads in that sense. That was never more evident than in a rematch with the Rams in Chicago on November 10. Stung by the whipping the Bears put on them in Los Angeles, the Rams were determined not to suffer a repeat. They were poised for the biggest upset of the year.

Coached by the old New York Giants linebacker Harland Svare, the Rams had some weapons that could make them dangerous on any given Sunday. Strong-armed quarterback Roman Gabriel could make trouble, as could running back Dick Bass.

From the hindsight of years later it seems surprising that given their personnel the Rams weren't more formidable on defense. Among those in their lineup were Merlin Olsen, Lamar Lundy, Rosey Grier, and Deacon Jones. A few years later, when George Allen became head coach of the Rams, he molded that group into a dominant unit. But for one day in '63 the Rams foreshadowed the future. The same team the Bears pounded for 52 points in October did not allow a touchdown in November.

Everything rested on kicker Roger LeClerc. LeClerc booted a 30-yard field goal in the first quarter and a 16-yard field goal in the third quarter, which was the only scoring the Bears did all game. Thankful once again to their defense they came out victorious with a final score of 6–0. It was the great escape. That magnificent Chicago defense didn't even let the Los Angeles offense breathe. The Rams gained only 59 yards rushing on 32 attempts and 66 total yards passing, with Gabriel going 7 for 23 on the day. This was Allen's masterpiece.

Defensive back J. C. Caroline said there seemed to be a failure around the NFL to understand just how much ability the Bears had on his unit. "People didn't realize we had pretty good athletic players on defense."

That helped explain the front line's ability to pressure the quarterback, the secondary's ability to intercept passes, and one of the best linebacker trios of all time, with Bill George, Joe Fortunato and Larry Morris.

The defenders also had an awareness that they were being counted on. The ferocious Chicago Bears; the "Monsters of the Midway"; Chicago's identity had long been built on defense. Whenever the Bears have been good, their defense has always been a big part of it. Chicago reveled in its image as a blue collar town, of being "the city of big shoulders," as poet Carl Sandburg once wrote. A brawny, hard-hitting football team fit the community's self-image. Chicago football fans would have been happy no matter what style the Bears used to win games, just as long as they would be contending for titles or winning them. But somehow it just felt better if the Bears left the other fellows black and blue and beat them on heart and gumption in a low-scoring game while rolling around in the mud.

"You are who you are," Caroline said. "People didn't think we had as many good players as we did."

10

PACKERS ON A STREAK

IT HAS BEEN almost fifty-five years since Bart Starr listened to Vince Lombardi's introductory speech to the lowly Green Bay Packers, and he can still recall the jolt-of-electricity reaction he felt when his new coach finished speaking.

"I'll always remember that first meeting," said Starr.

When Lombardi concluded his pep talk, a new coach talking to a holdover team coming off a 1–10–1 season, Starr said he could barely stay seated. His favorite line? "We're going to relentlessly chase perfection. In the process we'll achieve excellence. I'm not remotely interested in just being good."

Starr bolted from the locker room, found a pay phone, called his wife, and informed her that the Packers were about to become a winning team, something that was a foreign concept in the 1950s.

Vince Lombardi waited a lifetime for a head coaching opportunity. Green Bay waited a decade to find the right coach. The intersection of legendary coach, the smallest city in the National Football League, and the few dozen men who performed magnificently through the '60s produced magic for the ages.

Starr was there before Lombardi arrived and after he departed, but the years they overlapped produced some of the most impressive that football has ever seen. The other thing that impressed Starr when this burly man with a serious demeanor greeted his team was that he thanked them for having him, as if he had been invited to a private party.

"He thanked the Green Bay players for the opportunity to coach them," Starr said. "That tells you something about the man."

For some around the NFL, it told them Lombardi was crazy. To them, Green Bay looked like a dead-end job. Lombardi was the offensive coordinator of the New York Giants, regarded as a bit of a savant. He had a rock solid background as an assistant college coach, working at both Fordham University and West Point. It seemed as if he ought to be able to write his own ticket to coach a club in a bigger city, not get stuck with the lowly Packers.

The Packers were one of the foundation blocks of the NFL. Curly Lambeau started the team in 1919 and coached them for 31 seasons. Not only did he help Green Bay survive the retraction of teams around the league—including the ones that represented small cities—but he guided the franchise to six championships.

However, the moment Lambeau departed the team seemed to begin falling apart. For Green Bay, the 1950s were the equivalent of the European Dark Ages. As the club chewed up and spit out four head coaches—full-time or interim between 1950 and 1958—the Packers did not have one winning season:

1950: 3–9	1954: 4–8
1951: 3–9	1955: 6–6
1952: 6–6	1956: 4–8
1953: 2–9–1	1957: 3–9

In 1958, the team went 1–10–1, the worst since the team's founding in 1919.

Saint Vincent reversed the ugly trend. It seemed only minutes after he took over that the Packers finished 7–5 in '59, the club's first winning record since '47. A year later, Lombardi had the Packers in the NFL title game, though they lost to the Philadelphia Eagles. In '61, Green Bay went 11–3 in the regular season and crushed the New York Giants in the championship game, 37–0. And in '62, after a 13–1 season, the Packers topped the Giants again, this time by a score of 16–7.

There was no town in the country that loved its football team more than Green Bay; and under Lombardi, there was no team in the country that was playing better football. The suspension of Paul Hornung shook the Packers, but by the time the '63 season began a few months later they believed they could win a third consecutive crown without him.

In the season opener the Bears laid down the terms of engagement. Chicago won 10–3, throttling Green Bay's offensive. So that's how it was going to be. A second shot at the Bears was on the schedule for November 17, but with a win in hand and the head-to-head victory advantage the Packers knew they had to keep winning. After the season opener the Packers ripped off eight wins in a row, while the Bears dropped that single contest to San Francisco.

As November 17 approached, both teams were 8–1. Green Bay had been chasing Chicago since opening day, and a victory would propel the Packers into the lead in the standings for the first time all season.

The Packers were a team without a weakness. Teams start 11 men on offense and 11 men on defense. When the '63 season ended, 14 members of the Packers were chosen as all-stars by one organization or another. Ironically, Starr was not one of them. The Hall of Fame quarterback who owns five championship rings was hampered by injuries and missed several games that season. In Green Bay, or "Titletown," as the Northern Wisconsin city likes to call itself, just about everyone who started for the Packers that year became a household name. A true-blue Packer fan can probably name all of them fifty years later. Of the 22 starters on the team—plus Hornung and Robinson—10 have been elected to the Pro Football Hall of Fame, not to mention Lombardi.

No wonder they won a few games! Heck, it was a wonder they lost any games in '63. With Hornung off in Louisville selling houses during his gambling suspension Moore averaged 5.0 yards per carry as his substitute, but Starr still thinks Hornung was missed.

It's not all about numbers. Personalities make up a team, too, and Hornung could be a holler guy. Versatile abilities mesh to make the whole, and Hornung could kick as well as run and catch passes. Starr couldn't pinpoint a precise way to analyze in what way Hornung's absence was costly, but he feels it was.

"Of course," Starr said. "Hornung was a fabulous player. You miss out on having a guy like that. If you were an insider you would know."

The fact that the Bears were in first place from opening day on was more attributable to what the Bears were doing than what the Packers weren't doing. To most, the Packers seemed as good as ever, never mind overpowering most of their foes as they had done the previous two seasons; fielding a lineup so thick with all-stars that opposing coaches couldn't find a weakness to attack.

Lombardi inherited some of those stars, and helped develop them too. He also found new ones through the draft. You do not have to be a Green Bay groupie to believe that the man-for-man lineup the Packers fielded in the 1960s was the best group ever assembled. The reason, Hornung is sure, was Lombardi. The Packers didn't win before he got there, and they didn't win right after he left.

"He's still the guy they talk about," Hornung said of his old coach. "I am so happy that they have his name on the trophy—the Super Bowl trophy. That says it all."

After his career at Notre Dame, Hornung joined the Packers in '57—two seasons before Lombardi—but all of his greatest pro success came under him. In 1960 Hornung scored 176 points, which is still the second highest total in NFL history, topped only by the Chargers' LaDainian Tomlinson, who scored 31 touchdowns in 2006. The most amazing thing about Hornung's point total was that he did it in four fewer games.

"He did it in four more games," Hornung said of Tomlinson. "I would have scored 300 points in 16 games. Twelve games, that's a good record."

The Packers record under Lombardi was 89–29–4 in nine seasons. Two seasons were 12-game campaigns, with the rest being 14 games long. Green Bay won championships in '61, '62, '65, '66, and '67 under Lombardi's tutelage.

Lombardi was a lifetime New Yorker, a big-city guy transplanted to the Midwest. Yet he became an overnight hero and was touched by the way Green Bay residents received, treated, and adopted him. In 1962, the town threw him a testimonial dinner, and the hard-boiled coach revealed a soft-boiled interior in a grateful speech.

> *I feel it a privilege to bring a championship to Green Bay. No other city has its loyalty or its cooperation. It has been good to me. I'm glad to call it my hometown.*

When anyone produces championships—either over time or as quickly as Lombardi did—the copycat universe of the sports world wants to know how he did it. There are people who stand out as being unique; who have the gift to manage men with a special touch. Lombardi was one of those leaders and probably didn't even know why everything he did worked.

"I am restless, worrisome, demanding, sometimes impatient, and hot-tempered," Lombardi said once.

If another coach could find a recipe for success in that statement, more power to them. Whatever the mix of temperament and knowledge, it worked for Lombardi. Some viewed him from afar as a dictator or tyrant and none of his Packer players ever suggested that Lombardi made life easy for them. Defensive tackle Henry Jordan uttered the most famous quip of all from the players about Lombardi. "He treats us all the same, like dogs."

However, guard Jerry Kramer, author of two books about that era of Packers teams, wrote a commentary in the *New York Times* decades after Lombardi's death, insisting that his "genius was that he treated us all differently." One assumes they were both right in different ways. Jordan's statement seemed aimed at how Lombardi worked the Packers on the field. Kramer's comment seemed aimed at how Lombardi treated the players as individuals.

Like the best coaches, Lombardi recognized which players could handle his yelling or being made an example of and which players needed to be handled with a childlike touch. That's what Kramer was talking about. Kramer said that Lombardi's basic lessons were more about life than football, and his own favorite coach's comment was, "You don't do things right once in a while, you do them right all the time."

Lombardi understood how he was viewed by some outside of the Green Bay football world, and he could combine wit with a sharp tongue.

> *This is a game for madmen. In football, we're all mad. I have been called a tyrant, but I've also been called the coach of the simplest system in football, and I suppose there is some truth in both of those. The perfect name for the perfect coach would be Simple Simon Legree.*

Imagine being in the room when Lombardi merged a nursery rhyme and a fictional evil-doer to make a philosophical point. The only worthy follow-up question could be, "Are you the perfect coach?" Packer players who still hear Lombardi's voice reverberating in their heads more than forty years after he died would say yes. But Lombardi likely wouldn't answer that question, only reply with an enigmatic smile.

The defense's dominance was overlooked and shorted on praise. Behind Starr's precision passing, running the Lombardi sweep, and yardage eaters like fullback Jim Taylor partnering with Hornung, Moore, or Elijah Pitts in the backfield, Green Bay was going to score. But as good as their offense was, their defense was even better at stopping the other team.

- In 1960, when the Packers reached the NFL title game for the first time under Lombardi, they outscored foes 332–209
- In 1961, the margin was 391–223
- In 1962, it was a stupendous 415–148
- In 1963, the plus margin was 369–206.

Once Robinson moved into the linebacker corps the Packers had five Hall of Famers playing at the same time on defense. Willie Davis and Henry Jordan were on the line up front, Ray Nitschke was in the middle, and Herb Adderley and Willie Wood were in the backfield. As an offensive coordinator, who do you try to pick on?

Adderley ran an interception back for a touchdown in the second Super Bowl, had a knack for blocking kicks, and was employed as a kickoff return man by Lombardi.

During the '63 season in their week five game in October against the Minnesota Vikings, Fred Cox tried a 10-yard kick, Adderley blocked it, and Hank Gremminger caught it and ran it back 80 yards for a touchdown and 10-point swing that helped provide the Packers with a 37–28 win. Vikings coach Norm Van Brocklin called Adderley's deflection "close to superhuman." That play saved a victory that Green Bay needed to stay even with the Bears.

Adderley made a different kind of impact later in the season in the Packers' week 13 game against the Rams. He couldn't figure out why Los Angeles end Jim Phillips kicked him, but he wasn't going to let him get away with it. Adderley intercepted a Roman Gabriel pass and was hauled down 15 yards short of a touchdown by Phillips. After the play was dead Phillips kicked Adderley who responded with a carefully placed right cross to the jaw that stunned his opponent.

"I took my time with the punch," said Adderley later, recounting the blow as if he had been in a 10-rounder. "I didn't want to miss the opportunity." Both players missed the opportunity to play the rest of the game because the officials ejected them. Green Bay would end up winning, 31–14.

It seemed unlikely that any opposing player would ever pick a fight with defensive end Willie Davis. Davis was 6' 3" and weighed 245 pounds and was the fiercest pass rusher on the Packers. Although at the time no one was keeping track of sacks, historians later tried to piece together a total for him, estimating the total to exceed 100, and he might have even collected 120. It is not clear if quarterbacks were polled for comment.

As an undergrad, Davis, who later earned an MBA from the University of Chicago, attended Grambling State University, where he played for legendary coach Eddie Robinson. Historically, black football playing colleges were only periodically scouted by the NFL when Davis was coming out in '58, and he was barely noticed as a senior. However, Florida A&M was making ripples that year and scouts flocked to the Rattlers' game versus Grambling. Regardless of which players they came to see, they couldn't ignore Davis. He compiled 19 solo tackles and 16 assists that game. Still, that only got him a 17th-round look-see by the Cleveland Browns before he ended up in Green Bay where his talent was recognized. Davis felt he was just being dumped by the Browns, but Lombardi welcomed him with an inspiring, complimentary talk.

A five-time All-Pro, Davis combined uncommon speed with his size to terrorize offensive linemen on his way to the ball. Bears quarterback Billy Wade saw too much of Davis during his career. "Willie is the quickest defensive end in the business. He's not the strongest or the biggest, but he's always in there, always managing to get at least his arm in the way."

Davis definitely blossomed the way Lombardi envisioned, and he did so after as well, serving on numerous major corporation boards of directors.

Whether it was growing up, in college playing for Robinson, or in the pros playing for Lombardi, Davis wore his pride on his sleeve. For him, pride was an integral motivator to perform well, to achieve, and to win as a team and as an individual contributor to team. "You're less than a man if you let this guy win a battle when he shouldn't. Each man has to show his individual pride. I know one thing. I want to live with myself."

Bart Starr had not been hand-picked by Lombardi to be Green Bay's quarterback. It also meant that he was a bit tainted from being associated with the lousy teams of '56, '57, and '58. Lombardi wanted to build a winner; he didn't want a team full of losers. Just because you had experience in Green Bay didn't give you an edge. It may even have been a negative starting out with Lombardi.

Starr was grateful that the Packers picked him at all after a lost senior year at Alabama. He was sure that if he got into a pro training camp and was allowed to demonstrate his talent, he could play. But he needed the opportunity of the invite and the practice reps. In 1956, Starr appeared in nine games as Green

Bay's mop-up man. In '57, he started 11 games and completed 54.4 percent of his passes. In '58, Starr started eight games and had terrible numbers, including three touchdown passes against 12 interceptions. In his first three seasons in the league, Starr had a record of 3–15–1, and threw 13 touchdowns with 25 interceptions.

To even get a chance to survive the final cut, Starr had to impress Lombardi from the get-go. He made the team, but it was a long time before Starr was convinced he had earned Lombardi's trust. Starr was not flamboyant or someone who bragged. He worked hard and hoped the results made his case. He did not pretend he was a ready-made starter, but loved absorbing Lombardi's football knowledge. Eventually, each man, wary of the other to a degree at first, developed a warm relationship. It helped that Lombardi realized he did not have to go quarterback shopping; that he had the right man for his offense and his team in-house.

It may have been slow to take shape, but Green Bay tackle Steve Wright said aloud what the players understood after the first few seasons under Lombardi passed and the Lombardi-Starr relationship solidified. "The dirty little secret of those days was that during the week it was Lombardi's team, but on Sunday, it was really Starr's team."

Certainly, as the wins mounted up and the successful seasons passed, the whole world recognized Lombardi and Starr as symbiotic coworkers, one loud and forceful, the other more restrained. If the world wanted their quarterbacks to be swashbucklers, then Starr wasn't going to fit the stereotype. He was more cerebral and conservative than some felt an NFL gunslinger should be. If a whiskey company was looking for a name endorser, they would more likely call upon Bobby Layne or Joe Namath. If a fine wine vineyard was looking for the right guy, they might call Starr.

Often, with an older coach and a younger player, the relationship takes on overtones of father and son. In Starr's case, he offered the respect of a son and he reveled in learning from a mentor.

> *I loved going to meetings with Coach Lombardi. You never grew tired of [them] because of what a great teacher he was. It was always intellectually challenging and I enjoyed that aspect very much.*

The Packers were stung by the 10–3 opening-day defeat against the Bears, but since September they had played as well as ever, reeling off eight wins in a row. Chicago had shut down the vaunted Green Bay sweep and Starr's passing game, but if the Packer offense looked sickly in the opener it got well in a hurry.

In the eight games since Green Bay's lowest point total was 28. The Pack had scored 31, 31, 42, 37, 30, 34, 33, and 28 points in consecutive games. There was nothing much wrong with the defense either. Including the game with the Bears, the Packers' defense surrendered 10 or fewer points five times.

The November 17 Bears–Packers rematch was about to show that not all regular-season games were created equal—and for once, nobody was even pretending.

11

BEARS–PACKERS II

THE NIGHT BEFORE the second scheduled meeting of the Bears and Packers, Chicago linebacker Joe Fortunato was up late doing his homework when his telephone buzzed. It was around midnight.

Fortunato, the defensive signal-caller for the Bears, was giving the list of defensive options a last-minute once-over. He put his papers down and raised the phone. It was coach George Halas on the other end. In theory, neither man should have been awake. Halas dialed so he had to explain his reasoning. He said, "Joe, I've gotta ask you something. How's everything coming? How's the signals look?"

"Coach, I was still up when you called," said Fortunato. "The way the charts look, if they continue to do what they've been doing, we may shut them out." When Halas didn't say anything, Fortunato added, "We're going to do a good job and we'll beat them defensively."

That was a rarity, a coach calling a player for a pep talk. All Fortunato could figure out was that Halas had been really nervous with the Packers on tap and just wanted some reassurance; to hear exactly what Fortunato told him.

Halas and Fortunato were hardly the only men in Chicago with their minds on the football showdown.

Scalpers live on supply and demand and they knew the second Bears–Packers game offered the score of the season. As game day approached at Wrigley Field, tickets at face value of $5 were selling for $50.

The buzz in Chi-Town was louder than it had been for any sporting event in four years, or since the White Sox met the Los Angeles Dodgers in the 1959 World Series at Comiskey Park. In some ways this football game was like a heavyweight championship rematch. Could the Bears do it again? Could the Bears end the reign of their Wisconsin neighbor to the north?

Strictly speaking, nothing much tangible was at stake for the winner of the November 17 regular-season game. Everyone would wake up Monday morning and one team or another would have an additional W in the standings running in the sports pages of the *Chicago Tribune* or *Green Bay Press-Gazette*. No championships would be determined. No trophies would be presented.

Yet this was hardly just another game. What the coaches, players, and fans all recognized was that the winner had the upper hand to claim all of those rewards a month hence. Yes, there was a lot of football still to be played, but there had been no evidence offered throughout the season to indicate that anybody but the Packers or Bears could command the Western Division. But it was one or the other. They stood in each other's way, and this moment might settle it.

The Bears gained the upper hand on opening day with their 10–3 victory in Green Bay, and the Packers hadn't lost since.

The Bears stumbled against the 49ers, but that was their only stumble. It was quite a presumption to assume that both teams were going to win out after this encounter, but it could happen. If so, the result of this game would be magnified.

In actuality, the season was playing out as if it had been scripted by Halas. Those many, many months earlier when he announced that the road to the title led through Green Bay and his constant repetition that his team had to beat Green Bay twice was coming to a head.

> *There has to be a bigger charge for everybody this week. We haven't had one game that meant so much to us in a long time. Our boys are more attentive. They're on their toes, listening to everything that's said.*

Halas wanted Chicago excited. He wanted all senses attuned to the goings-on at Wrigley. He wanted home-field advantage to matter. It wasn't as if the Chicago fans needed exhorting, either. It had been announced that on Monday, the box office would open to sell remaining seats and Bears fans bundled up in the early-morning cold starting at 4 a.m. Those at the end of the block-long line bought standing room tickets for $20.

That left a few million interested fans locked out of the building. And worse, at that time, the National Football League enforced a 75-mile blackout area for television, so you couldn't even stay home in the living room and watch. Sensing a need, entrepreneurs announced they were running bus and train packages away from town to other cities beyond the 75-mile limit. Hotels in places such as South Bend, Indiana— home of Notre Dame—and located roughly 90 miles east of Chicago were renting out rooms, though they realized they were really just renting out television sets. Milwaukee got in on the action, too.

Taken together, it was probably the biggest excitement ever made over a Bears regular-season game in 42 years of play. Of course the scenario was intriguing. Fan behavior probably would not have been as frenzied if the opponent had been anyone else besides the Packers. And it would probably not have been as wild if the Packers had not become the goliaths of the league over the preceding few seasons. In addition, the craving for tickets would probably not have been as intense if it was not perceived that a championship would hang on the result. But the perfect storm of circumstances turned this little old regular season game into one of nationwide interest.

A few days before the teams' practices concluded, Halas was holding court at the Chicago American Quarterback Club luncheon when one of his questioners speculated that the game was so huge that maybe President John F. Kennedy would want to come. "Why don't you invite President Kennedy to the game?" someone piped up. And then after a brief pause added, "And if he can't come, I'd like his ticket."

JFK was as popular in Chicago as he was anywhere in the country—it being suggested by various sources that Mayor Richard J. Daley's assistance helped bring out the vote or at least the vote count by enough to put him over the top for the presidency ahead of Richard Nixon. Halas would have loved to host the president. "I think we could find a ticket for Jack if he came," said Halas.

No doubt, "Jack" being the noted football fan that he was wouldn't have minded a little Sunday afternoon diversion. However, JFK did not attend the game. If he could take the time away from concentrating on those evil empire Soviets, he was free to watch it on the tube since Washington D.C. was well outside the blackout zone. Some fans would have been pleased if by presidential decree he had lifted the NFL blackout, but in the absence of a direct citizen petition to the White House they did ask Halas to get it waived. "Can't," Halas said of the prospect of televising the game in Chicago, "because of the league rules."

What he did add was almost as interesting. The NFL was going to revisit those rules and might lift blackout restrictions in the coming seasons in the case of such sellouts. Indeed, that is exactly what happened.

Any Bears–Packers game was a big game, but the situation transformed this one into *the big game.*

"I'll tell you," said Chicago linebacker Joe Fortunato, "that was a special feeling. That's just the way it was."

"The second Packers game was really for the championship," said Bears defensive back Richie Petitbon. "The excitement in the crowd was something I'd never experienced."

Bears players were steeling themselves for a war. They knew how good the Packers were, but their certain belief that this was their year pumped them up. It was going to be a whale of a game, they felt, but they should win it because they knew how good they were, too.

"The second game against the Packers, oh yeah, it was a big one," said Bears defender Roosevelt Taylor. "The Packers had a solid ballplayer at every position. They were loaded. Lombardi put together a complete team. We had to beat them a second time."

For all of the buildup, despite the aura surrounding the game, all for all of its importance to the standings, there was one thing off that made the showdown almost unfair: The Packers were without Bart Starr. Starr, the man who held everything together for the Packers on offense, hadn't started a game since week six (October 20). Starr had broken his right hand—his throwing hand—on a play against the St. Louis Cardinals that day.

Green Bay won the Cardinals' game, anyway, and then with Starr sidelined and backup John Roach running the show, the Packers defeated the Baltimore Colts, Pittsburgh Steelers, and Minnesota Vikings without him. "I almost went crazy sitting it out," said Starr.

How long Starr would have to sit out was unknown. Wearing his dual hat as general manager, Vince Lombardi traded for another quarterback. Zeke Bratkowski, one of the many Bears QBs Halas had flirted with during the 1950s, was acquired to back up Roach in case of emergency. But Roach had been around for the '61 and '62 championship runs, so the team was in his hands.

Roach, who played his college ball at Southern Methodist, broke into the league with the then-Chicago Cardinals in '56, spent time with that franchise as it moved to St. Louis, and became a Packer in '61. He had been mostly sitting behind Starr ever since, but this was his turn to shine with a good team on the field in front of him—something he didn't have with the Cardinals. It would be gilding the results a bit to say that Roach did glow in his games as fill-in. The Packers continued to score, but Roach threw just four touchdown passes against eight interceptions while temporarily replacing Starr.

In that first game with Roach in charge against the Colts, the Packers were not only minus Starr, but were without Tom Moore at halfback, who had been filling in all season for the suspended Paul Hornung. Even so, Roach threw for 156 yards, the Pack rushed for 179 yards, and Elijah Pitts, the backup to the backup, ran for 74 yards, including a 34-yard touchdown.

The next week, the Packers rushed for 248 yards, with Pitts scoring two touchdowns and Jerry Kramer kicking four field goals for an easy 33–14 victory over Pittsburgh. Roach's finest moment as Starr's replacement came the next week against the Vikings, in which he threw three touchdown passes.

The Packers were not playing with a full deck, but had more raw talent at most positions than any other team in the league. Roach was now 3–0 as a starter; far from being unprepared.

Sometimes incredibly hyped games live up to expectations, with the result being decided as the clock runs out. Other times incredibly hyped games turn out much differently than conventional thinking allowed for during the build-up. This Bears–Packers game fell into that category. In one of their worst thrashings of the Lombardi era, the Packers were overrun and dominated by a hungry Bears team that felt it had much to prove. The Bears did a tap dance on the Packers' heads. They shut down the vaunted Green Bay running game, allowing just 71 yards on the ground, and intercepted five Packer passers while recovering two fumbles. The mighty Green Bay Packers committed seven turnovers. Ordinarily, they wouldn't do that in the entire month of November.

It was a mismatch from the first play and came close to being the shutout that Fortunato speculated upon. It was a toss-up of whether the emotions of the 48,000-plus fans inside Wrigley Field leaned more towards amazement or being delirious with joy. They watched their guys swarm the world champion Packers as if they were some NAIA team from Appleton, Wisconsin.

On that first play the Bears kicked off to the Packers, who sent Herb Adderley back to receive. Adderley was a Hall of Fame defensive back, but was also a dangerous kickoff return man at that stage of his career. J. C. Caroline, one of the fastest runners on the Bears and one of the team's most versatile performers, was on the coverage team. When Chicago kicked off, Caroline sprinted downfield with the speed of a rocket and leveled Adderley. Later he said that he heard whispers that Adderley proclaimed he was going to take a kickoff to the house on Caroline and Chicago. Caroline's answer was "Not in my house." It was a tone-setting play that had Bears players jumping up and down.

Chicago players were wearing emotion on their sleeves that day, and after the game was over and the W was in the bank, the team reviewed the films—just as it did every week after games at its training quarters. At this particular session, the entire team took note of how spectacularly Caroline played on special teams—that play and more.

"He had so many great plays that day that when the film was over everybody in the room stood up and gave him a standing ovation," said receiver Johnny Morris years later. "It was very emotional, all these players standing and cheering him. It's something I have never forgotten."

The slaughter was on after that, though it was more defensive domination than a massacre on the scoreboard. Green Bay used the run—and who wouldn't with star fullback Jim Taylor punishing tacklers—to set up its offense. But this was one day when Taylor got no traction. He could find no holes in the line, finishing with only 23 yards. There were only two games all season when the Packers did not score in double figures, and both of them were against the Bears. Against Chicago, Green Bay averaged five points a game. In their eight other games to that point in the season, Green Bay had averaged 33.25 points a game.

Taylor was a strong, 215-pound back out of LSU who rushed for 8,597 yards as a pro and ran up five 1,000+-yard seasons for the Packers. He was viewed as unstoppable over the course of a game, but the Bears stopped him.

"I played against Jimmy Taylor in high school and college," said Bears defensive back Richie Petitbon. "There was a lot of respect between the Bears and the Packers both ways. Those were hard-fought games, but they were clean."

Green Bay's offensive line was renowned, but on this day it was no match for the Bears. Between Stan Jones and Doug Atkins, the Bears had a couple of Hall of Famers in their defensive front.

"I remember all of our games were pretty tough against the Packers," said Atkins. "When you played against Lombardi, you knew it was gonna be a tough game."

They didn't run contests to determine such things, but Atkins may have been the strongest man in the NFL. The scuttlebutt had it that way, anyway. He was a huge man who was also extremely athletic, and the combination made it hard to keep him away from the ball. Atkins stood 6' 8" and weighed 275 pounds, and while he was attending the University of Tennessee in his home state, he became a high jump champion for the track team. Some offensive linemen thought there should be some kind of rule against Atkins' existence. He sometimes just tossed them aside and other times could just jump over them on his way to the quarterback.

Recruited to play basketball, the Tennessee athletic establishment recognized that Atkins' true calling was on the gridiron, and he ended up on a national champion Volunteers football team. Drafted by the Cleveland Browns, Atkins played on one NFL champ there before being traded to the Bears, where he became an eight-time Pro Bowl player during an exceptionally long 17-year career that culminated with the New Orleans Saints.

Atkins understood his body and what he needed to get into shape, and was a free thinker who liked to have a good time off the field as well as use his brute strength to heave opponents out of the way on it. There was just something inside Atkins that rebelled at the sight of George Halas. Atkins seemed to have an inordinate pleasure in driving Halas nuts. That might have involved ignoring curfew or running out of the locker room totally nude except for a football helmet on his head, doing a lap around the field, and running back into the locker room without uttering a word. Or, as fullback Rick Casares recounted, there was the time that Atkins was out drinking beer in Tennessee. "He'd call Halas up at midnight to curse him out," said Casares.

That was off the field. On the field, on the days when Atkins practiced hard, the Bears' offense didn't want to have anything to do with him. They saw the same Atkins that opposing teams faced.

"He was the strongest player I ever saw," said Casares. "You'd see him do things in practice that you couldn't believe, like just throw guys aside. He was like steel."

That was the Atkins that the Packers got in this game. He was a run clogger and pass rusher, and he did his best to get to know Mr. Roach up close and personal this day. The problem for Roach was that when the Packers' usual best running plays failed, he had to throw more and that wasn't working either. Not only was Atkins the king of the castle this game, but the formations the Bears set up on defense made it seem as if they were almost reading the Packers' minds about which direction the ball was headed.

Linebacker Fortunato was the man on the Bears defense who read the Green Bay formations and announced the defenses based on what he saw. This was one day when Fortunato read Green Bay's intentions as clearly as a road map. When the Packers planned to run right, the Bears were there. If the Packers planned to run left, the Bears were there.

"He was always a play ahead of Roach," said Bears defensive coordinator George Allen. "His judgment was perfect."

One of the biggest heroes of the day was someone who was barely mentioned in the lead-up to the game. Bears kicker Roger LeClerc began the game by scoring with a 29-yard field goal and then followed it up with a 46-yarder. Before the end of the quarter the Bears had added a touchdown on a 27-yard run by Willie Galimore and an extra point by Bob Jencks. It was 13–0 after one quarter, and everyone could see which way the wind was blowing— which at Wrigley Field was a common enough occurrence.

Everyone was thrilled, not only because of the big play, but because Galimore had made it. The native of St. Augustine, Florida, who distinguished himself playing for Florida A&M, was a speedy runner who kept getting slowed by leg injuries, including two knee surgeries. Ronnie Bull got his chance to start when Galimore was hurt, but Bull had an injured foot for this game. The fact that Galimore could turn on the afterburners again on his TD dash was good news; not only for this game, but for how the rest of the season boded. Galimore at top form had a chance to be a special weapon.

At halftime the Bears led 13–0, which didn't do justice to the control of the tempo Chicago had earned. In the Green Bay locker room, the Packers realized they had been manhandled, but took heart from the score. They were only down two touchdowns, a deficit not too daunting to overcome.

There was not much movement—in terms of yardage gained or points on the board—in the third period. LeClerc added a third field goal from 19 yards, which made the score 16–0, Chicago. Time was running out on the Packers, even if the score seemed deceptively close. As the fourth quarter opened and time ticked away, the Bears added another three points from LeClerc on his fourth field goal of the day, this one a 35-yarder.

It was four hits and two misses for LeClerc, though the misses didn't hurt the Bears any.

"I sure would have liked to have kicked six," said LeClerc. "One of my misses I hurried on and on another one Herb Adderley got in very fast." That was one of Adderley's trademark skills.

Chicago notched another touchdown in the fourth quarter, when Bennie McRae intercepted a Bratkowski pass (Roach had been benched by this point) and returned it 44 yards to the Packer five-yard-line. Quarterback Billy Wade ran it in.

It was probably McRae's biggest play of the season. A second-year man out of Michigan who had also been drafted by the AFL's Boston Patriots, McRae chose to play with the Bears. A year after being drafted he had worked his way into the starting lineup. McRae was a grand Bears success story for a few reasons.

There were skeptics who sniffed that he would not make it in the NFL because his six-foot height carried just 178 pounds. Also, when he was a junior track star for the Wolverines, McRae suffered a rare and dramatic leg injury running the low hurdles that put him into traction and prompted a doctor in the hospital to say he might never walk again.

"I was terrified," McRae said of the apparent muscle rip that sent him to the ground as if he had been shot. But the injury healed and he made a full recovery by the end of his senior year; one that was so thorough that George Allen took a quick look at McRae in his early days with the Bears and predicted he would become an All-Pro. Proving McRae's talent and Allen's acumen, McRae made that comment come true in 1965.

Wade's run made it 26–0, and it was obvious that the Packers weren't going to come back, even if they had a year of Sundays. Lombardi had grown impatient with Roach's inability to move the team, so although Bratkowski had only been around a short while, he was inserted at quarterback. Nothing helped. That only meant Bratkowski could throw his share of the interceptions—three to two over Roach.

In the waning minutes, Moore finally showed up and ran for an 11-yard touchdown, but that was all Green Bay would get. The Bears won 26–7, a very thorough thrashing. The victory made Chicago 9–1 in the standings and left Green Bay 8–2 and big losers in the tie-breaker of head-to-head play if it came to that. The Bears did nothing fancy; no trick plays, but piled up 248 yards rushing, the Chicago offensive line eating holes into the Green Bay defensive line.

Sports Illustrated's noted football writer Tex Maule reviewed the results and said:

The Bears have just proved themselves as physically powerful a football team as ever played the game. Their victory over the Packers was not the result of a particularly brilliant strategy or unusual tactics. It came because, in the series of man-to-man physical encounters that make up a football game, the Bears whipped the Packers in almost every instance.

Halas actually had the game plan written out and carried it in his pocket during the game. Afterwards, he shared pieces of it with one phrase particularly telling. It read, "Our defense will smother their championship offense." Which it did.

The Bears scored the first three times they had possession of the ball, and the Packers' main attack was safely punting the ball back to the Bears. Halas said he felt by the end of the first quarter that his team would prevail.

"I could sense the victory," Halas said. And if anyone doubted how much the win meant to him Halas added, "It was the biggest victory for us since the 1946 championship game."

The difference between this win and many of the others in Bears history was again the fact that no championship was won on this day. The win protected the Bears' division lead and extended it, but with four games still remaining on the regular-season schedule. Chicago may have looked unbeatable, but all the Bears had to do was think back to San Francisco to realize everyone was a threat.

Winning it all was more important than winning any single game—even against the Packers—but sweeping the Packers, as Halas had imagined long before the regular season, left him feeling pretty darn glad. Wade was pretty happy about the result as well, even though it wasn't one of his busiest passing days. Going with what they thought would work, the Bears' game plan relied on ball control, chewing up yards and clock at the same time. The goal was to keep the Packers' offense off the field and tire their defense.

"We played their type of game and beat them at it today," said Wade. "It may not be as spectacular, but you get results."

Tight end Mike Ditka was impressed by his own team's thoroughly dominating showing.

> *I mean we beat them up and down the line, at their own game—on offense—and on our own game—defense. You could feel the whole squad pulling together the minute we stepped on the field.*

Green Bay players were pretty surprised at how easily the Bears pushed them around. They were the two-time champs with a lot of pride and did not think there was another NFL team as good as they were or one that could beat them twice.

"If I were to answer for my ego, I would have to say no, the Bears are not a better, team," said Packer defensive tackle Henry Jordan. "But looking at the scores, I can't say anything but yes, the Bears are better. I was really impressed by their front line. Many times I was impressed right into the ground."

Could the Packers have been complacent? Lombardi never let the Packers get self-satisfied. Were the Bears hungrier to win this ball game than the Packers?

"We gave 100 percent," said Green Bay linebacker Bill Forrester. "But the trouble was the Bears gave 150 percent."

Mathematical conundrum aside, Forrester's answer to the question involved more than numbers: things that are measured less precisely, like will and determination. So were the Bears hungrier? Possibly so.

Lombardi, ever the realist, walked off the field, unhappy about what he had seen, but he was more aware than most that four more games of NFL football could be a minefield for the Bears. Chicago hadn't really won anything yet, except the psychological battle. That meant something in the Bears–Packers rivalry, but it didn't really mean a thing if the Bears had a letdown and went out and lost a couple to innocent bystanders during the race.

"It's not the end of the world," Lombardi said. "They beat us in the line both ways. But the season isn't over yet."

It definitely was not, though Lombardi might have been prompted to send Starr a get-well card.

12

DEFENSE AS A WEAPON

THE CHANT HAS become a cliché over the years, fans roaring "Dee-fense!" to lift their teams. New York Giants fans at Yankee Stadium in the late fifties were the ones who invented the cheer, but rarely has it been more appropriate for a team than the '63 Chicago Bears.

In a 14-game season, the Bears allowed 144 points, or around 10 per game, a touchdown, extra point and field goal on average. Chicago's defense recorded just one shutout—the 6–0 game against Los Angeles Rams—but seven times allowed a touchdown or less.

The Bears did not have the most explosive offense in the league, but even so, because of the defense's dominance, the team outgained opponents by about 1,000 yards total (996). Opponents were held to a 3.5-yard per carry average on the ground and just 110 yards per game.

Chicago allowed only 10 touchdowns through the air all season and seven via rushing. The Bears were not flashy on offense, but the defense made George Halas beam. From their earliest days, the Bears seemed to excel on defense, to almost have trademarked the black-and-blue style of playing the game. They were nicknamed "The Monsters of the Midway," and it wasn't for their short passing game.

As a team, the Bears intercepted 36 passes in the regular season, nine by Roosevelt Taylor, eight by Richie Petitbon, and six each by Bennie McRae and Dave Whitsell. In contrast, the Bears' quarterbacks Billy Wade (12) and Rudy Bukich (2) threw just 14.

When it came to fumbles, Taylor and linebacker Joe Fortunato each recovered three fumbles. Top to bottom it was a magnificent defensive tour de force.

"It was definitely a great defense," said Taylor, who played a huge part in it.

"Our defense was so good," said fullback Rick Casares, who was lucky enough to be able to watch them every week.

Right from the inception of the team as the Decatur Staleys, they played first-rate defense and didn't allow many points. It was a different type of ball game in the 1920s. The ball was fatter and rounder and couldn't be thrown as far. The rules inhibited passing. In general, game scores were lower. From 1920 through 1928, even though they played a dozen or more games, the Bears never allowed 100 points in a season. The season of '29 was an aberration (when they allowed 227), but the stinginess returned through '37. And then, playing the more wide-open style, the Bears romped to championships regularly in the 1940s with point differentials such as 396–147 in '41 and 376–84 in '42.

Defense always mattered in Chicago.

The longer the season went on in '63 and the better the Bears played, the defenders started increasing the ante on play in search of perfection. They challenged one another to shut down runners and receivers. They challenged themselves the same way. It began to be viewed as a personal insult if the other team moved the ball, accumulated too many first downs, or scored.

The attitude, according to defensive back J. C. Caroline became, "I'm not gonna be letting my man catch a pass. I don't want to be embarrassed in front of the fans." In the vast majority of things in life, there is no such thing as perfection. A baseball pitcher can throw a perfect game, a goalie can have a shutout, and a bowler can roll a perfect 300 game, but otherwise perfection is particularly lacking in sports. It's about doing the best you can and doing your best to win.

But the players could pretend they were seeking perfection. The thinking went, Caroline said, "They will not score on us. They will not get a first down."

George Allen instilled that belief in his defensive unit. He saw things that few other assistant coaches recognized, and he molded the defense into a stone wall. That quartet of defensive backs collected all of those interceptions, but they were the beneficiaries of the opposing quarterback's hurried throws, as well as their own sixth sense and ability to stick like glue to faking receivers.

The Bears' front four of Atkins, Bob Kilcullen, Stan Jones, and Earl Leggett were the main rushers and they mostly made do without the injured Ed O'Bradovich and Fred Williams.

Kilcullen, who came out of Texas Tech, was hanging out with Jones before the season opener, only to discover that the newspaper didn't think much of his chances of stopping the run. Still, he played 10 years, all with the Bears, through the 1966 season.

Leggett was the Bears' No. 1 draft pick out of Louisiana State in 1957, and he had an even longer career in the NFL. The 265-pound

Leggett took over for Williams in the beginning of the season when Big Fred injured his shoulder. Then with two games left in the season, Leggett ripped ligaments in his knee and was gone for the year. Williams, who had spent the previous few months rehabbing, returned to reclaim one of the defensive tackle spots.

Williams and Leggett were sharing an apartment—a jinxed one, apparently—and after Leggett returned home from a game, but before he had X-rays, Williams knew his roomie was in trouble.

"I was helping him in and out of bed," said Williams, "so I knew he couldn't be in very good shape."

Williams moved back into the starting lineup after missing 10 games and on the first play an opposing lineman smacked his injured shoulder. "I didn't think a thing about it until I got back into the huddle," Williams said, "and then I suddenly said, 'Gee, I must be all right.'"

It was remarkable that despite personnel moving in and out of the lineup the defense could lead the league in almost every category.

The secondary also did its job well. It was a breakthrough year for McRae with his six interceptions. Whitsell was already a three-year veteran when he came to the Bears in '61 from the Detroit Lions. Whitsell played 12 seasons and grabbed 46 interceptions and always said some of the most interesting and fun times he had in the game was as a teammate of Doug Atkins, Ed O'Bradovich, Roosevelt Taylor, and Earl Leggett. Playing with Atkins was like playing with a light brigade charger. "Atkins led just by saying, 'Boys, let's go get 'em!' Doug was so massive and could be so mean and tough when he said for us to 'go get 'em' we knew we had no choice but to do just that."

Whitsell, who operated a bar in retirement, always considered the '63 Bears defense to be an extraordinary one. "We came to play every day and every down. We never gave up and we didn't make many mistakes."

Overall, though, it was the men in the middle, the threesome linebacker corps of Joe Fortunato, Bill George, and Larry Morris and the combination of their smarts, ferocity, and terrific ability to blitz, to cover receivers, to tackle, and to fill holes created by blockers, that lifted the Bears above everyone else.

"The best there's ever been," Casares said of that trio in the middle. "George, Larry, and Joe, I mean the three of them, were just outstanding."

Bill George was a legend at linebacker. Born in 1929 in Waynesburg, Pennsylvania, the 6' 2" 230-pound George was a tackle at Wake Forest. The Bears drafted him in the second round in '51 and he was chosen first-team All-Pro eight times by his retirement after 15 seasons in '66.

Although coaches on various teams were experimenting with their defenses in the late fifties, George is often credited as being the man who invented the middle linebacker position and at the least he developed the role and showed how it could be played at the highest level. The breakthrough for the position occurred in a 1954 game against the Philadelphia Eagles, when George was playing alongside George Connor, who was the Bears' defensive captain. Bill George observed that if he dropped back into the open space between the line and the secondary, he would be in the way when the Eagles' quarterback attempted a dump-off pass over the middle. At the time, George—playing the position called middle guard—was required to make a move to rush over center before sloughing off into coverage. He figured that if he simply backed up he would ruin the Eagles' plans and plays. Connor responded favorably. "Why don't you go for the ball?"

On the ensuing snaps, George dropped back. The first time the Eagles attempted to throw over the middle the pass hit him in the stomach. It was not clear who was more surprised, George or the quarterback. The ball fell to the ground. The Eagle thrower, likely thinking the play was a fluke, tried a similar play soon after and this time George intercepted the ball. The middle guard disappeared from the lexicon and the middle linebacker became one of the most important players on the field.

Soon enough, not only George, but such prominent players as Sam Huff with the Giants, Chuck Bednarik with the Eagles, Joe Schmidt with the Lions, and Ray Nitschke with the Packers emerged as stars at the position.

"Bill George was the first great middle linebacker," said Abe Gibron, who coached the Bears from 1972–74. "He brought all of the romance and charisma to the position. He was like having a Clark Shaughnessy on the field. He called all the plays and had a special knack for it."

By moving backwards after the hike, rather than automatically charging forward, George essentially was no longer a fifth lineman; he fit into the 4-3-3 defensive alignment. At one point, George Halas had a radio transmitter implanted in George's helmet so the coach could call defensive signals from the sideline. That didn't last long, though, because commissioner Bert Bell ruled it illegal.

A few years later, when the San Francisco 49ers began to rely on the shotgun formation with the quarterback lining up several yards behind the center instead of reaching below his backside for the snap, George adapted again. He rushed as he used to when he played the middle guard position, perfecting the blitz from the middle linebacker spot.

"You've got to put constant pressure on the good quarterbacks," was George's philosophy. "You just can't let good quarterbacks get set."

George almost missed the '63 season entirely, nearly missing out on the fabulous season. In an automobile accident after the '61 season, George suffered neck damage between his fifth and sixth vertebrae. The impact was hard enough that George had to cope with stiffness and pain for more than a year. He played through that inconvenience in '62, but didn't know if he wanted to do so again.

He did end up returning to play in '63, but was surprised when Halas gave Fortunato the job of calling defensive signals on the field (minus the radio transmitter). Whether it was dissatisfaction with that move despite the success in '63, or a fresh perspective that encouraged him to investigate the employment landscape, one of the NFL's biggest defensive stars almost did the unthinkable after that season. George's contract was up and he floated his name and availability to the American Football League.

This was startling on all fronts. It bugged Halas to think that one of his foremost players might consider jumping leagues. It bothered the National Football League to think that it was possible one of its stars might flee to the competition. And surprisingly, it flummoxed AFL owners, who innately understood that if George carried his resume across the fence, the NFL might unleash nuclear weapons.

In January of '64, less than a month after the NFL season culminated, newspaper reports began appearing that George had made contact with at least five of the eight AFL teams inquiring about a job. George made it clear to the teams that he wanted to make more money after 12 years in the game. One might think that the AFL owners would jump at such an opportunity. That's what they were all about: stealing talent, putting names in uniform, right?

An anonymous AFL coach was quoted as saying, "Everybody wants to sign him, but is afraid to." An official, but unnamed spokesman for the league tried to explain the reticence which was uncharacteristic for the AFL. "There is no agreement between the two leagues," he said, "but even without talking they know what signing a player like George will mean. All-out-war. Something neither can afford."

Everyone in the AFL backed away and George re-signed with the Bears, where he stayed through the '65 season until the team give him his outright release. George played his last season with the Los Angeles Rams where George Allen, his Bears' defensive guru, had become the head coach.

"I just thought I had some football left in my bones," George said after the Bears released him. "The game gets into your system."

It was not many years after retiring that George was inducted into the Hall of Fame with the class of 1974. He said when he first received the phone call that he thought it was a prank from his old teammate, Fred Williams, about to tell him to send money in a hurry because his car was broken down. Then, when the Hall asked if he had artifacts of his career to donate for exhibition, George was at a loss for words. "The Hall of Fame people asked me if I had any mementoes of my career to donate. I looked around the house and all I could find was a very small jockstrap."

Apparently, it was too difficult to figure out a way to put the bruise marks from opposing ball carriers into a display, because that's how George frequently left his mark.

"He was one of the most intense football players I ever saw," said Bears receiver Johnny Morris. "He was the backbone of the Bears defense for so many years."

The entire linebacker group was the backbone of the Bears' defense in '63. Larry Morris came out of Georgia Tech where he had ascended to almost legendary stature through his high school and college performances, the latter which led him to the College Football Hall of Fame.

Morris was a wicked tackler who was nicknamed "The Brahma Bull," and also at times doubled as a center. There was a somewhat nonsensical photo of Morris accompanying a major feature on him in the *Atlanta Journal* that highlighted his center duties. Morris is bent over, hand on a football, wearing street clothes including a tie, with his three little children lined up in a row next to him in three-point stances as he is about to snap the ball to his wife on their lawn.

One remarkable aspect of Morris' career was that over a four-plus-year period, his high school and college teams all went undefeated. For decades, enthusiasm for professional football and public questions about the caliber of play persisted from those who preferred the so-called purity of amateurs playing the college game. By the 1950s it was felt the new appreciation for pro ball had finally spiked some of those issues; but whenever the participants in the Chicago Charities College All-Star Game scrimmaged against the Bears and whenever the Bears played any type of college group in an exhibition Halas demonstrated zeal in crushing them. He wanted to make sure that people comprehended how much better the pros were.

Still, into the 1960s that issue still came up. Morris, who was so identified with Georgia Tech in his home state, was drawn into such a discussion as he became one of the original Atlanta Falcons when that squad was an expansion team in 1966. Morris had this to say about the difference of the two games:

> We work harder. We put in five days of rugged practice every week. On Sunday we have to hit with everything we've got to survive. The pros collect the biggest, fastest, toughest and smartest players in the country, so the man you're facing is usually as good as you and he may be better, and you can bet he'll be knocking for keeps.

Morris was drafted out of college by the Los Angeles Rams, spent a little time with the Washington Redskins, and was with the Bears from '59–65. Morris loved taking direction from Clark Shaughnessy when he was defensive coordinator. He called Shaughnessy "truly a football genius. He had a simple theory about pass defense: First, it's easiest to knock down the passer; second, hold up the receiver; third, defend against the pass, but by then it may be too late."

There were times sports commentators noted that Morris terrorized quarterbacks, which means he was following Shaughnessy's instructions pretty closely. Morris never particularly made public that he hated quarterbacks or anything quite so extreme, but just felt obligated to run them over. At the end of his career, he even admitted that he admired some of them. It was actually ironic that during her husband's most attention-getting season in '63, Mrs. Morris early on said that it was no fair offensive players got all of the attention instead of the hard-working defensive players.

Morris mentioned Otto Graham, Charley Conerly, Y. A. Tittle, Bobby Layne, with an A-plus rating written next to Johnny Unitas' name as quarterbacks he respected. The same sportswriter asked about other linebackers whose work Morris appreciated and he did put in a word for the Lions' Joe Schmidt, but he emphasized the efforts of Bill George and Joe Fortunato, his Bears partners. It may have been loyalty, or it may have been reality, but when that threesome was together it was indisputably something special.

Over the years in Chicago Morris found working for George Halas fascinating. He sometimes stifled an inner chuckle when Halas, a never-give-the-other-guy-an-inch adherent, demonstrated some of his old-time distrust of enemy teams.

He's even more suspicious than most coaches. He goes to extremes to maintain security. Honestly, before the kickoff one day we had won the toss and I raised my hand showing how the wind was blowing. He actually grabbed my arm and told me not to let the opposition know which way the wind was blowing.

Of course, by mid-season of '63, there was not a lot of secrecy about which way the wind was blowing with the Bears. The defense was hounding teams into mistakes and they had such a smoothly meshing operation that not even the stream of injuries ran the train off the tracks.

The '63 season was Joe Fortunato's first as captain of the defense. Halas made the call to change captains. He took the authority for calling the defensive signals away from Bill George and because Stan Jones moved from offense to defense, he was out as cocaptain of the offense.

Fortunato graduated from Mississippi State, where he was an All-American, but was only a seventh-round draft pick of the Bears in '52. He was also a first-round draft pick of the United States Army, so he did not suit up for Chicago until '55. His first of five Pro Bowl selections was in '58, and he hit a hot streak in the early sixties, starting with a second-team All-Pro choice in '62. Fortunato was 6' 1" and played at 225 pounds, and was considered a mobile linebacker.

He excelled at search-and-destroy of quarterbacks and other ball carriers, which kind of dovetailed with his hobby of hunting in the off-season. Some of the same principles applied, though less so when Fortunato shifted more attention later in life to fishing.

Fortunato helped the Bears develop their reputation of featuring great linebackers; a status that linked him with Bill George and Larry Morris and continued through Dick Butkus and into the 2000s with Brian Urlacher. As a team, it is doubtful that the Bears or any other team had such a group of high achievers working simultaneously as Fortunato, George, and Morris. "It sure was a great trio," said Fortunato. "We played together so well."

Years later, Fortunato said one of the distinguishing characteristics of the entire Bears squad of '63 was the way everyone got along and how hard everyone worked to prepare for the season and in practice during the season. The common goal was a great unifier.

"We really had a lot of camaraderie. A lot of teams don't have that, but we had it."

Game by game throughout the '63 season the Bears' reputation on defense grew. They ended up leading the NFL in 10 defensive categories. To the degree Fortunato influenced the formations called, he tried to spread around the responsibility for sealing off offenses. Collectively, the Bears were as good as they had ever been opposite the ball.

"The biggest difference between our '63 defenses and those of other years was that we no longer were depending upon one or two individuals. When I called the plays I tried to avoid putting too much pressure on one man."

Chicago did not merely win the turnover battle, it overwhelmed foes with the defense's knack for stealing the ball; whether it was recovering fumbles or pilfering passes. The defense also avoided giving up big gainers; big plays that could energize another team and lead to fast points. The Bears made their opponents work for every yard, not gain them in big gulps.

"We eliminated the big mistake. What killed us before was the one big mistake. All of a sudden the other club would break a man open and it looked as though we didn't have anybody within 10 yards of him."

Once Fortunato got the nod from Halas to be the defensive signal-caller and the Bears followed with great success, it was as if all of the sports reporters in the universe discovered him at once. Suddenly, after years of high-caliber play in the league, there were stories being written about him citing how "brainy" he was and how his job called for "a computer mind."

In a story written by Brent Musburger, who in the sixties was a sports reporter for the *Chicago American* before becoming much more famous nationally as a sportscaster, what Fortunato had to do on a single play was dissected. The example used was from a game against the Packers when Bart Starr took the snap and handed off to fullback Jim Taylor. "On a single play," Musburger wrote, "Fortunato, who calls the Bears' defensive signals, must consider at least a dozen factors."

> *He must know what yard-line the ball is on and how far the ball is from the sidelines. He must know how many yards the opposition needs for a first down and how much time remains on the clock. He must recall what plays the quarterback has favored in this down and yardage situation in other games. He must know the physical condition of the opposing backfield and which players they have in the game. Joe might have to do three things himself on that single play. If the end comes at him he must fight him off. Then he must see if the running play is headed in his direction. Finally, he must be prepared to drop back and help out on pass coverage.*

Fortunato, who more than once sacrificed the health of his nose to a tackle of a ball-toting foe, otherwise stayed healthy until his final days with the Bears. With Shaughnessy—the defensive coordinator before George Allen—Fortunato was also held in high esteem. "Consistency is the word for him," said Shaughnessy. "He's very alert and reacts quickly. Instinct has a lot to do with it."

Yet even though Shaughnessy sounded like the president of the Joe Fortunato fan club, his promotion to defensive captain came after Allen took over from Shaughnessy. Because of his great respect for Bill George, Fortunato didn't want to see a change made. But maybe it was just time because Fortunato's ability to read opposing teams' intentions had become so good it was almost eerie.

"Instinct comes from experience," said Fortunato. "After a while you can almost smell a play coming. I have certain keys that I use."

No wonder Fortunato was picked to call the Bears defenses. Not only could he read the plays unfolding, he could smell them coming in advance. That's the way it looked all season long as the Bears shut down offense after offense. All season long, it just didn't seem possible to fool the Bears linebackers or the Bears defense.

13

JFK ASSASSINATED

DURING THE VICTORY over the Packers on November 17, Bears fullback Rick Casares was tackled by Green Bay linebacker Ray Nitschke in a fashion that lived up to Nitschke's self-description that he could sometimes be mean on the field.

Nitschke took down Casares and twisted a foot—and some yelled at him for the method being unnecessary, especially when Casares didn't rise from his carry. At first, people thought Casares had a broken ankle. Then the focus dropped a little bit lower to his heel. Five days later, Casares was in the hospital seeking an accurate diagnosis of what happened to his foot.

All of a sudden he heard several voices screaming in a hallway. The shouts came from nurses. They had just learned that the president of the United States, John F. Kennedy, had been shot in Dallas at 12:30 p.m., Central Standard Time.

"I was getting treatment," Casares said. "I was getting a cast put on."

Everything halted. Everyone stopped what they were doing.

Everyone who was of sufficient age remembers where they were when America lost its innocence. The assassination of JFK while riding in a presidential motorcade in an open-topped vehicle next to his wife, Jacqueline, while waving to thousands of cheering citizens lining a parade route, stopped time on the afternoon of November 22, 1963.

Nurses stopped forming a cast and wailed. Students in public schools were called back to their homerooms and sent home from school early on this Friday afternoon. Radios and television sets were turned on to hear breaking news that emanated from the Southwest in fragments. At first there were news bulletins and then there was nothing else except the news on the air.

It wasn't merely that regularly scheduled programming was interrupted. It was all replaced. Everything went off the air as the news departments of the three existing major networks—ABC, CBS, and NBC—took over all stations all of the time as history was being written.

In 1963, America was feeling pretty good about itself. The sleepy fifties were over and had produced an era of post–World War II prosperity. TV sets were in almost every home, Americans were buying houses in almost every suburb, and they were buying cars that allowed them to commute to the big city or to drive the open road.

There was plenty still to be fixed, particularly in terms of race relations and the Cold War with the Soviet Union, though an uneasy truce prevailed. There was a new, young, vigorous president in office; one who possessed charm and wit and was married to a beautiful wife whose clothing choices established styles for fascinated housewives. There were young children growing up in the White House and pundits told everyone that the United

States had entered an age of Camelot. The future looked pretty good, even if you were an African American seeking fairer application of your civil rights. That was coming . . . you could feel it.

No one realized when they woke up on November 22, 1963, that the elongated fifties would be over by lunchtime. An assassin's bullet fired from the window of the Texas School Book Depository at Dealey Plaza launched a fresh and more disturbing era; one that brought war, violence to the streets, assassinations (more than one), and upheaval to American society on a scale rarely seen. The sixties were a turning point in American history, accomplished in revolutionary fashion and the murder of the young president was only the first act.

Before the decade expired the United States was neck deep in a war against Communism half a world away in South Vietnam that few of its citizens wanted. Martin Luther King Jr., the most influential black leader of the twentieth century, was assassinated on the balcony of a Memphis hotel. Robert F. Kennedy, the former Attorney General of the United States, the slain president's brother, and himself a candidate for president, was assassinated in the kitchen of a Los Angeles hotel on a campaign stop. George Wallace, the governor of Alabama and proponent of separation of the races, was gunned down and spent the rest of his days in a wheelchair. Impatient for what was theirs, American blacks demonstrated in the streets for equality, riots churned in certain American cities, and a sexual revolution began the battle for women's rights in the United States.

From the moment a bullet struck JFK, the sixties were on fire.

John F. Kennedy, a senator from Massachusetts, won one of the closest presidential elections ever conducted over former vice president Richard M. Nixon in 1960. Kennedy's vice president

The most challenging year of long-time NFL commissioner Pete Rozelle's tenure began with him addressing a gambling scandal. Roselle suspended star players Paul Hornung and Alex Karras indefinitely, but also had to contend with the death of "Big Daddy" Lipscomb and the decision to play games on the weekend of president John F. Kennedy's assassination. *Photo courtesy of AP Images/Anthony Camerano*

The colorful and enigmatic defense tackle of the Pittsburgh Steelers, Eugene "Big Daddy" Lipscomb. He was an All-Star performer who died mysteriously in the spring before the 1963 season. *Photo courtesy of AP Images/NFL Photos*

Green Bay Packers All Star halfback Paul Hornung talks with Los Angeles Rams runner Jon Arnett (right) after a 1960 playoff victory. Hornung would be suspended for the 1963 season for gambling. *Photo courtesy of AP Images/Harold Matosian*

Detroit Lions defensive linesman Alex Karras, always resented being suspended for the 1963 season by commissioner Pete Roselle because of gambling allegations. *Photo courtesy of AP Images/ Preston Stroup*

The Pro Football Hall of Fame opened its doors in September of 1963, when it inducted its inaugural class of seventeen members in Canton, Ohio (top left, John "Blood" McNally, top right, George Halas, bottom, Curley Lambeau, Johnny "Blood" McNally, Cal Hubbard, and Don Hutson. *Photos courtesy of AP Images*

Legendary Green Bay Packers coach Vince Lombardi was feted by fans after winning the 1962 NFL Championship Game over the New York Giants. Lombardi's Packers were the main obstacle to the Bears title run in 1963. *Photo courtesy of AP Images*

Chicago Bears coach George Halas exults with players Bill George (61) and rookie Larry Glueck (43) after their team began the 1963 season with a victory over the rival and defending champion Green Bay Packers. *Photo courtesy of AP Images/Charles Knoblock*

Powerful fullback Jim Brown of the Cleveland Browns was the most dominant runner of his era. Both he and the Browns had a long-standing rivalry with the New York Giants, the team that beat them out for the Eastern Division title in 1963. *Photo courtesy of AP Images*

Halas was a stickler for tough practices, as can be seen in this image during preparation for a match-up against the Pittsburgh Steelers in November of 1963. (From left to right: halfback Ronnie Bull, quarterback Bill Wade, and tight end Mike Ditka) *Photo courtesy of AP Images*

The AFL was the brainchild of Dallas Texans founder Lamar Hunt (middle). He worked diligently to find money men like Houston Oilers owner Bud Adams (left) and New York Titans owner Harry Wismer (right) to buttress the reputation of the league. *Photo courtesy of AP Images/File*

Youthful coach and general manager Al Davis of the Oakland Raiders, who rebuilt a struggling team, poses with six squad members who were selected to the 1963 American Football League All Star team (From left to right: defensive halfback Tommy Morrow and Fred Williamson, linebacker Archie Matsos, halfback Clem Daniels, center Jim Otto, and end Art Powell.) *Photo courtesy of AP Images/Robert Klein*

Nick Buoniconti, the linebacker who was the heart and soul of the Boston Patriots defense during their run to the American Football League Eastern Division Championship. *Photo courtesy of AP Images*

San Diego offensive lineman Walt Sweeney, who was one of the core members of the Chargers 1963 American Football League championship team. *Photo courtesy of AP Images*

Two days after President John F. Kennedy was assassinated, the National Football League played on. Seen here mourning before their game against the Minnesota Vikings are Detroit Lions fullback Nick Pietrosante (33) and linebacker Wayne Walker (55). *Photo courtesy of AP Images*

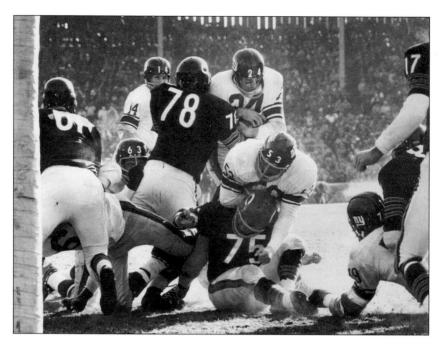

Bears defensive tackle Stan Jones (78) stuffs New York Giants halfback Phil King (24) at the goal line during the 1963 National Football League Championship Game in Chicago at Wrigley Field. *Photo courtesy of AP Images/NFL Photos*

A frustrated New York Giants quarterback, Y. A. Tittle, slams his helmet to the turf in the closing seconds of the 1963 National Football League Championship Game in Chicago after throwing an interception in the end zone to defensive back Richie Peitibon. *Photo courtesy of AP Images*

was the former Texas senator Lyndon Baines Johnson, a southerner intended to balance the ticket. Considered a liberal, while African Americans didn't believe he was moving quickly enough on civil rights measured, Kennedy was despised by whites who wished to retain the status quo holding blacks down and denying equal rights and dignity.

Kennedy was on a southern swing to make friends. He departed Washington, D.C. via Air Force One on November 21, and made stops in San Antonio and Houston before spending the night in Fort Worth. After a breakfast event, the very short flight to Dallas' Love Field took fifteen minutes. By the time the presidential party, which included Texas Governor John Connolly, left the airport for the Dallas Trade Mart, where Kennedy was scheduled to speak to a luncheon gathering, it was 11:40 a.m.

The crowds lining the motorcade route, which had been publicized, swelled to something on the order of 150,000 or more people and prompted Nellie Connolly, the governor's wife, also riding in the presidential limousine, to infamously say to JFK, "Mr. President, you can't say Dallas doesn't love you." Just seconds later, gunfire shattered the uplifting scene, the bullets wounding Mrs. Connolly's husband as well as delivering the mortal wounds to the president.

A scene of chaos ensued. Secret service agents swarmed the cars carrying dignitaries and dove in to protect Johnson. Mrs. Kennedy, resplendent in a pink suit, became hysterical, calling for help, trying to exit the vehicle, her blood-stained clothing visible to horrified witnesses. The limousine rushed to Parkland Hospital.

By 12:33 p.m., the police dispatchers in Dallas had their first reports of shots fired and were notifying Parkland that the president was being rushed to the site. Only minutes after the bullets were fired the first United Press International and Associated Press advisories were alerting the world that something major had happened in Dallas. Reporters, as usual, were traveling with the president, so they were already on the scene. The first UPI report came across the wire when little was known, but in part read, "Three shots were fired at President Kennedy's motorcade today in downtown Dallas . . ."

In 1963, the nation's most trusted newsman was CBS broadcaster Walter Cronkite. In later years, Cronkite would take on the look of a fatherly figure, hair going white, as he informed the United States at dinner time each weekday of what was going on in their world. In '63, Cronkite still had a head full of all-dark hair (not clear what color it was since the country's televisions showed black and white pictures), but he already had his air of credibility.

Cronkite was the first newsman on the air nationwide as CBS interrupted its soap opera *As the World Turns*. He read a bulletin and then the show resumed, but only briefly.

When he greeted the nation on this afternoon Cronkite looked like a working newsman. He sat at a desk—not a studio podium—with telephones clearly visible and other people in the CBS newsroom clearly working in the background. He did not have a sport coat on, but a long-sleeve shirt and tie. In part, Cronkite's first comments were:

> *There was an attempt on the life of President Kennedy. . . .*
> *He was wounded along with Governor Connolly. . . .*
> *He was taken to Parkland Hospital . . . where their condition is as yet unknown.*

Cronkite served on the air as the central gathering spot for correspondents on the ground in Dallas, funneling information. There was a report that the president was receiving a blood transfusion. There was another report that a priest had administered the last rites. Then reports began to flow in that JFK had died, but Cronkite formally added to each that they were unconfirmed. Finally, Cronkite said that CBS correspondent Dan Rather "has confirmed" that President Kennedy was dead. Throughout his commentary, Cronkite remained somber and professional, periodically donning his black-framed glasses and removing them. When he announced the fact of JFK's death, Cronkite perceptibly paused more than once, apparently to regain control of his emotions, before resuming his comments.

The rest of the world was not as calm. Shock was the prevailing emotion. Approximately seventy minutes after the shots were fired, and three miles from Dealey Plaza, Lee Harvey Oswald was arrested in connection with the shooting of police officer J. D. Tippett immediately after the assassination. Responding to a suspect description Tippett had pulled up next to Oswald in his patrol car and spoken to him. Then when he climbed out of the car Oswald shot him. Oswald fled, but witnesses saw him run into a movie theatre and called police. That's where he was apprehended after a minor struggle.

Much of the nation closed down that Friday afternoon. Businesses and offices shut their doors. Breadwinners went home to be with their families. Radios and televisions remained on as the populace sat riveted awaiting any news development. Lyndon Johnson was sworn in on Air Force One as the United States' 36th president and flown back to Washington.

Events unfolded with breathtaking speed. Kennedy was shot, rushed to the hospital, pronounced dead, a new president was sworn in, both LBJ and JFK's body were flown back to

Washington, a suspect was arrested, the murder weapon was found, Lee Harvey Oswald was charged, and all of this took place between lunchtime and early evening.

Stunned and depressed, the nation slipped into mourning. One by one, entertainment palaces shut down. Broadway closed. Officials that administered the National Basketball Association and the National Hockey League announced that games were being cancelled. Nobody felt much like having fun. Then the American Football League said no games would be played on Sunday. Yet no word came from National Football League headquarters.

Like the rest of their fellow citizens, pro football players were stunned, grasping to comprehend the magnitude of the national tragedy. Neither did they feel like going to work, either. Fifty years later, Chicago Bears defensive back Roosevelt Taylor can't remember for sure if the team practiced that Friday as it normally would have, or not, but he thinks it did. As far as the Bears knew, by the end of Friday, they still had a game to play against the Pittsburgh Steelers on Sunday, so why wouldn't they practice? The Bears did practice that day, but finished before hearing the news. Tight end Mike Ditka said, "We were shocked." Same as everyone else.

The country was in disbelief. Events of Friday, November 22, were difficult to digest and make sense out of as people went home and tried to explain to their children what was going on. It was a fair bet that the dinner table talk was not about football on that evening and that football was on almost no one's mind.

What to do, what was the right thing to do? Should the teams play on Sunday or should they stay home? Over in the AFL offices in New York City, Milt Woodard, the AFL's assistant commissioner, was monitoring events. Commissioner Joe Foss was not in the office. He was not in town. In fact, Woodard wasn't really sure where Foss was. It was hunting season in South Dakota, so he may have been out in the field somewhere. There were no cell phones in those days, so Woodard waited for Foss to call him in order to discuss the league's course of action.

Woodard actually called the NFL offices and asked to speak to Commissioner Pete Rozelle about what the senior league was going to do. Rozelle, Woodard recalled later, insisted the games would go on. "He said the National Football League definitely was going to play."

The afternoon ended and Woodard sat next to a silent telephone. No word from Foss. Dinnertime came and went. Woodard, the same as millions of Americans, followed the biggest news story of his life since World War II on television and radio. At 8 p.m., acting alone, taking the decision in his own hands, Woodard declared that the AFL was going to call off its scheduled football games. "It was in my mind that to play football would not have been smart or acceptable. Finally, I decided to announce, under Foss' name, that we were canceling the weekend's games."

When sports columnists wrote about the AFL decision, they praised Foss for making the right call. Woodard's role was pretty much unknown. There was vehement disagreement with the NFL choosing the opposite tactic to play despite the tragedy. Red Smith, one of the greatest sportswriters of all time, asked, "Which is the big league now?" The AFL, it seemed, was more in tune with the mood of the people.

On the Friday afternoon when President Kennedy was killed, San Diego Chargers defensive back Dick Westmoreland was on his way to practice. As an illustration of how unthinkable the news developments were when Westmoreland heard a snatch of a radio broadcast, he was confused.

> *I was in a gas station. I heard something on the radio and I thought they were talking about Abraham Lincoln. We practiced, but everybody was stunned. We sat around the locker room watching it on TV. We didn't want to play a game.*

Most, but not all, college football games were called off. It ended up with each school making its own decision and roughly a dozen played. One school that played was Oklahoma, scheduled for a confrontation with Nebraska. Oklahoma's coach was Bud Wilkinson, who served as head of JFK's national physical fitness program. Wilkinson telephoned Robert Kennedy to ask if the Sooners should play. Wilkinson said RFK gave him the go-ahead.

One of the first NFL figures to raise the issue of canceling games was Dan Rooney, the son of Pittsburgh Steelers founder Art Rooney, and one of the higher ranking family members in charge of the team at the time. Dan Rooney called Rozelle and said he didn't think the NFL should play that weekend. Cleveland Browns owner Art Modell did not want to play either—his team was scheduled to meet the Dallas Cowboys. But Cowboys general manager, Tex Schramm, wanted to play.

Rozelle was actually close to members of the Kennedy Administration, and knew Robert Kennedy personally. He also knew presidential press secretary Pierre Salinger very well, having known him for years dating back to a time period when they both worked in California. So Rozelle called Salinger to ask for advice on what to do.

JFK had been a football fan and his family was known for organizing highly publicized touch football games at the Kennedy retreat in Hyannis Port on Cape Cod. Rozelle did reach Salinger and quoted him as saying, "Jack would have wanted you to play the games." On that basis, Rozelle plunged forward with the plan to play. However, after consulting with the league's television network, CBS, it was decided that the games would not be televised.

The schedule for November 24 was as follows:

Baltimore Colts @ Los Angeles Rams
Dallas Cowboys @ Cleveland Browns
San Francisco 49ers @ Green Bay Packers
St. Louis Cardinals @ New York Giants
Chicago Bears @ Pittsburgh Steelers
Detroit Lions @ Minnesota Vikings
Washington Redskins @ Philadelphia Eagles

In Philadelphia, Eagles players contributed money into a pot for the family of slain Dallas police officer J. D. Tippett. The Browns beat the Cowboys, 27–17, at Cleveland Municipal Stadium. Quarterback Eddie LeBaron expected his Cowboys to get booed because they represented the city of the assassination. In what was already a tremendously tumultuous weekend, things got crazier when suspected assassin Lee Harvey Oswald was shot on live television Sunday morning when he was being transferred between jails. The Cowboys saw it happen on a small TV in the visitors' locker room.

"Put your helmets on and keep 'em on" is what LeBaron told his teammates. He expected irate fans would throw things at them, but that did not occur. The Cowboys were met by complete silence when they jogged out onto the field for the start of the game.

It may have been quiet that day, but for a long time afterwards, being a sports figure from Dallas—or anyone from Dallas traveling—was not very rewarding. "There was a stigma put on us," said LeBaron. "Someone would come up and ask, 'Where are you from?' We'd say, 'Dallas' and they'd say, 'Oh, you're the ones who shot the president.' It was a tough deal for a long time."

One concession was made to change the preplanned schedule. Ray Renfro, who had been a star wide receiver for the Browns, was back in town as an assistant coach for the Cowboys and the Browns had scheduled a "Ray Renfro Day" to honor him. That was postponed.

By Sunday morning—game day for the NFL—President Kennedy's body was in its flag-draped casket and rolling down Pennsylvania en route to the Capitol Rotunda where it would lie in state. Thousands would file past the coffin to pay their respects. Only forty-eight hours had passed since the assassin's bullets struck.

Back in Dallas, Oswald's jailers were moving him out of the county jail to police headquarters through a basement exit. Handcuffed with police surrounding him, Oswald was being led into an armored truck. The nation was watching on live TV to get a closer look at the man the Dallas police said murdered their president. Abruptly, from an angle slightly to Oswald's right, but almost head on, a man appeared on the screen wearing a dark sport coat and a fedora. Jack Ruby was dressed to blend in with the many other suit-wearing police officials. Before anyone reacted to his presence, the sound of a gunshot was audible and

Oswald flinched from Ruby's shot from a pistol at nearly point-blank range.

In a weekend of events that left the country reeling, an attentive United States had just witnessed a killing on television in real time, with the accused assassin crumpling from a shot to his stomach by a vigilante at 11:21 a.m., Central Standard Time. The intruder was quickly wrestled to the ground by a group of plainclothesmen and captured. Oswald was rushed to the hospital by ambulance where he died at 1:07 p.m., taking to the grave secrets and details of the JFK assassination case that have haunted Americans ever since.

The shooter was identified at Jack Ruby, a Dallas nightclub operator, who said he sought vengeance on Oswald to prevent Jacqueline Kennedy from having to endure a trial.

The nightmare of bizarre and terrible events was in its third day for Americans, as NFL football teams warmed up for their afternoon kickoffs around the country. The players, coaches and spectators—and there were plenty of them—were just about the only people not watching news developments on their TV screens. For those who believed no one would attend the games that Sunday, they were proven wrong. Attendance in Pittsburgh at Forbes Field for the Steelers–Bears contest was 36,465. Attendance in Wisconsin for the Packers–49ers game was 45,905.

Green Bay tackle Bob Skoronski remembers that everyone was affected by the assassination of the president, but not much conversation took place about whether or not the Packers should be playing the scheduled game.

"Lombardi was very concerned. He knew the Kennedys. If he was concerned we were concerned. It was a very tragic thing. It was a tough thing."

A lot of NFL players wished they were not suiting up that day.

"None of the ball players really wanted to play that week," said Roosevelt Taylor. "It was the week we played Pittsburgh. You could feel it all around you what was going on. It felt like a mistake to play. I was pretty much a youngster [25] at the time and I didn't have much to say about it."

Casares ended up having surgery and missing the rest of the season from the heel injury, so he was replaced in the lineup in Pittsburgh by Joe Marconi. Outside the football team atmosphere, Casares said the whole world seemed out of kilter.

"Everybody was spacey. People were going around saying, 'What happened?' It took you out of your normal routine."

Bears defensive back J. C. Caroline had the realistic outlook that if the league ordered the games to be played and his team was going to be playing, he would be with it. But that didn't mean he thought it was right.

"It wasn't our decision. If we were supposed to play the game we were going to play the game. You kind of wish you were able to stay home and watch it [the real-world news]. It was about respect for the president."

NFL football was played in the eleventh week of the season—as scheduled—in cities sprinkled around the land. It was almost the only time out the nation took from the relentlessly shocking and depressing events telescoped into the previous two days.

Appropriately enough, there was a chill in the air at Forbes Field when the Bears and Steelers kicked off. The temperature was 35 degrees and the wind was 15 mph. The Steelers were still years away from their greatest franchise achievements, but they were pretty good that season, with a 6–3–1 mark entering the contest. They may have been better still if they had been able to suit up the one major defensive figure they lost in the spring. Defensive tackle Big Daddy Lipscomb should have been in uniform for Pittsburgh. Instead, he was in the cold ground, dead for more than six months.

Halas recognized that the Steelers were no pushover; that they indeed could be very dangerous immediately after his team's emotional victory over the Packers. He told people he had circled that game on the schedule when it first came out and Pittsburgh was playing good ball 10 games into the season.

"The Steelers are at the top of their game right now and there could be a letdown by our players after that great win over Green Bay."

In fact, although they trailed the New York Giants by two games in the Eastern Division, the Steelers were not playing only to be spoilers. They still had a long-shot chance to catch New York.

This was a hard-fought game. Chicago took the early lead on a one-yard run by halfback Willie Galimore in the first quarter and Bob Jencks booted the extra point for a 7–0 lead. The Steelers tied the game in the second quarter on a six-yard run by Dick Hoak and an extra point by Lou Michaels. Michaels, like so many others at the time, was a part-time kicker who played a full-time position, in his case defensive end.

Chicago bounced back when Ronnie Bull took his turn out of the backfield with another one-yard TD run, culminated by a Jencks kick for a 14–7 lead in the second quarter. For once the vaunted Bears' defense couldn't make that stand up and the Steelers retaliated on a 31-yard touchdown pass to Roy Curry from Ed Brown. Brown was quite familiar with the Bears—he was another of Chicago's quarterbacks of the fifties during the fallow period when Halas was juggling signal-callers. Brown was a Bear from '54–61, and like several others of those discarded by Halas, found a starting job elsewhere.

Brown was one of the Bears rejects who felt he never got a chance to show what he could do, so he was not looking at this game as a special reunion to clap Papa Bear Halas on the back. "I want to beat them in the worst way," said Brown.

Yes, the Bears were sky-high after their critical triumph over the Packers, but that receded as a distraction following Kennedy being killed. That was foremost on everyone's mind. As Ronnie Bull recalled years later:

> *That was a tough day because of the assassination. We didn't know if we were going to play or not. Truthfully, none of us really wanted to play. Who wants to play football when something drastic like that happens? We went through the motions in practice. You know what they should have done was just moved the season back a week.*

Deadlocked at 14–14 going into the third quarter, whatever adjustments were discussed in the locker room at halftime did not work particularly well. Neither team moved the ball much in the second half, but in the fourth quarter, Michaels nailed an 11-yard field goal to give the Steelers the lead.

All these weeks, even months, the Bears had been nursing their lead in the Western Division standings over the Packers; whether it was a full game or on the head-to-head tie-breaker. A loss to the Steelers could change everything; it could cost the Bears the season.

On this day when many players wished they were like most other Americans sitting at home, and some of their weekend warrior luster had worn off, the player who probably most wanted to compete in this game for the Bears was Ditka. Ditka agreed with Rozelle that JFK probably would have wanted the games to continue, but Ditka wanted to continue for other reasons. This was a long-awaited homecoming for him. Pittsburgh was his home area and he hadn't played a game in the city since his senior year at the University of Pittsburgh in the fall of 1960. A large number of Ditka friends and relatives held tickets to the game.

This game that might have been postponed or called off turned out to be one of the finest in Ditka's playing career. All day long, quarterback Billy Wade found his man roaming free downfield. The totals for the afternoon would read seven catches for 146 yards; a huge performance. But despite Ditka's tremendous showing, the Bears were in trouble.

Pittsburgh led 17–14 when the Bears got the ball deep in their own territory, much closer to the goal line they were sworn to protect than the goal line they needed to cross to pull out a victory. Less than five minutes remained. Then things got worse. Chicago faced a 3rd and 33. The situation looked as bleak as the weather service's radar images just before a hurricane. Teams do not expect to make it on 3rd and 33. That happens about as often as Republicans and Democrats agree on anything.

Clearly the circumstances called for a pass and surely the Steelers knew that. But Ditka somehow beat the coverage, weaving in and out to grab a slightly-off Wade pass. He tucked the ball under his arm and ran for daylight . . . only there was no daylight. Within seconds, Pittsburgh defenders surrounded him. Six of them converged as Ditka swiveled his hips, used his strength to push off here and there, and turned a seemingly harmless catch into the pass play of his career. It was like a movie scene where the good guy is hopelessly surrounded by heavily armed bad guys, yet manages to get away. Ditka made his escape and dashed 63 yards for a spectacular first down and field position that set up the Bears for a possible touchdown.

"Ditka made an unbelievable play," said Bull.

"I think Ditka got hit by everybody on the Steelers," said Bears center Mike Pyle, "and some guys came back to hit him again. Finally, he just couldn't run anymore. He just collapsed. That was one of the greatest football plays I've ever seen in my life."

In those days, the NFL did not play overtime in regular-season games. The league had pretty much just discovered sudden-death overtime for the first time in its 1958 championship game. But ties did not hurt a team very badly in the standings, either, because they did not affect their won-loss percentage. The Bears were playing for the win and Wade twice threw into the end zone, the second pass hitting Bo Farrington in the hands before it fell to the grass.

Chicago still trailed, but kicker Roger LeClerc came in and booted an 18-yard field goal for the 17–17 tie, which is the way the game ended. It was definitely not as satisfying as a win, but the result counted almost as much in Chicago's favor. "Our future is still in our hands," said Halas. The Bears escaped with their status unscathed.

The same couldn't be said for Rozelle.

He was ripped in many quarters for having the temerity to inappropriately carry through with the games, and while that decision stuck to him forever and was viewed as a black mark on his reputation, Rozelle was able to live down the criticism and be viewed as one of the best commissioners of a league in U.S. pro sports history. However, he was haunted by his choice and later in life said he made a mistake. Even a close friend of Rozelle, Herb Siegel, recalled his feelings on the decision. "Pete was upset that he did it. He told me and said it publicly that was the one thing he regretted."

For a period of time, Rozelle explained his decision. Then he defended it. Then, eventually, he apologized for it. No, the NFL should not have played its regularly scheduled games two days after the president of the United States was assassinated and the country was in such turmoil, he admitted.

"I know it may sound corny," Rozelle said early on, "but Pierre [Salinger] told me we should play and that was the way Jack Kennedy would have wanted it."

Rozelle guided the NFL through difficult times, including the challenge from the American Football League and the plans that led to the merger. He felt he had made a difficult decision earlier in '63 by suspending Paul Hornung and Alex Karras for gambling. That is also one of the major decisive actions of Rozelle's 29-year career as commissioner that is always remembered, but not with as much feeling as the ruling to play on in the face of JFK's death.

Years later, Rozelle said he telephoned Salinger because he had known him for a long time, long before Salinger became identified with the administration, and in 1989 when Rozelle retired, he said that the worst mistake of his tenure was ordering that the games be played on that harrowing weekend in November of '63.

I really just wanted to talk it over with someone uniquely situated to guide me. Obviously, I had the greatest respect

*for the president. But there was so much made of it that I
regret that we played. It was a difficult decision because of
the emotional nature of a terrible tragedy.*

When Rozelle came under verbal attack, Salinger defended him
and never changed his mind.

*Absolutely, it was the right decision [to play]. I've never
questioned it. This country needed some normalcy, and football, which is a very important game in our society, helped
provide it.*

Many players that day disagreed with Salinger's take and did not
have a choice. There was no normalcy for them that Sunday.

Dick Hoak, one of the Steelers who scored a touchdown
against the Bears, said the team learned about the killing of
Oswald shortly before kickoff and that's what the players talked
about . . . not how to shut down the Bears.

New York Giants star linebacker Sam Huff, always a big name
in his home state of West Virginia, campaigned for JFK there
and was very upset to be playing.

*That was the only game I ever played on any level that I
didn't care about at all. There was no desire, no determination. I kept thinking, 'This is America?' America was a safe
haven. Then all of a sudden, it wasn't.*

Players spoke of being in a daze, of going through the motions,
just wishing and hoping the clock would tick faster. King Hill,
the Philadelphia quarterback, was from Texas and had Texas
license plates on his car. When he emerged from the stadium
after his game, someone had smashed his windows. He understood why.

Rozelle was repeatedly pressured to explain his decision.

It is tradition in sports for athletes to perform in times of great personal tragedy. Football was Mr. Kennedy's game. We would not—absolutely not—play the game if we really felt it would be showing disrespect.

A few months later when the Eagles were playing an exhibition game, a surprise guest appeared in the locker room. It was Robert F. Kennedy. The way Hill remembers that scene, "He came into our locker room and went around shaking our hands. He said he appreciated us playing the games that weekend."

It was not the type of gaffe that there would ever be a do-over for, that once-in-a-lifetime situation of national tragedy conflicting with football. That's how that Rozelle decision was viewed. Rozelle died in 1996 and indeed the NFL had never experienced a situation to approximate the November of '63 circumstances.

Until 2001, that is, when on September 11, terrorists unleashed a triple assault on the Pentagon in Washington, D.C., the World Trade Center twin towers in New York City, and on a jet plane that plunged to earth in a field in Pennsylvania. About 3,000 people were killed in all. Once again, the United States was paralyzed in horror.

The attacks occurred on a Tuesday. They completely disrupted Americans' daily lives. Major League Baseball suspended play. And this time, so did the National Football League. The games scheduled for the weekend of September 16 were postponed. As Ronnie Bull had made in a suggestion too late for 1963, the 2001 season was pushed back and completed a week late.

14

JIMMY BROWN AND THE REST OF THE GANG

FOR MOST OF the season, the Cleveland Browns were leading the NFL Eastern Division. Then by the season's eleventh week, with more attention on playing the games because of the presidential assassination than in what was going on in the games, the league woke up with a three-way tie for first in the East.

Cleveland, the New York Giants, and the St. Louis Cardinals were all sitting on 8–3 records.

The Giants and Browns were perennial powers, seemingly trading off first place regularly since the early fifties, when the Browns were absorbed by the NFL from the defunct All-America Football Conference.

Where did the Cardinals come from? Actually, the Cardinals came from Chicago, where they were based from 1920 when the league began, through the '59 season when they gave up competing for the hearts of Chicago fans against the Bears. The

Cardinals began play in St. Louis in 1960, at the same time the American Football League was formed. NFL owners looked at the switch as one way to keep the AFL away from another city.

But the Cardinals hadn't done much well on the field since '48, when they went 11–1. In their fourth season in St. Louis, the Cardinals had yet to record a winning record. Now, all of a sudden, they were in the hunt for a division title and a spot in the championship game.

The key to the Cardinals' sudden success under coach Wally Lemm was an explosive passing game. Quarterback Charlie Johnson threw for 3,280 yards and 28 touchdowns, and the Cardinals had the fourth highest-scoring team in the NFL. Bobby Joe Conrad caught 73 passes and Sonny Randle nabbed 51 (12 of them for touchdowns) and averaged 19.9 yards a catch. Tight end Jackie Smith was also a pretty good weapon, with 28 catches.

John David Crow, a Heisman Trophy winner out of Texas A&M, had been the team's steadiest ground gainer, but was hurt most of this season.

As it happened, this flirtation with first place didn't last long for the Cardinals. Just about the time the rest of the league got over reading the standings with the words St. Louis at the top, the Cards began losing. They dropped two of their final three games for the season, and fell to 9–5 and out of contention. So first place came down to a fight between the Browns and the Giants, a regular occurrence for a decade.

The Browns had an extraordinary history. In the handful of seasons the All-America Football Conference was in existence the Browns beat up on every team. In three AAFC seasons the Browns went 47–4–3. Their coach, Paul Brown, had proven to be an innovator in high school, at Ohio State, and when he coached the Great Lakes Training Center during World War II.

Paul Brown was the Browns, not only in name. He was creative on offense, recruited terrific talent, and in an exception for the time, didn't care if those players were African Americans. He sought out blacks Marion Motley and Bill Willis and gave them the chance to play on a prominent winning team. When the Browns shifted to the NFL with Otto Graham at quarterback, they were nearly as overpowering. Then they drafted a stunning running back out of Syracuse in 1957, who by coincidence also shared the last name of Brown—Jim Brown. Many today still consider him to be the finest player in NFL history.

At 6' 2" and 230 pounds, Brown was big, fast, and unstoppable. He played nine seasons in the NFL, retiring prematurely, and led the league in rushing eight times. He set records by scoring 126 touchdowns, rushing for 1,863 yards in a season, and 12,312 yards in a career.

Although the Bears were too busy worrying about what the Packers were up to, they didn't really want to deal with Brown in a single-game elimination championship. Years after Brown abruptly retired at age twenty-nine to go into the movies full-time, starting with *The Dirty Dozen*, one of his most vivid memories was of a play that he considered a mistake on his part. Somehow, it figured that the nearly perfect player remembered so clearly a play where he was less than perfect.

"They caught me from behind," said Brown of the play.

He still couldn't get over that someone had the gall to catch him from behind.

With the ball in his hands, the shifty and powerful Brown usually required a group to take him down. He also had a strong straight arm that brushed aside some of those would-be tacklers. Bill Glass, who would later become one of his Browns teammates, had previously played for the Detroit Lions, and was fully aware of what happened when you got in Brown's way. "He bashed me with his forearm and it was like being hit with a lead pipe. It gave you a headache."

Brown dished out headaches—literally and metaphorically—to every team he faced. He was a nightmare to defend and 1963 was his best season among all of the exceptional ones he recorded. That was the year he set the record with 1,863 yards and averaged 6.4 yards per carry. He was a walking first down.

As the '63 season wound down, and as the Cardinals fell by the wayside, the Eastern Division was a two-team battle between the Browns and Giants. After 12 weeks of play, both teams had 9–3 records, with the Browns personally polishing off the Cardinals on December 1 to create the separation.

Even before that, though, there had been a particularly nasty game against the Giants. On October 13, the Browns outlasted the Giants, 35–24. When Brown returned to that game years later in an autobiography, titled *Jim Brown Out of Bounds*, he accused the Giants' highly regarded defense of trying to injure him by poking their hands through the cross-bar and mesh of his helmet to get at his eyes.

> . . . *they're attacking my eyes. I wasn't happy, wasn't quite surprised. The Giants were sophisticated assassins. I had big respect for the Giants. They were football intellectuals, the smartest team in the league. Also the most calculating. Other teams would have one or two thugs who'd randomly*

jump you, hit you in the head. New York did nothing helter-skelter. Loose rules. Hard men. Not a lot of cash. It made the old NFL a primitive place.

Going after Jim Brown in any kind of personal way was normally risky business. You didn't want to make Jim Brown mad, because he always got even. He said that he sat alone during halftime of that game and stewed, but that he got payback with second-half touchdowns to make the Giants realize the futility of their assaults.

Brown said he was often baited by big defensive linemen who might have wanted to fight, but at the least sought to distract him. It was Brown's habit to rise from the turf very slowly when tackled, almost as if it was a big strain to get back to his feet. Foes learned quickly that it meant nothing. He wasn't hurt, just resting. It became a trademark. Brown said after retirement that although he was aware of trash talking, his concentration was usually intense enough to block it out.

The big man said he obtained revenge on some of his would-be hasslers by embarrassing them with his running. "I knew that if I ran over a man on Sunday, or misused him on a fake, made him look feeble, his coach would run that play more than once [in the film room the next day]."

Brown gave Cleveland an edge against anyone the Browns played, but the rest of the offense was more efficient than dynamite. Quarterback Frank Ryan threw for over 2,000 yards, but the ground game ruled. Halfback Ernie Green complemented Brown with 526 yards and averaged 6.0 a carry. The Browns defense could be fearsome, too, with Vince Costello, Paul Wiggin, Jim Shofner, and Bernie Parrish. Cleveland was a very good team that year, but just a tiny bit short of being good enough.

Two weeks after the game that was imprinted so strongly on Brown's mind, the Giants won a rematch, delivering a 33–6 thrashing that in the end was the most important win of the season for New York. The Giants obtained great satisfaction from that dominating win, not only on the scoreboard, but because it was one of the worst games of Brown's career. Not only was he held to only 40 yards rushing, but he was ejected from the game. When the Browns faltered against the Detroit Lions in the second to last game of the season, the Giants won their final two games to pull away and finish 11–3, one game ahead of Cleveland in the East.

The Giants began slowly. Sharing Yankee Stadium with the baseball team that had first dibs on playing dates meant that in 1963—as often occurred during that era—the Giants could not play at home until October, which was an ongoing nuisance for the team. The Yankees had a stranglehold on the American League pennant, and fans could pretty much book reservations for the World Series by July. Although it sounds remarkable in 2013, in an NFL season that opened on September 15, 1963, the Giants played four straight games on the road and did not visit their home stadium until that October 13 loss to the Browns.

However, the Giants ripped off five straight victories following that defeat as the offense jelled. Future Hall of Fame quarterback Y. A. Tittle, who had replaced the popular Charley Conerly, still had whiz-bang stuff in his right arm even if he looked older than Father Time (because he was bald).

The NFL was not really a passing league at the time. Most coaches believed that a decent ratio for the offense was about a

60–40 of running to passing plays, and nothing Jim Brown was doing in Cleveland or that the Green Bay Packers were doing with their sweep offered contradictory evidence. Yet in a hint of things to come, Yelberton Abraham Tittle, one of the most uniquely named players in NFL history, put together one of the most unique-to-date seasons for a quarterback in NFL history.

Already thirty-seven years old that season, Tittle completed 60.2 percent of his passes for 3,145 yards and a personal record of 36 touchdown passes and he did all of that while missing a game. The Giants were the flip side of the Browns on offense. While Phil King, Alex Webster, and Joe Morrison were capable backs, coach Allie Sherman—a former quarterback—was happy to let Tittle air it out. He made for a deadly combination with long-legged Del Shofner, who caught 64 passes for 1,181 yards.

Even at this late stage of his career, Tittle was a workaholic in practice. "If you can't hit your receivers in the middle of the week with no pressure," said Tittle, "how are you going to hit them in a ball game when it counts?"

The remarkable thing about Tittle was that he had been around the league, it seemed, since the football was as round as a basketball, and players were competing in leather helmets. It was approaching the halfway mark of the decade of the 1960s, and Tittle had been playing pro since 1948 in the All-America Conference. He spent most of his career with the San Francisco 49ers being the main man behind center in the city by the bay for the entire decade of the fifties. It was when he started to accumulate birthdays and the 49ers acquired John Brodie that management decided their senior citizen stalwart signal-caller was as passé as a passer as the waltz was compared to Elvis Presley.

Tittle did not want to retire, but it was obvious that he would never be more than an afterthought in San Francisco again as long as the talented and much younger Brodie was on the scene. On top of that, he had ended the 1960 season with a groin injury, so from a distance to anyone inquiring, he looked old and hurt. The first thing Tittle did was began the healing process and get himself back into top shape. He then readied for a training camp to show what he could still do. Somebody would trade for him, he felt. He hoped it was the Rams, as Los Angeles had a personal appeal for him.

Tittle was rooted in California. He owned an insurance business that was his post–playing-days security in San Francisco, so he didn't want to play ball 3,000 miles away on the east coast. He toyed with the idea of quitting, but admitted that he had too much pride to go out other than on his own terms.

The 49ers coach was Red Hickey and he had strong faith in the shotgun formation. That was an offense where it helped to have young legs and a scrambler playing quarterback, a job description that did not fit the drop-back passer that Tittle was.

Ironically, the turning point in Tittle's status came during a 49ers exhibition game against the Giants played in Portland, Oregon, leading up to the start of the '61 season. Tittle played well and nearly led the 49ers to a comeback win. Not long after that game Tittle was summoned to Hickey's office and informed that he had been traded to the Giants. They must have liked what they saw in him during that exhibition game.

"We have just traded you to the New York Giants for Lou Cordileone," Hickey informed Tittle.

Tittle thought, but did not say, *Who is Lou Cordileone?* It actually was a legitimate question, and decades later, Cordileone's main claim to football fame is as the answer to the trivia question of who the 49ers got in their trade of Tittle. That might be a little harsh, but it's not too far off. Cordileone was the Giants' No. 1 draft pick out of Clemson in 1960 and played guard. He spent only a season with San Francisco, but had a nine-year NFL career.

In the first of two autobiographies that Tittle later helped write, his comment on departing San Francisco was, "I had been shotgunned out of 'Frisco." That was true, but he did not realize at the moment that he was getting the best opportunity of his career. He had to tell himself, *You're not washed up.*

Not even close, as it turned out. Instead, Tittle was on the cusp of becoming the biggest star he had ever been in the league and on the biggest stage. He became the toast of New York, and as Conerly, who was even older (40), eased into retirement, Tittle became the focal point of the offense that drove the Giants to the top of the Eastern Division. Without Tittle, the Giants would have likely been a very different team in '61, '62, and '63.

Tittle and Conerly had a job share in '61, but the Giants won the East and met the Packers for the NFL title. In '62, the Giants were even better—Tittle tossed 33 touchdowns that year—won the East, and again faced the Packers for the NFL title.

The '63 season made three Eastern titles in a row for the Giants with Tittle under center. By then, Cordileone was playing for his third team since departing New York.

15

THE AFL IN '63

BY 1963, FOUR seasons into the grand experiment of the American Football League trying to bring the sport to more American cities, the league had taken some big losses.

Battles were lost, though by no means the war. Almost the moment the 1960 season ended the Los Angeles Chargers departed for San Diego. While that stung, the biggest defeat was the abandonment of Dallas by the Texans, which belonged to league shaker and mover Lamar Hunt. Creation of the AFL was Hunt's brainchild. He rounded up the owners, played a role in choosing the cities where teams located, and was the boss of the Texans. Starting the league and his own team was his response to being rebuffed by the NFL for an expansion franchise.

The NFL's response to Hunt after it became known that he was spearheading the new league and installing a team in Dallas where his family came from, and his father H. L. Hunt administered the clan's multimillions of dollars stemming from oil interests, was to rush the expansion Dallas Cowboys into existence.

Even though the Texans recorded better seasonal records on the field, Hunt gave up deluding himself about long-term victory when he realized the fans were always going to respond more to the NFL brand no matter how badly the Cowboys performed, never mind if they ever got good. What sealed the future for Hunt was when the Texans captured the '62 AFL title—and still drew under 20,000 to some home games.

Hunt was losing big bucks on the Texans in Dallas—not something that was unexpected—and he was able to write those losses off on his taxes, but for only five years. From his vantage point of winning a championship and still losing money, the immediate prospects did not look good against competition that was improving. Hunt was already toying with the idea of making a move to New Orleans or Kansas City when the Texans played their final regular-season home game in front of 18,364 fans. Worse, Hunt knew that probably only half of those fans purchased full-price tickets. So while the Texans were an artistic success, they were a financial failure.

It was a sad day for Hunt when he trucked his team to Kansas City, although that city made him an offer that was too good to refuse. At first, Hunt wanted to hold onto the Texans name, but he was easily persuaded how silly that would have been. The name Chiefs was chosen because of H. Roe Bartle, the mayor who had put on the full-court press to woo the franchise. Bartle was nicknamed "The Chief," but the name was also to honor the Native American heritage of the area, which is why the helmet insignia is an arrowhead. Hunt was guaranteed a certain amount of season tickets sold and other perks. There was also a ready-made stadium waiting for him.

"They're offering a nice deal up there," Hunt sighed.

Hunt made up his mind to leave Dallas only weeks after the Texans won the AFL title and started telling associates that it was going to happen. When he started the club, perhaps Hunt's best move was hiring an unheralded coach named Hank Stram to lead the team. Stram had been a loyal backer and fought in the trenches to sell the Texans to the populace and he delivered a championship. Stram loved the job and the place and was totally into the war. When Hunt broke the news to Stram, he was indeed disappointed, though when Hunt told him the details of the Kansas City offer, Stram said, "It's nice to be wanted."

Although it was pretty much a done deal that Hunt was moving off into the sunset, he snookered Cowboys owner Clint Murchison into paying him what was later estimated to be $300,000 to go away.

So in the fall of '63 the Dallas Texans were no more and the players woke up as the Kansas City Chiefs, moving north to Missouri to defend a title they won in Texas.

Training camp was conducted at William Jewell College in Liberty, Missouri, and many of the same faces were on the roster. But the team did not play as well. The season of '63 was not the Chiefs' year. The first season in Kansas City the Chiefs finished 5–7–2. The fans were happy to have them, but not everything went as smoothly. As explosive as the Chiefs could be, they hit a stretch in midseason where they lost six out of seven with one tie. That was the story of the year.

Quarterback Len Dawson was the rock of the offense. After floundering for several years on the benches of the Pittsburgh Steelers and Cleveland Browns, he gained new life with the

Texans and was All-AFL in '62. In '63, Dawson threw 26 touchdown passes and fullback Curtis McClinton surpassed Abner Haynes as the No. 1 rusher.

Dawson's was a remarkable story. He had been a first-round draft pick out of Purdue in 1957, and the Steelers barely let him take a snap. Ditto with the Browns. He was suffering more than a crisis of confidence when he surfaced with the Texans—he was one baby step from retirement.

Instead, Dawson became a six-time AFL All-Star, led the Chiefs to league championships and a Super Bowl title, and was enshrined in the Pro Football Hall of Fame in 1987. Paul Brown, the usually astute judge of talent running the Browns, even told Dawson that no one was going to pick him when he was put on waivers. By then, Dawson and Stram had spoken, and Stram was rarin' to give Dawson another chance. There was a good reason why Stram felt warmly towards Dawson— he had recruited him out of high school for Purdue—where he was an assistant coach and an alum—and seen the guy play well in college. Dawson was totally demoralized, but once he got a chance to play again, he thrived. "I had spent five years in the NFL with the Steelers and Browns and had started two games," Dawson said. "Had never started and finished a game. Never played two games in a row."

Once Dawson became a Texan, the team couldn't get him out of the lineup even when he was injured. It was one of the all-time pro football rags to riches stories.

Morphing from the Dallas Texans into the Kansas City Chiefs was one of the story lines of the AFL's '63 season, but the drop-off by the Chiefs provided opportunities for other teams to thrive. The Denver Broncos still couldn't get over their striped socks and the fashion faux pas may have dragged them down. Denver was the one team in the Western Division that finished below the Chiefs, with a 2–11–1 record.

Midway through the '62 season, the Broncos appeared to be a coming powerhouse, starting the season 7–2. Then they lost their last five games in a row, and when Coach Jack Faulkner left camp in '63, he had 14 rookies on the roster. Some of them proved to be good ball players, like fullback Billy Joe, halfback Hewritt Dixon, and defensive back Willie Brown, but the rest of the squad was raw.

Denver's philosophy that season, as it had been since the inception of the team, was to throw to tight end Lionel Taylor. Taylor had played all of eight games for the Chicago Bears before he joined the AFL, and in '63, he put together his fourth straight humongous receiving season with 78 catches for 1,101 yards and 10 touchdowns.

Outside of gazing at the Rocky Mountains beyond the walls of the home stadium, Taylor was the best show in town. Taylor had a 12-catch game in '62 against the Boston Patriots, which the Broncos still lost, 41–16. It was a given that Taylor did not have as much speed as some pro coaches might have desired, but although his hands were not exceptionally large, it was as if they were greased with glue. Taylor said he practiced strengthening his hands.

"I work at palming a basketball rather than doing things like push-ups," said Taylor. "It keeps my fingers flexible."

The Broncos lived in the Western Division basement, the Chiefs were stuck in mediocrity, and the San Diego Chargers never spent a minute out of first place. They won in week one and were tied with Kansas City and the Oakland Raiders. They won in week two and the three squads were still even. But after they moved to 3–0 no one caught them. Oakland chased them all season long, yet finished a game out.

Oakland was awful in '62, finishing 1–13. Searching for a new coach, Oakland management hired Al Davis off Sid Gillman's staff in San Diego, and Davis led the Raiders to an amazing turnaround, finishing 10–4. Not only that, but Davis introduced new uniform colors for his club—silver and black. Davis was chosen coach of the year. As he always said, "Just win, baby!" and that would make everything all right.

One reason things improved so much for the Raiders was the growth of running back Clemon Daniels and his league-leading 1,099 yards rushing, which was more than 300 yards better than his previous total (766).

Although Oakland hung around, the Chargers never faltered and would not be caught. The standings were tighter in the Eastern Division, even if the teams were not playing as well as either the Chargers or the Raiders that season.

The New York Jets were at the bottom at 5–8–1, with the Houston Oilers at 6–8. Tied for first were the Boston Patriots and the Buffalo Bills, both at 7–6–1.

One thing the Jets were not anymore was the Titans. New management had dispensed with that nickname after the previous season, but the Jets were not a very explosive offensive team with a limited number of stars (notably Bake Turner with 71 receptions and Don Maynard with 38 catches, who was better in years before and after '63). Probably the No. 1 asset the Jets had was head coach Weeb Ewbank, who had won championships with the Baltimore Colts after building that team up from nothing. He was about to repeat that feat in New York.

To a major degree, the Houston Oilers were the class of the AFL during its first three seasons. Houston won the first two titles and lost in the '62 championship game to the Dallas Texans in double overtime. But the Oilers just didn't have it in '63.

Another thing the Oilers were noted for was signing the first position player away from an NFL team. Willard Dewveall left the Chicago Bears for the Oilers in '62, and Bears teammate Richie Petitbon remembers that as causing somewhat of a stir, seeing that the Bears players who had been around for several years were familiar with George Blanda's story and how he had become a sensation in the new league after being snubbed by George Halas.

Dewveall was a 1959 second-round draft pick for the Bears out of Southern Methodist University. He was 6' 4" and weighed 225 pounds.

"He was good," said Petitbon.

However, Dewveall was behind Mike Ditka on the depth chart at tight end in Chicago, and it appeared he might spend eternity there. That was a good motivator to look for other employment. Plus, Dewveall chose Blanda's team. As it so happened, in a six-year career during which Dewveall caught 204 passes for 27 touchdowns, his signature moment occurred when someone else was manning the quarterback spot for Houston. Dewveall caught a then-pro football record 98-yard touchdown pass from Jacky Lee in '62.

At the top of the East were the Patriots and Bills with so-so records, but one of them had to win the division in order to provide an opponent for the championship game. While Buffalo was fighting for a spot, their best days were still looming, as they would win the AFL title in '64 and '65 and later appeared in four consecutive Super Bowls (although they lost them all).

In 1963, it made sense that the Bills' record was around .500, as they scored almost the same amount of points as they surrendered. Jack Kemp was a solid leader at quarterback and Cookie Gilchrist was a load coming out of the backfield, but the defense was porous. It didn't help any that the other key running back, Wray Carlton, was hurt most of the season and that coach Lou Saban kept feeling a tug to use younger quarterback Daryle Lamonica as well as Kemp. Receivers Elbert Dubenion (53 catches) and Bill Miller (69) didn't care who was putting the ball in the air, they grabbed it anyway.

Although Buffalo was the preseason favorite for the division, they started 0–3–1 and wouldn't even have been able to tie the Patriots if Boston hadn't been thumped, 35–3, in the last regular-season game. The Patriots put 11 men on the All-Star team: Tom Addison, Houston Antwine, Nick Buoniconti, Ron Hall, Bob Dee and Larry Eisenhauer on defense, kicker-end Gino Cappelletti, and running back Larry Garron, Charlie Long, Billy Neighbors and Babe Parilli on offense. It made people wonder a little if the Patriots hadn't underachieved a bit under coach Mike Holovak.

Cappelletti was one of those AFL stars fortunate that the league came along to rescue him from a life that may never have otherwise been involved with pro football.

Cappelletti played college ball at the University of Minnesota, but was not drafted by the NFL coming out of school. He was playing touch football and working at his brother's bar in Minneapolis when the Patriots called.

When the Eastern teams tied, a pre-championship playoff game was set for War Memorial Stadium in Buffalo on December 28, 1963. Cappelletti worried about how the Patriots would play against the hot Bills after getting creamed by Kansas City.

"It's hard to get your confidence up for a playoff game getting whipped like that," said Cappelletti.

It was typical wintry weather for upstate New York in December with the temperature at 20 degrees for kickoff. There was just enough of a breeze to make the air feel like 9 degrees with the wind-chill. One distinctive memory for Cappelletti about the weather was that the field was frozen so the Patriots wore sneakers instead of spikes.

The Patriots roughed up the Bills early and often and won easily, 26–8, with Cappelletti, one of the AFL's great players, being the pivotal figure. He kicked field goals of 28, 12, 33, and 36 yards, as well as two extra points. The Patriots led 10–0 after the first quarter and 16–0 at halftime.

In the third quarter, Buffalo stunned Boston with a 93-yard TD pass from Lamonica to Dubenion, and then Saban employed one of the AFL innovations borrowed from the college game. At the time in the NFL, teams could not attempt two-point conversions. The AFL, devoted to a more wide-open style, chose to emulate the colleges, and Buffalo scored its two-pointer. That meant entering the fourth quarter, the Bills needed just one touchdown with an additional two-point conversion for the tie.

That was the Buffalo wishful thinking, anyway. Instead the Patriots rallied again and added 10 points. Garron caught a 17-yard scoring pass from Parilli and Cappelletti made his last field goal.

"We beat 'em and we beat 'em good," said Cappelletti.

The victory gave the Patriots a more respectable 8–6–1 record with the looming assignment of facing those 11–3 Chargers for the AFL title.

One thing the Chargers could do well was score. They piled up a league-leading 399 points that season. What was so impressive about the Chargers was how they employed the passing game. From the vantage point of a half-century later that would not be surprising, as San Diego's coach was Sid Gillman, and Gillman is regarded as perhaps the most brilliant passing game innovator in history. He was still building his reputation at the time, though.

When the American Football League was formed in 1960, one of the Western Division teams was the Los Angeles Chargers. Given the competition from the wildly popular and entrenched Los Angeles Rams, it was swiftly apparent (faster than it was obvious in Dallas) that if the Chargers were to thrive, it wouldn't be in LA. The lack of attention was hurtful—just as it was in Dallas—because the Chargers were an on-field success, going 10–4 that first season and playing in the first AFL title game (they lost 24–16 to the Oilers). They were entertaining as all get-out, or at least as entertaining as the circus, if anyone cared to watch.

The Chargers and Gillman transferred their act to San Diego in time for the '61 season, and they were even better. That season, San Diego finished 12–2 and advanced to the title game again, albeit losing again to the Oilers, 10–3. That killed Gillman, as the Chargers had a 396–217 point differential during the regular season.

A dismal 4–10 '62 season was tucked in the middle, but by '63, the Chargers were back on top in the West. Dick Vermeil, who later hired Gillman as an assistant coach with the Philadelphia

Eagles, explained that Gillman was successful because he never sat still, was always trying to dream up new plays.

Sid was always looking for or trying to create something for the offense that hadn't been done. He loved to be the first coach to do something new, something creative. If he got a good idea from someone else, with very little effort, he could improve on it. He never lost his thirst for knowledge.

One of the Chargers' and Gillman's offensive stars was running back Keith Lincoln, who shunned the Chicago Bears' offer for San Diego coming out of college. He said Gillman had a gift. "Sid was one of the first people to lengthen the field and he worked hard at it," said Lincoln.

Decades after the Chargers' success, Lincoln was asked why the team was so good and said it was a no-brainer. "It has to start with Sid Gillman. I really think he has to be one of the top half-dozen coaches of all time. And he surrounded himself with talent [assistant coaches]."

Players, too, Lincoln added. "He had a good eye for talent. The things we had."

So much talent at so many positions, talent that Gillman drafted and discovered and molded, and all of it provided the weapons needed to win his first pro title after coming close two years in a row.

The Chargers were anxious and thrilled to be heading back to their third AFL championship game. Bring on the Patriots. They had played twice during the regular season and the contests were close. Yes, San Diego won both of those games, but by a combined total of five points. Sure the Chargers earned those two wins, but they had come hard. A third meeting promised to be just as challenging.

16

NO EASY GAMES

CLOSE CALL.

That's what the game against the Steelers was for the Chicago Bears. Mike Ditka's nerve-wracking, enervating, and clutch 63-yard pass play saved a tie. Who knew that the scenario would practically repeat itself a week later?

It was all the Bears could manage again in their next game, a second 17–17 tie, this time against the Minnesota Vikings. Once again, the Bears had to come from behind to earn the tie and stay in what seemed to be the equivalent of a half-inch ahead of the Green Bay Packers in the NFL's Western Division standings.

The Vikings were a mediocre team, one that had a 4–7 record coming into the matchup. The game was in Chicago at Wrigley Field and the temperature was 23 degrees, something that was supposed to help the Bears. Yet this game was a struggle from the start. Chicago played distracted, allowing four sacks and fumbling four times, three of which were lost. The Bears were atrocious on the ground, rushing 33 times for only 67 yards.

Minnesota started the scoring with a 16-yard field goal by Fred Cox in the first quarter, and the Bears answered with a 16-yard field goal by Roger LeClerc before the period ended. The Chicago fans started to get grumpy in the second quarter when the Vikings scored two touchdowns—one rushing and one passing—to lead 17–3 at the half.

During the halftime break there was a brouhaha in the Bears' locker room that was fairly typical of the relationship between George Halas and Doug Atkins, one of his star defenders. Halas had a rule against players drinking carbonated beverages like Coca Cola at halftime, but when the team entered the locker room, Atkins grabbed a Coke. When Halas saw it he began hectoring Atkins to give it to him. Atkins refused. Back and forth this argument went as the intermission ticked away. The Great Coca Cola Fiasco killed halftime discussions from Halas about adjustments.

"They had argued the whole time halftime and he didn't have a chance to talk to the team," said Roger LeClerc.

Atkins was a dominating player, but he could definitely drive Halas crazy. While many viewed Halas as a league treasure and revered him for his part in organizing the league, Atkins was enrolled in the school of thought that believed Halas should have retired as coach because the game had passed him by.

He was good in his day. When football changed, coach Halas didn't change too much. He kept the same old people around. He knew his football, but when people are changing things, if you don't change with them it hurts you a little bit. He kept the same old people around him, whether they did a good job or a bad job, it didn't make any difference. When he gave the old folks a raise he gave them a title. That was all they wanted. They worshipped Mr. Halas.

Atkins was a bona fide star on his way to the Hall of Fame, but he didn't remember Halas praising him much. "I think a few times he gave me compliments. Wasn't too many. It was more the other way than it was compliments. He always wanted something more out of you, you know. He always wanted more and more. I don't know. He was a different man."

At one point during his lengthy stay with the Bears, the *Chicago Tribune* wrote a story about Atkins that was headlined "Doug Atkins Says What He Thinks." That was accurate and it was also clear that Halas was rarely happy to hear what Atkins thought.

In that tense tie with the Steelers, Atkins went berserk on the sideline—and in Halas' face—when a bad pass from Wade nearly prompted a heart attack in the big defender. The pass was incomplete, not an interception, no harm done, but Atkins couldn't keep quiet about it. "What kind of stupid pass was that?" Atkins growled. "I'm out there getting my tail mussed up on every play and the minute I go off the field the offense nearly throws the game away!"

Such internecine verbal flagrancy is frowned upon on sports teams, and Halas' frown aimed at Atkins spoke as loudly as a shout. There was no telling just what Atkins would say in a given circumstance, though the sports reporters had to love his candor. Atkins was a powerful man and even the best offensive linemen had difficulty preventing him from entering their backfield without knocking on the door. In one game, Atkins smeared Eagles quarterback King Hill, and was surprised to learn that Hill was sent to the hospital following the collision.

"Heck, I didn't think I hit him hard enough to hurt a flea," said Atkins.

Opposing teams just hated trying to block Atkins. Emlen Tunnell, a star for the New York Giants and then at the very end of his career with the Green Bay Packers, said Atkins was a nightmare to stop. "Atkins is not easy to get out of there. For his size, Doug's amazingly agile. He jumps and hurdles and if he's not on top of the passer he's so close it's nerve-wracking."

That's why Halas kept Atkins around. Atkins may have irritated Halas because he didn't act like a Boy Scout, but he was too valuable to trade. So what if he had a personality quirk where he just had to bug Halas? It was worth it to hear that Vince Lombardi, coach of the arch-nemesis Packers told his offensive linemen, "I don't care what you guys do out there, just don't get Atkins mad."

For all the troubles the Bears had operating on offense against the Vikings, Wade dragged them back into the game. He scored on a one-yard run in the third quarter and threw for an eight-yard touchdown pass to fullback Joe Marconi in the fourth that led to the tie. Marconi had subbed for the injured Rick Casares.

Marconi was an eight-year veteran drafted in 1956 out of West Virginia who spent his first six seasons with the Los Angeles Rams. Hardly ever a feature back during his career, the 6' 2" 225-pound Marconi was solid in heft and ability and led the Bears in rushing in '63 with 446 yards on the ground while also making 28 catches (for 335 yards). Halas was known to say that he thought Marconi was every bit the ballplayer as

Casares, and Marconi's play was a major reason why the Bears never lost after Casares was knocked out for the season with a nagging foot injury, which he said sometimes still bothers him fifty years later.

The irony was that a tie was all the Bears needed to keep pace with the Packers, because a few days earlier on Thanksgiving, Green Bay and the Detroit Lions ended in a 13–13 tie, and the Packers still had the dreaded West Coast trip of back-to-back games in California looming on their schedule.

As the season wore on, there was a growing recognition that Wade was the difference maker for the Bears, making things happen and steering a sometimes listing ship back on course when circumstances demanded it. It was after the season ended that a probing sportswriter was trying to figure out the Bears season. What the team did on defense was obvious. Wade, for one, was glad he wasn't playing against it. "I've studied and studied our defense and I'm convinced there is no way you can beat them except with luck."

But there were subtle differences incorporated into the offense. Just who, it was wondered, made the choices and decisions to open up the offensive style rather than always stick to the grind-it-out game? A Chicago sports columnist attributed the comments to an unnamed player, but this is how it came out: "Are you kidding? It was Billy Wade's offense. A great majority of the time we were running what Wade wanted us to run."

And a great majority of the time it worked. In a season when the Bears were so focused on besting Green Bay twice, it couldn't be overlooked that they also had to win other games. They had some challenges, and after the first meeting of the season when they topped the Vikings, the dynamic inside the locker room took a turn that allowed people to understand that it was quickly becoming Wade's locker room.

It was Ditka who proposed giving the Minnesota game ball to Wade, and others immediately agreed. "He called a great game today by sticking to the stuff we knew would work," said Chicago guard Bob Wetsoka. "Sometimes we deviate too much from our game pattern. Today we took the field with a plan and we followed it."

Wade had spent time as a backup with the Rams prior to being traded to Chicago and was afraid the clock would tick away on his career if he didn't take charge immediately with the Bears. He was only in his early thirties, but sports reporters kept coming back to the fact that there was gray showing in his hair.

"I will work twenty-four hours a day, if necessary, to play quarterback for the Bears," said Wade. It may not have taken around-the-clock work to became the man, but Wade met his goal.

During the early sixties there was much less emphasis on the kicking game than there is today, when an attempt is rarely missed. Kickers now use the so-called soccer style, and more and more distance is sought from a kicker's leg. Before the age of specialization it was nice if a team had a good kicker, but that kicker had to be able to play another position, too, to be kept on the 33-man roster. The most unusual aspect of the Bears' team in '63 is that it had two guys splitting the kicking who didn't otherwise play regularly. Roger LeClerc made some big boots, but Bobby Jencks pretty much only kicked extra points.

Jencks was 6' 5", 227 pounds, and was a tight end, which put him behind Ditka on the depth chart. He began the season as the field-goal kicker, but after going 1–10, LeClerc took over. Jencks played for Miami of Ohio and kicked two field goals and two extra points in the Chicago Charities College All-Star Game against the Packers. In college, Jencks tied the then-NCAA record with 17 field goals.

His booting style was also unique because he was bow-legged. "They say I have a little different way of kicking. People have always laughed when I set up for a kick. But it doesn't bother me. They stop laughing when the ball goes through."

It was Jencks who s topped laughing when the ball stopped going through the uprights on his early-season field-goal attempts. After his slump Jencks was excellent on conversions and that's the role he played for the rest of the season.

Wade, more than Halas, understood the growing impact passing was having on the sport, and was anxious to make the acquaintance of more receivers. One of the key guys on the Bears' offense was receiver Johnny Morris, who played the position which in that day was referred to as the flanker. The flanker was what used to be the third running back in the backfield and had become a third wide receiver.

At 5' 10" and 180 pounds, Morris was hardly the largest pass catcher around, but he got open with his speed and Wade zinged the passes in to him. Morris was a track and field sprinter out of Long Beach, California, who competed in the 50-yard dash. One reason for that was how slim he was. It took almost two years after Morris began attending the University of California Santa Barbara for him to top 160 pounds. A friend who saw him starring at touch football urged him to go out for the team and he became all-league.

Somehow Morris got on radar screens long enough to become a 12th-round draft pick for the Bears in 1958. He said it was a bit scary when he showed up for training camp and everyone was a famous All-American, a grizzled veteran, or a huge-looking player standing next to him. "I was dwarfed, engulfed," said Morris. "I stood there not knowing what to do. I felt like an unnoticed little shrimp." It was somewhat miraculous that Morris didn't get cut after fumbling three times in one exhibition game, but his energy and passion set him apart from other wannabes and Morris made the final roster.

It took some time after that to become a contributor. Morris, who played his entire career for the Bears, was a part-time running back, but the team's dangerous return man before gaining a regular spot as a receiver. He led the NFL in punt-return average in '59 at 12.2, and that season averaged a career high of 25.8 yards per kickoff return.

Moving to flanker, where Morris initially did not want to play, made his career. "I felt like I was out in the pasture. Then I found out that the position was tailor-made for me."

Speed and shiftiness made Morris a risky man to surround by foes, and if he saw daylight, he was gone. "You use the head fakes and hip fakes, but it's not a standard thing," said Morris. "I mean each defensive man seems to react differently to the fakes and no two of them will watch the same things." That pretty much made it sound as if mental telepathy took care of the rest for Morris.

Morris gave more credit to playing time than natural skills as his catches mounted up (he was on his way to a career high of 93 for 1,200 yards in '64).

*If I've improved as a receiver it's probably due to a combi-
nation of experience and practice. You learn how to set up
patterns. You learn ways to weave in and out of the linebackers and watch them out of the corner of your eye.*

Although the two consecutive ties did not hurt the Bears in
the standings, not winning was a bad habit the team needed to
break. On December 8, Chicago hosted the San Francisco 49ers
at Wrigley Field. This was a grudge match, as the 49ers were the
only team all season to defeat the Bears.

Showing what a fluke the game in California was, the 49ers
had remained on a losing path and carried a 2–10 record
into the game. It was easy enough to predict the content of
Halas' pep talk, reminding his charges that they owed one to
San Francisco and should have won the first time. The Bears
scored 14 points in the first quarter, with Willie Galimore
bursting free on a 51-yard jaunt and Marconi scoring on a
19-yard run. The game was really over by then, though the
49ers scored a TD on a three-yard rush by fullback J. D. Smith
in the second quarter. That closed the gap to one touchdown,
but the margin didn't last long. Wade scored on a three-yard
run before the end of the third quarter, and Roosevelt Taylor
pushed the spread to 28–7 with a 30-yard touchdown on an
interception.

The 5' 11", 185-pound Taylor was a third-year man out of
Grambling State, and was having his best season with nine interceptions, although he had led the team in tackles in '62. Early in
his career, Taylor played the role of the strong, silent type, and
he did so by design, watching and learning at safety. "People
don't know much about me because I'm quiet. I let my actions

on the field speak for me. I have as much pride as anybody, but I'm not going to do a lot of talking."

After his big season in '63, Taylor did open up a little. He revealed his love for rock music, though he said Ray Charles was his favorite singer. Being an all-city basketball player in New Orleans with great leaping ability helped his defensive coverage. Chicago defensive coordinator George Allen initially traveled to Grambling to scout the gargantuan Ernie Ladd for the defensive line, but returned home with a belief in Taylor.

Success usually loosens guys up, but even the best are motivated by a failure or haunted by a memory that lingers about something that went wrong. Taylor had no trouble picking out such an embarrassing moment from early in his life as an NFL defensive back.

> *I'll never forget the first touchdown pass that ever went over my head as a pro. It was during my rookie year and Tommy McDonald of the Eagles caught it. Not only did he catch it, but I fell while trying to bat the ball down, bloodied my nose and got dirt in my eyes. When I got up, everybody was staring at me.*

It was easy enough to understand why that stuck in Taylor's mind. It was probably never going to get any worse than that moment in his pro career. Really, most things got a whole lot better from there.

Entering the last week of the regular season, the Bears' record was 10–1–2, and they were scheduled to finish the season against the Detroit Lions. The Lions were 5–7–1 after playing the season without defensive tackle Alex Karras, who was suspended for the year by Commissioner Pete Rozelle in the preseason betting scandal.

Green Bay, the two-time defending NFL champs, had played extraordinary football without star running back Paul Hornung, in exile for the same reason as Karras. The Packers were 10–2–1, and had to face the San Francisco 49ers in the finale in San Francisco. The Packers had polished off the Los Angeles Rams a week earlier in the first half of the West Coast swing, and they held on to beat the 49ers, 21–17, to complete the regular season with an 11–2–1 record, with their only two losses to the Bears. If the Bears won their game versus Detroit, they would be Western Division champs.

The Lions–Bears showdown was at Wrigley Field on a day that was an advertisement for domed stadiums. The air temperature was 1 degree and with 11 mph winds, the wind-chill was -15. This was the Ice Bowl before the Ice Bowl. Considering the weather the Bears hung onto the ball well with no fumbles and Wade was able to move the team through the air surprisingly well.

However, the Lions were affected by an in-team tragedy. Future Hall of Fame defensive back Dick "Night Train" Lane was married to singer Dinah Washington. Sometime in the middle of the night as Detroit prepared to depart for the game, she passed away in her sleep at the age of thirty-nine. A shocked and distraught Lane did not accompany the team to Chicago.

Chicago opened the scoring with a 20-yard LeClerc field goal in the first quarter. Wade made a mistake in the second quarter, and Detroit's Larry Vargo ran an interception back 42 yards for a touchdown. It was 7–3 Detroit at the half. The Bears made their move in the third quarter. They took the lead on a 51-yard pass from Wade to Morris, and added to it on a 22-yard pass from Wade to Mike Ditka. The third quarter would end with

Chicago leading, 17–7. Morris had a phenomenal day, catching eight passes for 171 yards.

All the Bears had to do was hold on to the lead for 15 more minutes of play and they would clinch the Western Division crown, but Detroit wasn't finished. Terry Barr caught a four-yard touchdown pass from Earl Morrall and the Lions trailed 17–14. Then things got truly scary for Chicago. In the fourth quarter, the Lions were driving down the field for the go-ahead score. Instead, Chicago defensive back Dave Whitsell jumped in on a route, stole a Morrall pass, and ran it back 39 yards for the Bears' game-sealing touchdown. They would win the game, 24–14. Ditka called Whitsell's interception runback "the biggest play of the year."

The months-long race was finally over, and the Bears were going on to the NFL title game for the first time since '56. For months they played with the looming presence of the formidable Green Bay Packers on their shoulders, who were just waiting for a misstep. Chicago played with major pressure every minute from opening day till the final whistle of the regular season, and prevailed.

"When I looked up and saw the ball coming toward me, I couldn't believe it," said Whitsell. "I said, 'This one belongs to me.'"

The Bears could say the same about the division crown.

17

NO GO IN GREEN BAY

FOR THOSE WHO believed that Vince Lombardi's team was invincible—especially the fans in Green Bay—it was difficult to fathom that the Packers would not be participating in the NFL championship game in 1963.

The Packers were the two-time defending league champions and had appeared in three title games in a row. Plus, it wasn't as if they had fallen off the radar screen. They had the second-best record in the league at 11–2–1. Green Bay seemed as good as it had ever been with the basic problem being that the only team in the NFL that had a better record was its all-time rival in the same Western Division.

Playoffs today revolve around multiple division winners and Wild Cards teams, but in '63, there was only one way to qualify for the championship game—the one-game playoff—and that was by winning your division title, being the best in the division regardless of record.

So for the Packers, the season ended on December 15. See you next year.

This seemed all wrong to the Packers, who believed they were still the best team in football, though they wouldn't get the chance to prove it. They were not fortune tellers, so the Packers had no idea what was in store for them and Lombardi during the remaining years of the sixties when they would win three more championships. For now, in '63, their run was over after the preceding three years of success. In reality, someone had merely hit the pause button on their dynasty, but the players could not know that then.

Fifty years later, Green Bay quarterback Bart Starr has trouble assimilating how his team could compile a record of 11–2–1 and not win its division.

"Those losses came to the Bears," said Starr.

For a long time, for many years, Starr said, "there was a tendency" to look at that season with some disbelief. The Packers played so well all season, lost just two out of 14 games, and still couldn't place first. Only gradually, over time, was it possible to cope with those losses and handle being shut out of the title game in '63.

Finally, Starr said, a certain type of peace was accommodated with the near miss. "Hey, it didn't happen [for us]."

Tackle Bob Skoronski, who also made a Pro Bowl, said the Bears were very good. "I can't take anything away from any of those guys," he said. Yet like Starr, he said it was tough to cope with the idea that the champion Packers were not going to be in the championship game to defend and it was all because of the two losses to the Bears.

"I know for everyone it was difficult to get over."

The Packers of '63 had no major drop-off in performance from the Packers of the previous three seasons. The '60 team finished 8–4 and lost to the Philadelphia Eagles in the title game. The '61 team finished 11–3 and defeated the New York Giants in the title game. And the '62 team finished 13–1 and again defeated the Giants in the titlè game.

In '63, Jim Taylor led the team in rushing with 1,018 yards and Tom Moore gained 658 more on the ground. Although Starr missed four games with injury, he still completed 54.1 percent of his passes for 15 touchdowns against 10 interceptions. Boyd Dowler, Max McGee, and Ron Kramer were the primary receivers. Herb Adderley and Willie Wood still ruled in the secondary. The defense was certainly still sound, with Hall of Famers galore in that unit. Not to mention a rookie linebacker named Dave Robinson came along that year who became a Hall of Famer as well.

Yes, the Packers missed the suspended Paul Hornung, but you couldn't pinpoint a specific moment in the two losses and one tie where he surely would have made the difference. Yet Hall of Fame guard Forrest Gregg always wondered if not being able to suit up Hornung that season was the difference and decades later in his autobiography he raised the issue.

> *We finished with an 11–2–1 record, while the Bears were 11–1–2. You can't help but wonder what does a player mean to a football team? What does a Hall of Fame player mean to a football team? It's difficult putting into words what not having Paul meant to us. He was an integral piece of the Packers—the champion Packers. He might have made a difference in one of those Bears games, potentially altering the fortunes for both teams.*

Hornung supposed that if anyone was going to win the Western Division besides the Packers, it would be the Bears and he wouldn't feel as bad if it provided the avenue for one more title for Papa Bear George Halas.

> *The greatest man in the history of the league was a Bear. I believe any player who ever played in the league should get down on their knees and thank George Halas for what he did for them.*

The greatest sports rivalries are not one-sided. What heightens the drama and anticipation when the games are contested is the belief that either team has the chance to win and can offer hope to its fans. The Chicago–Green Bay rivalry dates back to the beginnings of the NFL in the 1920s, and the teams always play twice a year. The Bears and the Packers are the franchises that have won the most championships, but the teams are not always at their best at the same time. Often they have been, but there have definitely been periods of years where that wasn't so.

It was obvious as the sixties began that the Packers had the upper hand. They did not see the Bears coming in '63 and would not have believed that anyone could have beaten them out in the standings that season. However, other teams, certainly not the Bears, and fans were unaware of what was on the horizon. Soon enough, Lombardi's Packers would collect more jewelry—lots more jewelry—by winning three straight championships in '65, '66, and '67, including gaining additional glory by winning the first two title games against the American Football League in the contest that came to be known as the Super Bowl.

Collectively, the sixties belonged to the Packers. But temporarily, '63 belonged to the Bears. In Packer lore, in Packer minds, 1963 represented the one that got away. How can a team play so well, win that often, and not even reach the title game? It was not easy to explain from the Green Bay side. The admission had to come that it was the Bears who earned the bragging rights on the field with two key victories, beating the Packers in Green Bay and in Chicago when they had to.

With the passage of time, though, the 1960s are lumped together as the decade that Green Bay owned and the description is unimpeachable. The case is convincing that the Green Bay Packers under Vince Lombardi during that era were the best football team of all time.

"That's hard to say," Starr said, not wanting to sound too boastful. "But I would like to think so and because of our fabulous coach you had to think so."

The league thought the Packers were pretty darned good in '63, with 14 players—same as the years before when they were the champs—being chosen for all-star recognition. It was unreal really that somebody found a way to honor Herb Adderley, Dan Currie, Willie Davis, Bill Forester, Forrest Gregg, Henry Jordan, Jerry Kramer, Ron Kramer, Ray Nitschke, Fuzzy Thurston, Jim Ringo, Bart Starr, Jim Taylor, and Willie Wood. The team was close and the players respected one another.

"That was the biggest thing about the whole thing," said Skoronski. "We had a great group of guys. We had a lot of love for each other. And we had a heck of a lot of talent."

Actually, if there was a genuine off-year during the Packers sixties run, it was the next season, 1964, when Green Bay was no better than 8–5–1 for second place in the West.

For those whose memories aren't long enough, the Packers whiffed on the title game two years in a row, but returned with a vengeance in '65. Although many of the top players remained the same from 1959 when Lombardi arrived in Green Bay through the fifth title season culminating with the January of 1968 Super Bowl, there were some key changes in personnel, too.

The credit for Green Bay's great achievements, said Starr, who was part of them all, goes to Lombardi. Having a brilliant coach pulled everything together.

"I think he had the confidence and self-esteem and abilities that he knew he could make it work. The confidence factor came to the forefront."

When they were part of it and in the years that followed as they aged into retirement and senior citizen-hood, the Packers who played for Lombardi and who were part of the Green Bay dynasty realized they were part of something special and that might not ever be duplicated.

While there may be a feeling that the '62 team that finished 13–1 was the best of the bunch, the Packer reign is generally considered collectively under the umbrella of "The Lombardi Era." Still, after crushing the Giants 37–0 in the '61 title game, the Packers eked out the win in the rematch in '62, winning just 16–7. On a frigid day in New York, Taylor was probably the pivotal player, grinding out 85 yards against an inspired Giants defense.

Middle linebacker Sam Huff had been lifted from anonymity playing defense and deposited into the minds of even the most casual football fans by a television special called "The Violent World of Sam Huff." He was also the focal point of a Giants defense hungry for revenge following the '61 beating. One of the most colorful stories Packer runner Jim Taylor ever told was how in the '62 title game Huff dumped him on a running play and said, "Taylor, you stink." Taylor promptly scored a touchdown on another run into the end zone and said, "Hey Sam, how do I smell from here?"

Compared to Wood and Adderley in the defensive backfield, Jesse Whittenton did not draw much attention. He was one of the holdover players who suffered through the 1–10–1 season before Lombardi was hired, but was good enough to keep. Whittenton once said his favorite game was a regular-season win against the Giants when the Packers had to win to capture the Western Division. At that time, New York's passing game with Y. A. Tittle throwing to Del Shofner, was the premier air attack around.

Also at that time, before he was famous for his pivotal role on *Monday Night Football*, Howard Cosell reported on the Giants out of New York. Leading up to the game, he told his audience that Whittenton couldn't cover Shofner with a blanket, which wasn't a bad line, but was indeed an insult. Cosell was wrong. Whittenton shut down Shofner in the clutch. Part of what earned Cosell both fans and enemies was his arrogance behind the microphone.

However, Whittenton said Cosell made a point of seeking him out later and said, "I'm never wrong, but I was wrong about you . . . and I want to apologize." Whittenton gleefully said, "I made Howard Cosell apologize."

Actually, the Packers made anyone apologize who ever doubted them in the sixties, assuming you could find any such misplaced belief other than in the most diehard opposition. The Packers had talent at the top in Lombardi. They had a star quarterback in Starr. They did everything well, from blocking to tackling, from advancing the ball to stopping the other guys from advancing the ball.

Lombardi fostered loyalty— he wanted men of character, as well as ability—but he had a strong hold on his Packers as both coach and general manager. He controlled their playing time and how much money they made. Packer management didn't have to worry about Lombardi squandering the palace funds. He was as hard-nosed with dispensing the cash as he was about devising strategy to defeat opponents.

The famous story about Lombardi revolving around his role as GM was the time that All-Star center Jim Ringo showed up with a lawyer to represent him in contract negotiations. Ringo was ahead of his time bringing representation. Apparently, Lombardi asked them to wait a minute, went into another room, made a call and then returned to address Ringo and the attorney and told them they could now go negotiate with the Philadelphia Eagles because that team was Ringo's new employer.

Nitschke was adored by Lombardi as a player and Nitschke admired Lombardi as a coach, but they didn't exactly have jovial contract negotiations.

I always had some differences of opinion myself with Lombardi at contract time. But I did my own arguing. I rather looked forward to it. Our discussions would get pretty loud. Each year, the girls in the office would see me go into his office and sit back waiting to hear the yelling start. We'd get sore at each other. But it was all part of the game and as long as I was the one doing the yelling instead of some lawyer who didn't know a red dog from a pink poodle, Lombardi never sent me to Philadelphia.

Forrest Gregg, one of the All-Star offensive linemen who later coached the Packers, said he came into the league at the right time and that just as Green Bay started winning the entire country was growing fascinated by pro football through the expansion of television coverage. He said he could tell the difference between the amount of attention received from 1960–62. The Packers won titles just as America was tuning in to watch more games, so Green Bay, Gregg, and his fellow players became much better known on the sporting landscape.

Everyone felt good about winning the first championship, but the bane of many teams that have the talent to do so, but fail to repeat, is how they get distracted, lose motivation, or lose their edge. From the start of training camp in '62 Lombardi refused to let the Packers do that.

"You're the motivation for other teams to play well," Gregg quoted Lombardi as saying. "Everybody is coming for you."

Surely they were, but with few exceptions teams couldn't find ways to take advantage. In their 13–1 season the Lions did. Although the final score was only 26–14, the Lions laid a bigger hurt on the Packers than that, dominating with a defense that swarmed everyone, pounded Starr, and did it all on national TV on Thanksgiving Day. This was one of those beatings where it wouldn't have surprised the audience if Alex Karras and his 300-pound defensive tackle partner Roger Brown each held a Starr leg, dangled him upside down, and said "Make a wish." A football fan might have walked away from that game with the thought, *Those Packers aren't so good.* But that was Green Bay's only loss all season.

The next year, the Bears beat the Pack twice; coming for the Packers with targeted ideas and plans, and that was the difference in the entire season. The Packers' sixties reign spanned the era of NFL single-game postseason championships and the dawn of the Super Bowl era. It was the Packers that went beyond the NFL championship games the first two times, as there was still another game to play versus the AFL in order to be declared "world champion."

One of the by-products of the gradual merger of the NFL and AFL was a postseason game played by the winners of each league. The idea to name the game the Super Bowl came from Lamar Hunt, who in turn got the idea from watching his daughter play with a popular toy of the time called a super ball. The game was more than just a game. The Packers were considered the finest football team on the planet, and the Kansas City Chiefs represented the upstart league. Green Bay had to win to defend the honor of the older league.

Bob Skoronski said winning Super Bowl I was his favorite victory among all of those championships. There was a lot of buzz about how important the game was. He remembers a lot of league higher-ups talking about how the Packers had to play well so the league would look good. "There was a lot of talk about who was the better league. There was a lot of feeling about who was the best. It was serious business."

NFL players kept a close eye on the AFL doings, he said. The NFL guys knew their teams were chasing some of the same players who signed with AFL clubs.

"We talked about them. We watched them play. There was a lot of good talent. There was plenty of good coaching."

The Chiefs had to do better than be blown out to show that the newer league played a good brand of football. It pretty much worked out to fill the needs of both sides. The Packers won

35–10 on January 15, 1967. Green Bay's lead was only 14–10 at the first intermission, but the Packers pulled away in the second half. No shame accrued to either side from the result.

Green Bay's resident philosopher and chronicler of those teams was guard Jerry Kramer, who wrote the best-selling book *Instant Replay* and later *Distant Replay*. Kramer kept a diary that ran to more than 100,000 words and worked with the late Dick Schaap, editor of *Sport Magazine* and other claims to journalism fame, to produce the final documents.

Kramer predated Lombardi's arrival in Green Bay by a season and he chose to focus his diary on one season—1967—the end of the run. That season included the Ice Bowl victory over the Dallas Cowboys. He recounted a celebration of the win spent having drinks with the guys. He said he got a bit carried away and barely remembered the night later except that he and Fuzzy Thurston, the Packers' offensive guard, completed the evening "with toasts, toasts to the two greatest guards in the history of the whole world."

It seemed that Thurston was often underrated and not always appreciated by the whole world. At 6' 1" and 245 pounds, Thurston was not huge for a guard by NFL standards, though he looked tough enough with his buzz cut and extra large jaw. He played college at small Valparaiso University in Indiana, and was a 5th-round draft pick of the Philadelphia Eagles in 1956, but didn't make the team and then went into the Army. When he came out of the service, Thurston took another shot with the Eagles in '58 but again did not make it. He almost stuck in Winnipeg in the Canadian Football League, but the Baltimore Colts called looking for emergency help because of injuries.

Thurston caught on with the Colts and played sparingly. It was also his good fortune to be on the Colts' roster when they won the NFL title. Combined with his tenure on the Packers, that made Thurston a six-time champion. About that best-guards-in-the-world designation, Kramer mentioned, as crowded as the NFL all-star teams were with Packers, it was tough for some guys to get in the door, but Thurston was a two-time selection. After all of his ups and downs to be named all-league was some kind of special for Thurston.

"It's an honor I only dreamed about. I never thought it would actually happen."

The honor did not exactly go to his head. Thurston never lost his sense of humor, and whenever he appeared at one of the many dinners and luncheons Wisconsin fans invited players to after they began winning titles Thurston was self-deprecating. "This is Fat Fuzz," he said, "the man who made Paul Hornung." He was not quite half-serious. Indeed, Thurston was the one on the team who could lift fellow players' moods and relieve tension. A famous *Sport Magazine* story about Thurston even referred to him as "Joker and Hyde."

Thurston was beloved by the people of Green Bay and Wisconsin as a whole because of that outgoing personality. Thurston helped lead the Packer runners on the sweep, but he had an even more endearing way of talking that busted up the fans. After the 1967 Ice Bowl, Thurston said the only way he could stay warm was by drinking ten vodkas. No one knew whether or not to believe him, but for years, until recently, Thurston would tell you about it at his Fuzzy's bar.

One might say Thurston was born for that raconteur role. In 1962, Thurston put on a good show for a visiting writer, singing to the crowd in a Green Bay drinking establishment after the Packers won the world championship over the Giants and jumping up on top of the bar to dance. It was easy to chuckle when Thurston told a tale or acted one out, but he had to be taken very seriously on the football field when he was throwing blocks.

Thurston was a character for sure, one minute keeping the hands of greedy pass rushers off his quarterback despite being out-weighed by 40 pounds, and playing hurt while doing so. During his career Thurston played with shoulder and ankle injuries that ordinarily would have sidelined others for weeks. But by playing with pain he felt he was living up to his part of the bargain of being a good teammate and doing his best to win a championship.

"When all is said and done, this is what my game is. I know the other guys are doing their job and I know it's going to look pretty bad if I don't do mine."

That was Thurston's bluecollar, responsible-sounding outlook, sort of an aw-shucks, low-key hero approach to playing with pain. Yet the next minute Thurston could be acting out what seemed to be the type of roles later portrayed in *Animal House*. Once, Thurston was asked about the veracity of a story that he had actually devoured a copy of the Green Bay newspaper reporting the story of the Packers' '62 title. Thurston said that he didn't remember doing that, but "don't bet against it." It could often be said in the presence of Thurston's company: And a good time was had by all.

The occasion of Kramer's toast to himself and Thurston followed the Packers' third straight NFL championship and advanced them to their second straight Super Bowl, this time against the Oakland Raiders. Kramer wrote of a week's worth of practice in Northern Wisconsin, where the temperatures either registered as minus or in single digits. The Super Bowl was to be played in Florida, though, and Kramer did take note of how crushed the team was to be changing climates.

"The temperature was seven degrees below zero and when we landed in Florida the temperature was 75." Kramer had said on national television that Lombardi had created an atmosphere of Camelot; a perfect place for the team to win. On the flight to Florida, Kramer said, Marie Lombardi, the coach's wife, came over to him and gave him a kiss for saying it.

The Packers, of course, polished off the Raiders to win their second consecutive Super Bowl and their fifth championship of the decade. It was a grand time to be a Packer and it was special to play under Lombardi.

"He was a magnificent guy, and a bright guy," said Skoronski. "He loved to win and he made it contagious. He forced it to be contagious. There was only one way in Green Bay and it was his way and that was okay."

Although the passage of the years has winnowed the number of ex-Packers who competed during the championship days because of old age, the surviving players return to Green Bay for a Packer alumni weekend each season. Skoronski is a regular and recognizes that those teammates shared a lot and accomplished a lot. But while they were playing, Skoronski said it was slow to dawn on the team how the entire nation was getting to know them.

"We didn't realize the national impact that the team had."

Decades after all of those Green Bay players retired, Hornung is like Starr. He believes the Packers of their era—from 1960–68—did constitute the best professional football team of all time.

"There's been some good ones, but naturally I think so."

Even if one more ring got away in '63.

18

BEARS–GIANTS, 1956

PROFESSIONAL ATHLETES AND coaches have memories that make elephants seem like they're suffering from amnesia. Every result, every play, every slight accumulates and sticks in the mind for as long as it takes to obtain revenge. Oh, the player or coach might not admit it, but vengeance for a disappointing loss or harsh injury is always a nickel shy of payback.

In certain leagues teams play irregularly and in others they play twice a year. Less frequently does it happen that teams must face one another with a championship on the line or with the stakes of being able to advance into the playoffs.

Sometimes poetic justice arrives when least expected. Sometimes it never arrives at all and eats at the soul for a lifetime. When the pairing was set for the '63 National Football League title game, the Chicago Bears and the New York Giants had different thoughts on their minds.

This was the third straight championship game appearance for the Giants. They were the victims of the Green Bay

Packers in '61 and '62, and a large percentage of the Giants roster was the same as it had been in those two years. The Giants would have preferred a third shot at the Packers, but paramount was winning the darned thing regardless of who the foe was.

The Bears did not have the same frame of reference, as they had expended tremendous mental and physical energy throughout the regular season keeping the Packers from overtaking them. Chicago's season had been all about beating Green Bay twice, and about getting ahead of the Packers from day one and staying ahead. They were the hunted all autumn long, and they rose to the occasion not only when necessary against the Packers, but by beating enough other teams along the way to capture the Western Division and shut the Packers out of the postseason.

It was an exhausting achievement and it might have worn the Bears down and might well have produced a mental letdown. The long pennant race was over and the Bears prevailed over the Packers. Great going! Great job! Mission accomplished! Of course, Bears coach George Halas could talk like that longer than a Congressional filibuster to make sure his players didn't have their judgment clouded, if he thought it necessary.

It would have been easy to believe that the hard part of the season was over. That type of thinking is usually fatal. It may well have been suicide to think that way. The Packers had been disposed of and now Halas' reminders were about the next task: the big game coming up on December 29. This championship date with the Giants was what they had sweated and slaved for, had elbowed the Packers aside for, and they knew it, but if you're a coach, you just want to make sure.

There was something else that Halas could bring up, and if he didn't, the oldest members of the team would and did. All they had to do was mention a number to pique the interest of younger teammates and to rev up their own juices. The number consisted of four digits and it was a year—1956. On December 30, 1956, the New York Giants embarrassed the Chicago Bears, 47–7, at Yankee Stadium. That was the last time the Bears had advanced to the championship game.

Not only was the score embarrassing to live with, but the manner by which it was accomplished made it worse. That day was very cold and wintry. The Giants drew 56,836 fans, wearing the finest in cold-weather fashion, but how the Giants were outfitted made more difference than how the spectators were adorned. In one of the stranger ways that history repeated itself in the NFL, the Giants made the same adjustment to beat the Bears for the crown as they had in 1934.

In 1934, the Bears were 13–0 in the regular season; an offensive juggernaut rolling over foes. Running back Beattie Feathers rushed for 1,004 yards, the first runner in NFL history to break the 1,000-yard barrier. He was injured by the time of the title game, though. But New York's starting quarterback, Harry Newman, was out as well. Few expected the Giants to put up a major challenge since they had lost twice to Chicago in the regular season and their overall record was 8–5.

As in 1956, December 9, 1934, was another frigid day in New York City, especially for the 35,000 fans sitting in the stands. For the first half of the title showdown at the Polo Grounds the Bears had their way, building a 10–3 lead on a field coated in ice and as slippery as an oil slick. Standing in the locker room at the intermission was clubhouse attendant Abe Cohen, who was also associated part-time with Manhattan College. Giants coach Steve Owen asked Cohen if he could rush across town and come up with enough sneakers to help his team cope with the footing.

Cohen carried a large bag, rounded up nine pairs of sneakers, and made his way back to the Polo Grounds with the fourth quarter still to go. Once many of the Giants were shod differently, their play was transformed. The coach on the other sideline witnessing the turn of fortune was an unhappy, hoodwinked George Halas. He was furious and protested, but the Giants were doing nothing illegal. In a comment famously ascribed to Halas, he ordered his players to step on the tennis-shoe-clad Giants with their spikes, but as a defensive strategy that did not work.

Oh was Halas steaming. He referred to the loss of a title because of sneakers as "That goddamn rubber shoes game."

New York made a late-game comeback, running off 27 straight points. With the Giants' players running on the frozen grass with confidence they won the championship 30–13. In NFL lore this became known as "The Sneaker Game." Boy that hurt Halas. "I wish I could forget the fourth quarter," he said many years later.

After that debacle Halas said his players would never go into a game without backup equipment of two pairs of tennis shoes per player. That made even more peculiar what transpired in '56. It was not as if the circumstances presented themselves every week. In fact, twenty-two years passed until the Bears were again playing on a frozen field in New York against the Giants for a championship. Who would ever imagine that there would be two sneaker games between the same foes?

Of course more than two decades later when the situation repeated itself only Halas was left as an active participant from the first game. It's likely that none of his players were very familiar with the details of the '34 loss. When the Bears came out to prepare for the kickoff for the '56 championship game, fullback Rick Casares jogged onto the field.

"I was one of the first guys out there when we came out to warm up," said Casares. "I fell right on my face."

In theory, Halas was the living embodiment of institutional memory for the National Football League, and while he was involved as owner on one of his temporary hiatuses from coaching in favor of Paddy Driscoll, he was still around. But somehow he let the sneaker game remembrance elude his focus when another December presented his players with more ice than they had ever seen outside their barroom glasses.

It was the Giants, not the Bears, who learned from historical precedent. New York planned ahead. Giants' star defensive end Andy Robustelli owned a sporting goods store in Connecticut, and was quite conscious of the temperature and the weather forecast. "I've been thinking that if the weather stays this cold we'll be playing Sunday's game on cement."

Rather than wait for an emergency SOS to be sent out after the Giants reached Yankee Stadium, Robustelli toted dozens of pairs of sneakers of all sizes to the field. The '56 Giants were prepared from the start of the game and once again the Bears might as well have been Shoeless Joe Jackson times eleven. During the regular season the teams tied 17–17, so the title game figured to be a close one.

It wasn't.

The Bears got clobbered, 47–7. The Giants were ready for football or ice hockey, whatever broke out, in capturing their first title since 1938.

"It lasted forever" is how Casares viewed the day's activities. "They just beat the heck out of us in the frozen field game. That [the sneakers] was the difference in the ball game."

Casares scored Chicago's only touchdown on a nine-yard run after a fumble recovery. Ironically, the Bears brought in George Blanda in relief at quarterback. So before Halas decided he was worthless, Blanda had been tasked with rescuing the Bears in a championship game and threw for 150 yards.

Qualifying as bulletin board material, even though the Giants mounted it on their clubhouse door, was a postcard sent to New York management. Coach Jim Lee Howell gave his players four days off over Christmas, which the newspapers had noted. The message on the postcard was: "Merry Christmas, but you won't have a Happy New Year." The signature was simple: "A Bears fan."

New York quarterback Charley Conerly threw two touchdown passes and Ben Agajanian, a kicker who had four toes crushed on his kicking foot in an industrial accident in college, booted two field goals and five extra points. Agajanian was nicknamed "The Toeless Wonder," and on this day he pretty much was. The Giants were ahead 34–7 at halftime.

Whether anyone believed Driscoll or not he said the Giants' tennis shoes didn't matter. Maybe he was just trying to be polite and give credit to the Giants. "The frozen field and their sneakers had nothing to do with it," said Driscoll. "We carry sneakers all the time. Our shoes were just as suitable as their sneakers. It was the same for both sides."

That was not true; it was not the same for both sides. The Giants were smart enough to put their sneakers on their feet. Driscoll must have missed New York's litmus test. Before the game Howell sent one player, Gene Filipski, out onto the field wearing sneakers, and another player, Ed Hughes, wearing spikes. Hughes took a couple of steps and catapulted onto his butt because of the slippery surface. Filipski had no difficulty moving around on the frozen ground. Howell evaluated the results rather logically. "Everyone wears sneakers," he informed the team.

The years went by and the Bears did not return to the title game. The Giants made it twice, losing to the Packers. By 1963, many of the players who participated in the '56 championship game had retired or been traded off. But both were veteran squads virtually littered with big-name players of longevity, several of whom were on their way to the newly opened Hall of Fame after their retirements.

Among the Giants, tackle Roosevelt Brown, kicker Don Chandler, receiver Frank Gifford, linebacker Sam Huff, defensive end Jim Katcavage, defensive back Jimmy Patton, guard Jack Stroud, fullback Alex Webster, and Robustelli were still active from the bunch that took it to the Bears in '56.

Among the Bears still active who were on the roster in '56 were defensive end Doug Atkins, defensive back J. C. Caroline, linebacker Joe Fortunato, linebacker Bill George, lineman Stan Jones, lineman Fred Williams, and Casares. And, of course, Halas was still around, the man on the sidelines who had been present for not only the '56 loss, but the '34 one as well. Jim Dooley, who played on the team in '56, was an assistant coach in '63.

There was plenty of seasoning in the Giants lineup, mostly guys whose contributions were harder to quantify by yardage totals (except for Gifford and Webster). Brown was considered one of the greatest tackles in NFL history and he was a virtual unknown coming out of college.

Brown was 6' 3", weighed 255 pounds, and attended Morgan State, a predominantly black school, before departing in 1953. At that time, the pros had little pipeline to the black schools and no one really knew how good Brown was. The Giants selected him with their 27th pick in the draft back when the draft lasted a lot longer and had a lot more teams winging it the longer it went. For the results Brown produced—and given how ridiculously deep in the draft he was taken—he may have been the biggest draft day bargain in history. It's not as if the Giants had done much more homework than any other team. Someone in the front office saw Brown's name on the list of Black All Americans and took the wild and crazy risk of spending the 27th-round pick.

Some years later, after Brown had become a perennial All-Star in his 13-year career, Giants owner Wellington Mara said, "We had nothing to lose." The observation was certainly an understatement.

Brown was precocious in ability, but also in other ways. When he was a youngster growing up in Charlottesville, Virginia, he was not simply enrolled in school, but took a placement exam. He did so well on it that the local authorities put him in the third grade, skipping those earliest years. As a result, he graduated from high school at fifteen and college at nineteen, and said he was twenty when he played his first game for the Giants. When he began playing football in high school, his dad didn't like it, so Roosevelt and his brother had to sneak onto the team. Since his involvement paid off with a football scholarship, it was time well-invested.

The odds were very high against Brown becoming a successful pro after being the 321st player selected in the draft, but he had a sculpted body and a good attitude. It didn't take long for him to prove he was way above average in talent, too. Brown became an iron man, almost never missing a game. There was one time when he was sandwiched between Baltimore's Gino Marchetti and Big Daddy Lipscomb and suffered a fractured cheek bone and missed one game, but except for a sprained ankle that cost him two more, he missed no other games because of injury. It would be a different type of understatement to say that Brown was passionate about the game.

"It's been my whole life," Brown said of football. "The friendships I've made, the good times, the championships we've won."

The Giants player least likely to be around for the '63 title game was Gifford. In many ways, Gifford has led a charmed life. He was a huge star at the University of Southern California, where he acted in Hollywood as a part-time job. Gifford's reputation was the opposite of Brown's in college. Everyone knew who the dashing and handsome All-American was. In New York, he was a first-class runner and was the toast of the town after being the toast of the town in LA. Gifford became an eight-time Pro Bowl selection in his career.

However, in 1960, that career was almost truncated. In one of the most famous and well-remembered hits in NFL history, Gifford was leveled by Philadelphia Eagles' linebacker Chuck Bednarik, and lay flat on the turf, unconscious. The hit knocked him out for the rest of the season and led him to retire. After missing the '61 campaign, Gifford did return to football and the Giants and moved to a receiver position in '62. Gifford had spent the year scouting for the Giants, but still had the itch to play. He was an easy choice for comeback player of the year.

"What did matter was the excitement of being part of it all," said Gifford. "I should never have retired. It was a big mistake."

In 1963, Gifford was still a major offensive threat, catching 42 passes for seven touchdowns.

One of the key plays that propelled the Giants to the Eastern Division title in '63 came in a late-season game against the Pittsburgh Steelers. In the last game of the regular season when New York beat Pittsburgh to finish a game ahead of the Cleveland Browns in the standings, Y. A. Tittle aimed a pass at Gifford. It seemed to sail off target, and Gifford, fearing an interception, leapt sideways to swat it away. "All I was trying to do was bat the ball in the air," said Gifford, "and it stuck in my hand."

Stuck in his hand. Sounds pretty much like a miracle catch and given that it was made in a full-out dive in the prone position that was probably a fair assessment. The Giants were leading 16–10 at the time and Gifford's grab kept the ball away from Pittsburgh. New York went on to the 33–17 victory that propelled the Giants into the title game against the Bears. Coach Allie Sherman, who moved Gifford to flanker in a position swap with the versatile Joe Morrison and made it easier for Gifford to return from his brief retirement, was pleased to see his man become the hero in the clutch.

"That guy they were burying not long ago made it great for us, didn't he?"

Steelers coach Buddy Parker said Gifford's play was the game-changer and Gifford also picked up his share of kudos in the Giants' locker room postgame. One thing the Steelers foolishly did before the game was rile up Sam Huff. Whether Huff was searching for motivation or not, he interpreted quotes by

Pittsburgh players in the newspapers leading into the game as saying the Giants were scared to play them.

"We beat them on team balance," said Huff.

Against many teams Huff represented the creation of imbalance. He grew up poor in West Virginia without much to his name and becoming a pro out of the University of West Virginia raised his financial status considerably. He may have been the best-known defensive player of his time because of the TV documentary about him, but he was a five-time Pro Bowl selection and an eventual Hall of Famer. There was not a lot of mystery to Huff and how he played middle linebacker.

> *Football is a game of body contact. You either love it or you don't. There's no in-between. We don't get paid to look fancy. The idea is to stop the runner the best way you can. I like to get right inside their helmets and think like they do. It's too late to tackle a man after he's made his move.*

The most unusual thing about Huff's career is that he was well-known as a guard who protected ball carriers at West Virginia and the Giants chose him to be a guard in the NFL. In 1956, however, New York had a shortage of linebackers and they shifted Huff to that role. It turned out to be the best idea since someone matched peanut butter and jelly. As it so happened, tackling runners, not blocking for them, was Huff's true forte.

New York was pretty proud of its defense and several of those holdovers from '56 played on that unit. Not the least of the returnees to the Bears wars was Robustelli, the sneaker man of '56. A Connecticut native, Robustelli played his college football at a small local school named Arnold after serving in the Navy during World War II.

Robustelli was just about as overlooked as Roosevelt Brown. The Los Angeles Rams drafted Robustelli in the 19th round of the 1951 draft. A two-time All Pro for the Rams, Robustelli wanted to return to the East and was traded to New York, where he was chosen All-Pro five more times.

"The only way to play this game is to play it as hard and tough as you can," said Robustelli.

Robustelli was on the winning '56 title team and he and some of the other old-timers of the Giants squad wanted to earn one more ring before they retired. In Chicago, those old-timers just wanted to win one ring and they couldn't think of a better way to obtain it than by beating the Giants.

19

THE AFL CHAMPIONSHIP GAME

BY **1963 THE** San Diego Chargers wanted to win the American Football League championship trophy so badly they didn't care if it resembled a tin cup or an ugly candlestick.

The Chargers were the close-call team in the early days of the AFL and were sick of winning honorable mention. The league was founded in 1960 and that first season the then-Los Angeles Chargers won the Western Division and advanced to the title game where they lost to the Houston Oilers, 24–16. In '61, same deal. The Chargers won the West and lost to the Oilers in the championship game, this time by a score of 10–3. That just about drove Coach Sid Gillman into film-viewing seclusion, trying to figure out where things went wrong.

In '63, the explosive Chargers—who led the league in offense—just wanted to be known as the best. In San Diego they lived in perpetual sunshine, but they wanted just a minute or two to bask in it in front of the world. The Chargers finished 11–3 and scored 399 points. The Boston Patriots—their championship opponent—should not be able to stop them.

"We had an awesome team," said defensive back Dick West-moreland.

One reason the Chargers played so well was the guidance of Gillman. Gillman had a better eye for talent than a Hollywood casting agent, though he was really renowned for the way he experimented with the passing game to make it ever more dangerous. Gillman was a Charger before the players were Chargers and even presided over one of those come-one, come-all tryout camps that new teams sponsor to show their new community how much they like them. They stem from the theme "You Too Can Play Pro Football," though in reality the guys in the front offices have to work overtime to keep the smirks off their faces when the hopefuls show up that haven't played a down of organization football since Pop Warner league.

> *I remember that first tryout camp we had. Every bartender in Los Angeles thought he could play football. These gorillas would be outside every day standing in their cleats, lined up for inspection.*

Gillman culled the herd, pretty much allowing the wannabes their 15 minutes of fame, and then went shopping for players in more reliable places rather than the discount bin.

It was the Patriots that sometimes felt as if they couldn't afford to shop anywhere but the discount bin. Boston was not as well-heeled as most of the other franchises. Owner Billy Sullivan had journalism ink in his veins. The son of a newspaperman, Sullivan worked as a public relations man for Boston College, his alma mater, Notre Dame, and the Boston Braves. Displaying the work ethic he would need during his near-three decades of Patriots ownership, Sullivan churned out press releases for his causes as swiftly as he could type. Famed sports columnist Red Smith reflected on Sullivan's productivity in handing out those purple-ink copies and called him the "Maitre de Mimeograph."

Sullivan did not possess pockets nearly as deep as some millionaire AFL owners—like the Hunts and Hiltons—but his biggest problem in Boston was the lack of a permanent stadium for home games. The Patriots changed addresses as often as college students did dorms, switching off between Fenway Park, Nickerson Field, Harvard Stadium, and Boston College. If your building had bleachers and a hot dog stand chances were Sullivan would come knocking asking to borrow the keys.

Yet Sullivan was able to piece together reliably decent teams. Fans may have had to check the master schedule to see where the team was playing, but the product on the field was entertaining. During the first few years of the league the Patriots played well enough, but couldn't stop the Houston Oilers or Buffalo Bills. In 1963, they outlasted the Bills in a single-game playoff to reach their first championship game.

During the regular season, the Chargers and Patriots met twice. In September, the Chargers won, 17–13, at Balboa Stadium. In November, the Chargers won 7–6 in Fenway Park. The Patriots pretty much tamed the Charger offense. Given the regular-season backdrop, the championship game figured to be tight.

"We played them that year twice and they were tough ball games," said San Diego fullback Keith Lincoln. "We thought, 'It's gonna be a close game.'"

The Patriots could score, averaging 23.4 points per game, but defense was their team's strength.

On offense, Boston started the old Kentucky babe, Babe Parilli, at quarterback and he threw for 2,345 yards to a solid group of receivers, including flanker Jim Colclough, kicker-catcher Gino Cappelletti, tight end Tony Romeo, and rookie wide receiver Art Graham.

Graham was a big get for the Patriots. He was a local from nearby Somerville and was a star at Boston College. The 6' 1" 205-pound Graham was the team's No. 1 draft pick. The Cleveland Browns wanted him, too, but Graham slipped to the 11th round in the NFL draft because teams felt he was surely going to stay home to play. They were right, but it wasn't preordained.

The AFL draft was held in late December of 1962, about 60 seconds after the college football season had ended. In those days, Boston College still played Holy Cross—one of its rivals—before the programs chose different directions of big-time growth (BC) and staying smaller time (HC). They played in early December and that was Graham's last college game.

"I got off the field and someone told me right there, 'You're the No. 1 draft choice of the Patriots.'" He replied, "No kidding?"

Graham had been surreptitiously approached by a few pro teams gauging his interest in their operations.

Three or four teams contacted me during the AFL-NFL wars. Then word got out that I signed under the table so I dropped to the 11th round with the Browns. But I hadn't signed. I think Billy Sullivan started the rumor. One reason I hadn't signed was that I wanted to play baseball for BC in the spring.

Meanwhile, the talent wars raged and Graham heard the stories about teams babysitting draft picks so they couldn't even negotiate with teams in the other league, or even chat. Buck

Buchanan, the huge defensive tackle out of Grambling, was a coveted pick for Kansas City that year and was spirited away to be hidden in a hotel room. Chiefs owner Lamar Hunt won that battle, but he also told a story on himself when he was pursuing Roman Gabriel, a quarterback out of North Carolina State. Hunt said he finally got Gabriel to pick up the phone in his dorm room and talked to him for a half hour trying to sell him on joining the AFL. Hunt found out much later that the person on the other end of the line was the Los Angeles Rams' general manager Tom Fears, not Gabriel. Gabriel signed with the Rams.

That was typical of what the NFL was doing at the time. It actually had a secret program going where it deployed employees all over the country to prevent draft choices from making contact with the enemy. It was called "Operation Hand Holding."

The Rams lost a draft choice to the Raiders when lineman Harry Schuh of Memphis State was scooped up and flown away, along with his wife, to Las Vegas and beyond. The Cowboys invited receiver prospect Otis Taylor to Dallas for Thanksgiving and then held him and several other players as virtual hostages as they were moved around to four hotels.

"They didn't even want you talking to anyone in the lobby," said Taylor. "Once they knew you'd talked to somebody, they'd move you to another hotel."

As crazy as that was, a Chiefs scout, Lloyd Wells, who must have been part-bloodhound, tracked Taylor down anyway. Wells approached Taylor's room from the back of the motel, climbed a fence, knocked on his window, and talked him into leaving with him. Taylor ended up signing with the Chiefs. That was one of the more memorable tales from the draft wars.

In Graham's case, he was not as hotly pursued because he was viewed as a lost cause to the NFL. Not that the Patriots were taking any chances. At the moment it was possible to sign Graham, the Pats were on the scene. Early on a Monday morning, about 7:30 a.m., there was a knock on Graham's dormitory door. His roommate answered and saw this middle-aged man whom he didn't recognize. "Who are you?" the young man asked Billy Sullivan.

Graham had been advised by former Boston College star, and All-Pro defensive lineman, Art Donovan to ask for at least $10,000. He signed for $15,000. Graham caught 21 passes in 1963, but the bang for the buck was enormous, as he averaged 26.2 yards per catch while scoring five touchdowns.

The Patriots carried their 8–6–1 record into the championship game feeling pretty good after some rocky times during the regular season.

"We had ups and downs," said Graham. "We won early and lost a few games in the middle."

Graham also remembers the '63 season as being plagued by bad weather. Games were played in the mud, cities were hit by unexpected fall snowstorms, and so were practices.

"It was one of those winters where it snowed early and it never left," said Graham. Notable among the hassles was the final regular-season game when the Patriots were torched 35–3 by the Chiefs in Kansas City that forced them into a one-game playoff with the Buffalo Bills. When the team landed, Graham said, the players were supposed to board busses. But the temperature was frigid and the busses were all stalled out, so hauling its gear the team piled into a group of taxis. The Patriots were asked, "Who are you people?"

On game day, the kickoff was delayed for 15 or 20 minutes because of more bad weather. Then the Patriots played just about their worst game of the season.

After all the miserable weather all fall, when the Patriots arrived in San Diego for the championship game, they just about sweated to death. Their hotel was like a sauna and the temperature got up to 85 degrees at Balboa Stadium. It seemed to take about five minutes for the Patriots to become dehydrated. Everything felt as if it was moving in slow motion and the players were heavy-legged.

"It was like we were running on mattresses," said Graham.

While Babe Parilli, who had been coached by Bear Bryant at Kentucky, was most inclined to throw, the Patriots' offense was aided by back Larry Garron, who rushed for 750 yards and caught 26 passes (for 418 yards) as well. But the reality was Boston's best avenue for success was relying on the defense and its ability to contain the Chargers. In the two previous regular-season games, the defense had done its job, holding San Diego down.

There were some big-time defenders on the Patriots' unit. Linebacker Tommy Addison was tough and defensive lineman Houston Antwine was probably tougher. Defensive end Bob Dee was an original Patriot, playing in 112 straight games and becoming a four-time All-Star selection after he had a cameo with the Washington Redskins in the late 1950s. And his defensive end partner Larry Eisenhauer was ferocious.

Eisenhauer was from Long Island, New York, but also attended Boston College. He would utter such comments as "I hate quarterbacks," and his teammates nicknamed the four-time All-Star "Wild Man." Eisenhauer said he earned the nickname by revving his emotions and adrenalin up to thousands of rpms per minute and never slowing down his charges at the quarterback in the pocket. Oh yes, to psych himself up in the locker room before games, Eisenhauer occasionally tore one apart, bashing lockers, walls, partitions, or anything else standing with his arms, shoulders or helmeted head. "I know I'm a very emotional player. But before every game I have to get ready to play and I do this by slamming locker doors, belting my teammates, hitting walls and just doing all the damage I can. I put a hole in the wall in the Bills' dressing room [with his head]."

Patriots teammates learned to stay out of Eisenhauer's way and the team may have been looking to keep a jack-of-all-trades repair man on the payroll. One season, Eisenhauer sent five opposing quarterbacks to the bench for doctor visits, including both Jack Kemp and Tom Flores of Buffalo in the same game.

"Eisenhauer hit me harder than I've ever been hit before in my life," said Kemp. The wall in the dressing room had no comment.

The reason the 6' 5" 250-pound Eisenhauer signed with the Patriots instead of bothering with the NFL was opportunity. He knew there were openings on Boston's roster, and besides, the team was right down the street from Boston College.

"This was a new league, but I felt it was big time," said Eisenhauer. "It was just exciting to be part of it."

So did Tom Yewcic. Yewcic was the Patriots' backup quarterback and punter in '63. He didn't get much chance to throw, although he did start one game Parilli missed, but he did kick all season. Yewcic was older than most of the players on the team. He was already thirty-one, despite only a few years of football experience, because of the unusual arc of his career. The odds were much higher that Yewcic was going to be playing pro ball in Boston for the Red Sox than the Patriots.

While at Michigan State Yewcic was a first-class baseball player who was voted the most outstanding player in the 1954 College World Series. He signed a professional baseball contract and spent seven years in the minors, with one of the briefest Major League cameo appearances of all time. Yewcic caught one game for the Detroit Tigers in 1957 and came to the plate once without a hit. His stats practically reflected the real-life character played by Burt Lancaster in the movie *Field of Dreams*.

Giving up his dream of making it in baseball, in 1960, Yewcic hooked on with the Toronto Argonauts of the Canadian Football League, where if only briefly he spent time in the backfield with Cookie Gilchrist, a soon to be AFL star. Yewcic had a nice showing in a unique exhibition game between the Argonauts and the NFL's Pittsburgh Steelers, where they used compromises in setting the rules and that gained him "a look-see" with the Steelers.

"They were pretty well set, though," Yewcic said of the Steelers. "They wanted me to be a defensive corner and I didn't have the speed for that. In the American Football League they were looking for guys who could do more than one thing."

Versatility—not including calling pitches—got Yewcic a job with the Patriots. He would sign with them in '61 where he remained until 1966. With Boston, Yewcic was always a second-string quarterback and first-string punter, but would occasionally go out for passes. In an odd categorization, Yewcic and Tom Brady are the only players in team history to have punted, thrown for a touchdown pass, run for a touchdown, and caught a pass. There are a couple of those tasks that few fans will remember each man doing.

Yewcic talked to the New York Titans as well, which were on their way to bankruptcy court and emerging to become the Jets. It was Yewcic's good fortune that he joined the Patriots at the right time, when he fit perfectly and the team was at its peak and on its way to the '63 championship game. The Chargers played flashier football, but the Patriots played a determined, hard-nosed style.

"The reason we were good," said Yewcic, "was we had a lot of good athletes."

That may have been so, but the Chargers are better remembered for having great athletes and some with the most colorful of backgrounds.

As a group, San Diego not only led the AFL in offensive production that season, but led the league in defensive stinginess, too. One reason for that was a guy on the defensive line who was so large he just about took up two positions. In 1963, pro football was not densely populated with 300-pound linemen as it is now. A Fuzzy Thurston could be a star blocker at 245. A Stan Jones could be a star defensive tackle at 255. What the Chargers had was a player who was agile and strong, yet was also much bigger. If anyone ever selects the All-Time Pro Football Entertaining Team, Ernie Ladd will hold down one of the two defensive tackle spots. Ladd stood 6' 9" and after a meal weighed about 320 pounds. A native of Louisiana, Ladd, who became nearly as famous in the world of pro wrestling as he was in the world of pro football, played college ball for Grambling. In 1961, Ladd was drafted by both the Chargers and the Chicago Bears. Interestingly, the Bears seemed to value him much more, picking Ladd in the 4th round while San Diego waited until the 15th round.

Outspoken, concerned with African American civil rights, and a man with a sense of humor, it takes some imagination to see Ladd fitting hand and glove with George Halas. It would have been something else again, however, to imagine him on a pass rushing line with Doug Atkins. Stan Jones would have stayed on offense and Ladd and Atkins would have totaled so many quarterback sacks the category would have been invented earlier.

For those who enjoy their football players less than homogenized, The Ernie Ladd Story was one for the ages. He was bigger than life and everyone else around him—and that included Big Daddy Lipscomb. Plus he had an appetite to boot and could probably eat more than Joey Chestnut and Takeru Kobayashi combined. He just didn't bother with silly competitive eating rules restrictions most of the time. Various sources cite witnesses confirming that Ladd was perfectly capable of turning every meal into a buffet. Maybe Ernie was just trying to make a good impression, but the report from his first breakfast at Chargers training camp upon arrival listed his menu contents as the following: ten eggs, eight pieces of toast, three glasses of juice, four cartons of milk. That did not last Ladd all day. For lunch he deposited two hamburger steaks, beef stroganoff over rice, and a few side dishes into his stomach account. There were additional sightings of Ladd downing a personal record of 130 pancakes at a sitting. He also at least once lunched on ten pork chops, three helpings of rice and green beans, and a sweet mix of desserts that included three peach cobblers, three dishes of ice cream, and a half-gallon of milk. Someone forgot the partridge and the pear tree.

As an aside in a book about Sid Gillman, the author reported an occasion when Ladd was showing off for sportswriters in New York and ate four 16-ounce steaks for the main course, but the steaks were not lonely on the plate, either. Ladd added two shrimp cocktails, three servings of cole slaw, three helpings of spinach, three baked potatoes, eight rolls with butter, a half-gallon of milk (the milk mustache seems pretty consistent from meal to meal) and three desserts. It was then said that a Chargers player named Irv Robertson commented, "He's lost his appetite. You should see him eat when nobody is watching." And at least once Ladd did engage in an official eating contest against a hefty fisherman in the Golden West Eating Classic in San Diego. It was estimated that they combined to ingest 22,000 calories of food that included everything from spaghetti and meatballs and fried chicken to hams, prime rib, sirloin steak, cake and ice cream. Ladd eked out the victory by a margin of three ounces of leftover food.

Did these guys know how to have fun, or what?

The amazing thing is that Ladd could eat in this manner and still retain muscle and mobility. But he did. Otherwise his nickname would not have been "The Big Cat" (although that was used more in wrestling). All but a very small number of football players in the early sixties could avoid taking off-season jobs. Ladd got the idea he might be good at professional wrestling and he began a new career in that element in 1961, one that he continued until '86.

While Ladd was generally viewed as a nice guy, he made hay in his wrestling career as a villain. He made the choice, theorizing that he was too big for fans to identify with, so he had better options as a bad guy. "I was too big to get sympathy by being beat on, so I made a much better heel."

Ladd talked trash galore about opponents, but faced many of the top names, including Andre the Giant, Bob Backlund, and Bruno Sammartino. Typical of Ladd's insult humor in the wrestling game was calling Andre the Giant "The Big Fat, French Fry" and Wahoo McDaniel (another dual football-wrestling guy) "The Drunken Indian."

Ladd reportedly made $100,000 a year wrestling when he was probably taking down something approximating $25,000 a year for football—as a four-time All-Star.

While the Bears missed out on Ladd, Ladd didn't miss out on the Bears. He had a top-notch running mate on the Chargers' defensive line in Earl Faison. A former Indiana University All-American, Faison was a five-time AFL All-Star who checked in at 6' 5" and 265 pounds. It was a pick-your-poison emphasis for foes' offensive lines on which guy to concentrate most, since it was impossible to double-team both Faison and Ladd. Faison was one of those players from a challenging upbringing in Newport News, Virginia, living with little money without a father, who was able to change his life because of sports.

"If it weren't for football," he said, "I'd probably be back there now working in the shipyards."

No one could sneer at the Chargers on the other side of the line, either. The offensive front was anchored by Ron Mix, who was San Diego's No. 1 draft pick in 1960. Mix was an All-American at the University of Southern California and was also a No. 1 pick of the Baltimore Colts, but chose to stay in the sunshine rather than swap coasts. He said he was offered

$8,500 by Baltimore and $12,000 by San Diego. Mix was a nine-time AFL All-Star; the best offensive tackle in the 10-year history of the expansion league. Mix was 6' 5" and 270 pounds and his secret weapon was a devotion to weight lifting, something that was not yet viewed as appropriate exercise for a football player.

Mix also got smarter the longer he played—and there were indications he was pretty smart in general since immediately after he retired from football he became an attorney.

> *At one time I believed experience was overrated. There was no substitute for brute strength and quickness. Since then, I've played against players who are stronger and quicker and my experience has helped.*

Charger players did not all love coach Sid Gillman. Gillman was a tough taskmaster, could whip players with a sharp tongue, and drill them repeatedly. But even those who didn't consider him to be a warm and fuzzy father figure respected his knowledge of the sport. Gillman was a coaching lifer, with a resume longer than his pants inseam. Gillman coached at Miami of Ohio, the University of Cincinnati, and the Los Angeles Rams before the Chargers and worked at numerous assistant coaching jobs.

Gillman brought supreme organization to his practices and introduced fresh concepts in the passing game and offensive formations over his entire career—he couldn't help himself from jotting down new ideas on napkins or hotel message pads. He learned from every football game he watched and he taught anyone willing to listen. He was a pioneer in the use of game film. When Gillman was growing up in Minneapolis, a family member owned a movie theatre and he got him to splice the football newsreel pictures together for use at home on the $15 projector Gillman invested in when he and his wife barely had enough money to eat.

Billy Sullivan, the boss of the team the Chargers faced for the title in '63 said of Gillman: "He taught us how to go big league."

Not every opponent appreciated Gillman's methods, though. He was known as a fussbudget who could say the wrong thing to annoy people and periodically, for reasons of his own, he did not call off the dogs when his club was routing someone. Sonny Werblin, the man who bought the New York franchise out of bankruptcy and went on to spend big money on Joe Namath once said of Gillman: "The milk of human kindness has turned to yogurt in Sid Gillman."

Gillman was addicted to the nuances of the passing game the way some people are addicted to chocolate cake, and the Chargers, who wore lightning bolts on their helmets, did have an electrifying offense. Not that Gillman looked at Lance Alworth, Don Norton, Dave Kocourek, and Paul Maguire as anything but human beings, but they were also his toys in a sense, the way some guys love to stockpile fishing tackle or hunting gear.

"He was the best passing coach ever," said Kocourek. "He had films of all the great receivers and he'd devote a reel to each particular pattern."

The Patriots may have played the Chargers pretty much even during the regular season, but that didn't mean they were going to face the same Chargers a third time.

Alworth, the brilliant receiver nicknamed "Bambi," and the first AFL player inducted into the Pro Football Hall of Fame, was the beneficiary of Gillman's genius and Gillman was the beneficiary of Alworth's fast feet and great hands.

"Every week Sid would draw up a game plan and he knew it would work, and we knew it would work, and so did the guys we were playing."

That's partially what happened on January 5, 1964. The Charger players realized about an instant after kickoff that Gillman had drawn up a winning game plan. The Patriots apparently had not thought that far ahead. They probably felt they knew what the Chargers could do and there was no indication they were ready for what the Chargers did.

It did not help the Patriots much that the night before the championship game when several players went out for dinner they returned to their hotel and got sick to their stomachs. Yewcic did not know for sure if it was food poisoning, but the effect was the same.

"We had a bunch of guys get sick the night before the game by going out to eat," said Yewcic, who did not get ill.

That is, Yewcic did not get sick until he watched the way the Chargers came out. The game turned into a showcase for every San Diego offensive star, from quarterback Tobin Rote, the old veteran of the Green Bay Packers, to Alworth and Norton, Lincoln and halfback Paul Lowe.

"We were running around like nuts," said Boston receiver Art Graham. Actually, the Chargers were running circles around the Patriots, driving them nuts.

Gillman, as he was in the habit of doing, added some wrinkles to his already powerful offense and that fooled the Boston defense.

"We showed some motion that we had not shown before," said Lincoln. "It allowed us to get a jump on them. We got a half step ahead of them. You get that momentum and it goes from there."

San Diego owned the first quarter. Rote scored on a two-yard run and George Blair booted the extra point for a quick 7–0 lead. Lincoln then escaped on a 67-yarder for a TD, and capped by the extra point it was now a 14–0 lead. The Patriots next got on the scoreboard with a seven-yard run by Larry Garron. But then Lowe burst free for a 58-yard touchdown on a sweep to make it 21–7 after one quarter.

Mix led the interference for Lowe and in the home team's radio booth the announcer nearly hit his head on the ceiling in excitement as he proclaimed, "I think I just saw Ron Mix take out three Patriots on that run."

The big lead was nice, but the Chargers did not take victory for granted that early in the contest.

"It doesn't mean you're going to win the game," said Lincoln.

However, it did not take much longer for the Chargers to realize that yes, they were going to win the game. Blair banged an 11-yard field goal in the second quarter, but Boston's Gino Cappelletti retaliated with a 15-yarder. It was 24–10 when Norton caught a Rote heave on a 14-yard pass play for another San Diego touchdown before halftime. Trailing 31–10 going into the locker room at the intermission was a morale crusher for Boston.

This was the end of defensive back Dick Westmoreland's rookie year and he earned his chops against Parilli's arm and Boston's army of receivers. "They were coming after me. Their offensive coordinator had to be thinking, *The new guy.*

But we had an awesome team and a smart team. Chuck Noll was our defensive coach and he made things plain as day for me."

As defensive coordinator, Noll presided over the No. 1 ranked defense in the AFL that year and it was merely part of his training en route to becoming a four-time Super Bowl champion coach, leading the Pittsburgh Steelers.

Westmoreland said Noll had the Chargers completely prepared for the Patriots, who did not add any twists to their scheme. When the game got started and the Boston plays unfolded, Westmoreland said he thought, *Oh, here they come. It was just like we practiced.*

Maybe the Patriots thought a pep talk from coach Mike Holovak at halftime would help, but it didn't. The Chargers slowed down the pace of their scoring in the second half, but the Patriots never got into the end zone again. The only scoring in the third quarter was a 48-yard TD pass from Rote to Alworth.

Alworth was 6 feet tall and weighed about 185 pounds, which sounds sturdy enough, but sometimes it seemed as if a strong wind would blow him over. It was a deceptive picture broadcast in a league dominated by bigger men, but Alworth had always been a remarkable athlete. He grew up in Mississippi and earned 15 high school sports letters. At the University of Arkansas, Alworth played well enough to later be inducted into the College Football Hall of Fame.

The NFL loved Alworth more than the AFL did. The San Francisco 49ers made him their first-round draft pick in 1962. It was the Oakland Raiders—not the Chargers—that drafted

Alworth in the 2nd round, but traded him to San Diego for three players, including Bo Roberson. As it turned out, the high price was not high enough.

Alworth was more surprised than anyone that two different pro leagues thought so highly of him.

"Heck, I never even expected to play pro football. I thought I was too small."

Some around the pro game thought he might be too, but that didn't last for long. Alworth was all-league seven years in a row and caught 542 passes for more than 10,000 yards and 85 touchdowns. Alworth caught passes in 96 straight games and went over 1,000 yards receiving seven times (leading the league three times). It would have been a surprise if Alworth didn't catch a touchdown pass against the Patriots.

That was Alworth's first championship. His second one, which few remember, came at the end of his career when he left San Diego and won a Super Bowl with the Dallas Cowboys. That was after the AFL-NFL merger and it represented a kind of career symmetry for Alworth. He caught a touchdown pass in Super Bowl VI against the Miami Dolphins.

"Parity with the NFL was always on my mind. For the most part people just refused to compare the leagues. It was a putdown."

In the fourth quarter the Chargers added two touchdowns, one on a 25-yard Lincoln catch from backup quarterback John Hadl and the other on a one-yard run by Hadl. That made the score 51–10 and finished off Boston.

On a day when the Chargers gained 610 yards in total offense, the 6' 1" 215-pound Lincoln had one of the greatest offensive games of any pro football player in a regular-season or playoff contest. He rushed for 206 yards on 13 carries and gained 123 yards on seven receptions for 329 yards gained—plus a 20-yard gain on a pass he threw. It was a mind-bending performance.

"We never thought the score would be like that," Lincoln said years after the thumping of Boston.

The first quarter set the tone and the second half was the punctuation mark. At no time did the Patriots threaten San Diego on that day.

"They had a great defense, but Sid Gillman solved their defense," said Westmoreland. "We were running motion plays and they were befuddled. It really went on all day. We knew we had an explosive team and if things went our way we knew we would be kicking butt."

Lincoln was a lightweight coming out of high school, but added poundage at Washington State and kept improving his early years in the AFL when he was healthy. Keeping his body in one piece was a problem for Lincoln during his nine years in the league. When quizzed for an in-house question-and-answer session after he was traded to the Buffalo Bills, Lincoln listed his injuries as a broken collar bone, four broken ribs, five broken fingers, an uncounted number of broken knuckles, two broken ankles, an injured knee, three pulled hamstrings, a dozen hip pointers, and three or four knockout blows to the head that would classify as concussions.

In-between, Lincoln rushed for 3,383 yards at 4.5 yards per carry and caught 165 passes.

Either immediately after the title game, over the summer, or leading into the next season, just about every English-language sports publication did a story on Lincoln. Coaches and defensive players called him just about the best back in the wide world this side of Jim Brown. Lincoln did not join the chorus and when asked to recount this stupendous game, he said he guessed he did all right.

A half century later, with the exception of quarterbacks who now run up the yards as if they are totaled on pinball machines, there has never been a one-man show by a back in a pro football championship game to match Keith Lincoln's awesome outing.

20

HALAS BACK IN TITLE GAME

SEVENTEEN YEARS AFTER his Chicago Bears last won the NFL championship, George Halas was getting another shot. At his age, sixty-eight, the challenge of coaching was growing, and while he would never say so publicly, knew he had to be approaching the twilight of his career. If he didn't have the energy to stomp up and down the sidelines it wouldn't be worth it. Just maybe this was his last chance at a title.

A lot of people called Halas "the old man," though never to his face. He had been around as long as there had been a National Football League. Some believed that Halas may have been losing his sharpness in recent years, but here he was in '63 all over again, turning in a coach-of-the-year effort and leading his team to the cusp of one more championship.

The man who founded the Bears won titles in '21, '32, '33, '40, '41, '43, and '46. Going 17 long years without a championship was frustrating and could classify as an eternity in franchise years.

In the interim, between his last championship and '63, Halas had gone from middle-aged to senior citizen. The NFL had matured from unwanted foster child—compared to college football—to take center stage. The players were bigger and faster, the helmets had transformed from leather to hard shell. The All-America Football Conference had gone and the American Football League had come.

The Bears quarterback in '46 was Sid Luckman, probably Halas' favorite player of all time. In the intervening years, the Bears had gone through Johnny Lujack, George Blanda, Bobby Layne, Zeke Bratskowski, Rudy Bukich, and Ed Brown to get to Billy Wade.

What Halas proved in '63, not only with his long-range planning leading into the year, but his handling of the troops when players got injured, was that he still had his coaching chops. He had worked the angle from training camp through the regular season that if they beat out the Green Bay Packers they would get to and win a championship. For months, the two-time defending Packers lurked just over the Bears' shoulders, but Chicago held them off and Halas' faith and perseverance was proven correct.

"We were at the top of the league on defense," Halas grunted in satisfaction and pointed out that while Chicago intercepted an NFL-leading 36 passes, it also allowed just eight touchdown passes through the air all year.

Halas was as much a curmudgeon as ever. He was the lion that roared. He burned to win. And if he had to get tough with his players, he did. He was as old school as they come, but Halas was a prophet to his players. They felt obligated to listen to someone that predicted victory over Green Bay and prepared the game plans to beat them twice. Sometimes the players wanted to tune out Halas' grouch demeanor. They almost always wanted to tune out negotiating sessions over new contracts. But they also respected him, his football knowledge, and all he had done for the league.

The Bears had outdistanced the Packers and had put them in the rearview mirror for '63. Only the New York Giants remained on the schedule. Giants and Bears, these were two of the oldest teams in the NFL. Halas was in his twenties when he first met the Mara family. They were old-timers of the league, too.

New York won its first league championship in 1927, and won again in '34 over the Bears and again in '38. They also reached the title game in '35 and '39, though they lost both games. In 1941, the Giants lost to the Bears and then defeated them in the '56 title game. New York dominated the Eastern Division over the next several years, playing for the championship in '58 and '59 against the Baltimore Colts and in '61 and '62 against the Packers. New York lost all four of those championship games. So as much as Halas wanted to make up for the second sneaker game of '56, the Giants hungered mightily to make up for all kinds of recent close calls.

Halas took a couple of sabbaticals from the sidelines during the decades that he ran the Bears and was not on the sidelines (Paddy Driscoll was) when New York pulled off that win in '56. The bitter loss led Halas to return to coaching once more. "I wasn't sure I could do any better than Paddy, but at least I was in a position to do something. And anyway I was tired of sitting on my hands and watching the other guys have all the fun."

Now Halas had the Bears back in the championship game for the first time since '56. Of course, when you are old enough to qualify for Social Security and are still active in pro sports, people are forever asking when you're going to retire. Halas was not interested in such discussions. "I feel the same way," Halas said, compared to his younger days. "Right now I'm not sixty-eight. After beating the Lions Sunday, I feel just like I did when I was thirty-eight."

Maybe Halas looked the same to outsiders, too. Around the time of the title game, one journalist described him this way:

> *George Halas, geriatrics' gift to professional football, is a man who looks as if he was never born, he was simply cast from iron. At his gracious best, he exudes all the warmth of breaking bones. He smiles as if it hurts his feet.*

Okay, so maybe Halas was sixty-eight, but he seemed to have retained the appearance of ruggedness.

Halas jokingly dismissed the age question, but maybe he knew this was a last-chance team, his one-for-the-road team. There was no question the Packers were still dangerous and they would be getting Paul Hornung back the next season. The slow passage of those 17 seasons taught Halas that you couldn't just throw a team out there and expect to win a championship. For Halas, it had been like being Moses wandering in the dessert for forty years. Halas was parched, desperate for another championship.

Some newspapermen even played the hypothetical game of matching the '46 Bears against the '63 Bears, trying to guess who would win. It was just a frivolous exercise, but even members of the '46 team admitted that the Bears defense of '63 was better than theirs.

The players changed, the times changed, but Halas didn't change and he didn't think the fundamental reasons why fans liked the sport had changed either.

What we had going for us was the great, bursting enthusiasm of the players, their liking for the game and the bruising contact. That hasn't changed. The players of the present are just as intense. And that is why the game has come as far as it has. Fans in the early days responded to the all-out effort of the players. Fans now respond just the same, but in greater numbers.

Halas had seen it all from the 1920s to the 1960s; from guys playing bare-headed to guys playing with leather helmets to guys playing with hard plastic helmets. He was around the sport when everyone ran and few attempted passes regularly. He helped implement new rules that opened up scoring and encouraged throwing, but he also recognized because of those changes that defenses had to be more sophisticated.

Football is so much more complicated today than it was in the old days, even though the basic requirements are still good blocking and tackling. All the coaches spend hours going over game movies. The defenses are so much stronger now. In the old days we used to spend one day a week on defense, now it's 50-50, offense and defense.

One of the ways Halas was resistant to change was his belief that he could run up and down the sideline screaming without constraints. The NFL had outlawed that freedom, but Halas typically felt no need to be constrained to life between the 40-yard-lines. A rule restricting coaches from moving beyond 10 yards on either side of their bench was in effect by the late 1950s. It just wasn't always enforced, in particular against Halas, opposing coaches thought.

Another way Halas hadn't changed was in his devotion to protecting the team coffers. In fact, he seemed to want to pay the same salaries to Bears in the 1960s that he paid in the 1940s. Larry Morris, one of his outstanding linebackers in '63, admitted that he fought with Halas over wages, but put aside the pecuniary interests when it was football time. "We had our salary scrimmages, but I have utmost respect for Coach Halas. Pro Football owes him a lot. He's the only one of the original franchise owners still in the NFL and don't let anyone tell you he doesn't know how to run the show . . ."

Halas always was ready to sacrifice for the good of the NFL, but he was never willing to give an inch if it benefited an opponent on the field. He also thought everyone else was like him, seeking out the tiniest advantage and going to great lengths to obtain it.

When you own the team and coach it, the players don't have much leverage, and neither does anyone else. However, when the Bears slumped a few years before their ascension to glory again in '63, the fans made their own statement—at least some of them did. Halas dummies were hung in effigy, pointedly indicating they thought he should retire. Those people weren't toasting him. Sure enough, he hung around long enough to convert the critics.

If Halas was stung by a growing chorus of football people suggesting that the Bears were losing because of him (or in the case of some .500-plus seasons not winning titles) because he got old and the game got younger and faster, 1963 was his reply to show that he still had it; could still produce a champion. There were a fair number of Halas and Bears renaissance stories written between the end of the regular season and the showdown with the Giants.

One thing was certain, though, even if those outside the team didn't recognize that the Bears were going to be for real in '63—the players were on board. Halas worked on the players from the beginning of training camp; drumming into them that they had to beat the Packers. Well, they did—twice—and here they were playing for the title. Halas had worked them into exhaustion and psyched them to the heavens, but he spoke the truth.

Like Morris, the other Bears looked past their salary wrestling matches and focused on football. They blinded themselves to Halas traits that aggravated them and accepted his iron fisted leadership on football matters.

"Halas was a tough guy, but he was fair," said linebacker Joe Fortunato.

Many people said Halas actually ran the NFL even though others served as commissioners through the years. Opposing coaches felt Halas could get away with berating the officials in ways they couldn't. That he could even talk officials into changing their calls. A lot of people said Halas could even determine who would referee his games.

Call it influence, power, stature, or intimidation, but by the 1960s, Halas had clout. He was the last man standing from his era. Bears defensive back Roosevelt Taylor doesn't profess to know much about what Halas did behind the scenes, but in his mind Halas ran the NFL so he could pretty much get away with what he wanted to do.

"He wasn't the easiest guy to get along with," Bears fullback Rick Casares said of Halas.

Definitely not in his office when talking money, and sometimes not on the field where Halas was a dictator, but players found out that Halas had the knack of coming through in the clutch if something bad happened and if they needed money for an emergency.

"If you needed Halas, he'd make sure he was there," said J. C. Caroline. "If you had financial trouble, he'd make sure you got that help. You could always call Halas—he could be in California—and he would call you back. But in practice, if he told you to do something, you'd better do it."

The Bears always felt they deserved more money than Halas was willing to pay. That's not uncommon among athletes assessing their self-worth, but long before pro football was a big-money game and before free agency, players believed Halas was such a tightwad they got smaller paychecks than players on other teams.

"Well, we didn't make much money, but we did have a lot of stories," said lineman Stan Jones. "He came up the hard way, trying to make payrolls, going through the Depression. It would have been a little tough. He did have a big bark, and also a big bite, but he had a soft core. You knew he really cared about you."

After Jones retired he was an assistant coach for 27 years. One year, Jones was scouting at the Blue-Gray Game in Montgomery, Alabama, over Christmas, and his phone rang. Jim Dooley, a former Bears player who became a coach with the team, was on the other end of the line. After making small talk for a while, Jones asked what the purpose of Dooley's call was. "Well, to be honest," Dooley said, "Coach Halas asked me to call you to see how you were doing."

To Jones that meant, "You were never going to be less than family there."

Jones was one of the holdover players from the '56 Bears team that lost that championship game to the Giants and he said the guys who had been around had been treating that defeat like an open wound that would never quite heal.

> *Going against the Giants was always a big game, because they always had a lot of publicity being in New York and they had all those super stars on the team. We had played the Giants in 1956 and lost to them bad in Yankee Stadium. There were a few of us around that still remembered that game. There was a feeling of having something to settle with them.*

In the days leading up to the championship game, Halas made light of the weather. It was supposed to be very cold on game day.

> *They tell me we might get some snow in a couple of days, but you know, I can't spend much time worrying about the weather. I suppose it's going to be cold Sunday. You may remember we played in 16-degree weather in our final game against the Lions last week and we found it, ah, just delightful. Especially after we won.*

There was a suggestion that high winds might bother the Giants more because they relied so much on quarterback Y. A. Tittle's passes, but Halas wouldn't buy into that perspective.

> *I don't see the weather as any particular factor either way. It may be gusty, sure. I guess the Giants had trouble with that in New York last year against the Packers. Yes, they depend a lot on Y. A. Tittle's passes, but we throw the ball some, too. I'm asked if the Bears' defense is going to have to win it.*

Well, you can't win without scoring. We're satisfied we've got enough offense to win.

There were enough Giants still on the roster to remember '56 and there were plenty of Giants on the roster who remembered losing two straight title games to the Packers. Some Bears wanted revenge on the Giants. The Giants wanted revenge on anybody, as long as they walked out of the building carrying the championship trophy. They had two swings and misses in the sixties and didn't want to strike out.

A youthful feeling and rejuvenated, George Halas had his best chance to win his first NFL crown in 17 years and, for all he knew, it would be the last chance of his career. He couldn't help but be thinking, *We took care of the Packers, now the Giants.*

Now the Giants.

21

THE CHAMPS

THE COLD WAS very real. It was 11 degrees at kickoff, and blower heaters were fanning air to try to warm up chilled players on the Wrigley Field sidelines on December 29, 1963. Winds of 11 mph didn't help the battle. The Tennessee State Marching Band was lucky it did not suffer from mass lip frostbite during the playing of the National Anthem.

These are the kinds of days in the pro football world where macho linemen trot out on the field in short sleeves even as skill players blow on their fingers to eradicate numbness. The fans who don't have proper footwear or carry bottles of Old Homicide in their pockets and sip every first down are the ones who suffer the most. At least players are engaged, trying to win a championship.

Players felt the frigidity in their bones when hard hits were delivered and it was the growling Bears who made the hardest hits and the man they hit the hardest had creaking bones to begin with. New York Giant quarterback Y. A. Tittle had passed from thirty-six to thirty-seven years old during the regular season in which he threw a record 36 touchdown passes. That was old going on ancient for an All-Star. Tittle and receiver Del Shofner had a special chemistry. Tittle seemed to be able to find Shofner amidst crowds of defenders as if they had telepathy. At one point, Shofner was disturbed by a rumor going around that he might be traded for the suspended Paul Hornung. Coach Allie Sherman took time to reassure Shofner, saying that he wouldn't trade him for Hornung "and all of his girl-friends." Giants defensive tackle Dick Mozelewski overheard that comment and said, "Hey, let's vote on that."

For Tittle, the Sunday matinee game was nightmarish. While he was leading the No. 1 ranked offense in the NFL that season, the Chicago Bears were winning raves for the No. 1 defense. While the Giants scored 448 points, an average of 32 per game for 14 games, the Bears surrendered just 144 points, or an average of 10.2 per game. This was the game where the Bears would solidify their reputation, hounding Tittle with the front four and linebackers, blanketing New York's receivers with their agile secondary.

"It was their offense against our defense," said Bears halfback Ronnie Bull. "Our defense did a pretty good job of making it that way."

On body damage alone, the Bears won the war. Between the opening kick-off and final gun, the Bears harassed Giants Tom Scott (broken arm), Phil King (sprained ankle), and Bookie Bolin (general distress) out of the game and hurt Tittle's left leg badly enough that he limped through the second half.

"Our defense really won the championship for us that year," said Bears fullback Rick Casares, who had to sit out the title game with his injured ankle.

The Bears got the ball first and halfback Willie Galimore gained two yards on a run right. On second down, Joe Marconi, the sub for Casares, rushed for three yards. The Bears seemed to be moving with a five-yard offside penalty against the Giants and a 12-yard scramble by quarterback Billy Wade that would have put the ball on the Bears' 41-yard-line. But Wade fumbled at the end of his run and New York defensive back Erich Barnes recovered.

The 6' 2" 200-pound Barnes came out of Purdue University to join the Bears in 1958, but was traded to the Giants in '61. He knew and was friendly with many of the Bears, but he was the enemy this day. Barnes was a ball hawk, though more often on interceptions. His philosophy of guarding receivers included a belief that he had at least an equal right to the thrown ball. "Every time a ball leaves the quarterback's hand, I feel I'm the receiver, and the offensive man is on defense."

New York started its first possession in Chicago territory as the 45,801 fans moaned. Runs by Joe Morrison and Phil King, plus a Tittle-to-Morrison 11-yard pass drove the ball to the Bears' 14-yard-line. On 2nd and 8, Tittle faded back and fired to Frank Gifford in the end zone. Gifford out-faked Bennie McRae and was open. When Don Chandler kicked the extra point it was 7–0 Giants at 7:22 of the first quarter.

Not much yardage was gained by either side on their next possessions, and then Chicago had another fright. At the end of a seven-yard gain, Galimore fumbled and safety Dick Pesonen not only recovered, but picked the ball up and ran it back to the Bears' 24-yard-line. Turnovers kill championship hopes, and Halas was beside himself as this early offensive disaster unfolded with the biggest of mistakes on the simplest of plays. This was precisely how the first Giants touchdown was set up and a looming 14–0 lead would have been demoralizing, particularly against a team not noted for big comebacks or high scoring.

The first quarter was not even over yet and the turning point of the game seemed to be at hand. Tittle aired it out on first down, throwing to his favorite receiver, Shofner. Shofner was an All-Star who ran with the shiftiness of Lance Alworth. He got free in the end zone, the ball zipped towards him—and he dropped it.

Tittle and New York had relied heavily on the screen pass all season as a compromise between a solid running game and the long ball. On 2nd and 10 from the 31-yard-line, Tittle dropped back again. He didn't look deep this time, but sought King coming out of the backfield. Bears defensive end Ed O'Bradovich was steaming in from a corner to collar Tittle, but the QB got the throw off. The Bears had watched more and longer movies of the Giants than if they had gone to see a double feature of *Lawrence of Arabia* and *Mutiny on the Bounty*, two of the real best-picture nominees at the Academy Awards in '63. Only the Bears got more out of their screening of the Giants' habits than they ever would have out of studying Peter O'Toole or Marlon Brando.

"We were taught to read screen when Tittle set up, and then dropped back another two or three yards," said O'Bradovich.

This attempted screen landed not in King's hands, but in linebacker Larry Morris' big paws. Morris tucked the ball to his side and took off downfield. Not until 61 yards later did Giants guard Darrell Dess catch up to him and save a touchdown.

That was probably the longest distance Morris had run since high school, and at 6' 2" and 226 pounds, his body was more designed for slamming than sprinting. He couldn't quite outdistance all potential Giant tacklers.

"I was so tired I knew I was going to get caught," said Morris.

Morris, Joe Fortunato, and Bill George made for a fearsome trio of linebackers, and they sometimes traded off over who was playing best in a given game. This day belonged to Morris. The Bears were particularly rich and spoiled at linebacker compared to all other positions, so when Coach George Halas complimented Morris' performance, it was not throwaway praise.

"Morris played the best game of any linebacker I've seen," said Halas.

Instead of facing the explosive Giants offense deep in their own territory, the Bears had an opportunity—Morris had run the ball back to the New York five. On first down, Ronnie Bull gained three yards rushing. It was 2nd and goal at the two-yard-line. Wade kept the ball this time and plunged in for six points. When Bob Jencks kicked the extra point, the score was even at 7–7.

Whether the Bears realized it or not on the touchdown pass to Gifford, a Morris hit on Tittle had injured the quarterback's knee. He promptly informed Coach Allie Sherman, but said he didn't think the damage was too bad. "I'll walk around on it for a while and see how it feels," said Tittle. "I think it will be all right."

Sherman, who was forty years old at the time, grew up in Brooklyn and played pro ball briefly as a quarterback for the Philadelphia Eagles. He had reinvented the Giants under Tittle, presiding over the last days of Charley Conerly's leadership and then opened the offense wide for the best years of Tittle's long career. Sherman was old enough, however, that as a kid he sneaked into the Bears–Giants title game at the Polo Grounds in 1934.

"I was always a football nut," said Sherman. When he said that he elaborated by indicating he was not a passionate follower of one team, but of the sport. "I just watched the execution of the plays. That fascinated me more than the score. Maybe it was then that I had the first inkling I might someday be a coach." It was also true that he was not enormously talented and wouldn't be as good a player as many of those he coached. In a self-deprecating joke Sherman said, "I was the league's best left-hand ball holder for place kicks."

But he was a good coach and designed explosive offenses that thrived with strong throwing quarterbacks. Sherman needed Tittle. After the worrisome hit and limping along the sideline for a little bit, it was determined that the knee wasn't enough of a problem for Tittle to stay out. When the Giants got the ball back, Tittle was calling the signals.

The Bears almost matched the Giants on breaks as the quarter was coming to an end. When Jencks kicked off following the touchdown, Charley Killett bobbled the ball and Chicago recovered the fumble on the New York six, only the Bears were whistled for off-sides on the boot and had to re-kick.

That meant the second quarter began with a kickoff from Jencks. Bears luck did not repeat, and the Giants had a first down on their own 38-yard-line. Morrison and King took turns making small gains on the ground, but once again Tittle caught the Bears defense off-guard and hit backup tight end Aaron Thomas with a pass that covered 36 yards. Soon it was 3rd and 6 on the outskirts of the Bears' goal line. A Tittle pass to King failed, and Chandler kicked a 13-yard field goal to give the Giants a 10–7 lead at 5:11 of the second quarter.

The ease with which New York moved the ball could have disconcerted the Bears' defense, but what no one knew at the time was that the Giants would not score again. The Bears had allowed their season's average on the scoreboard and tightened their belt buckles. It's not as if the Bears were nervous early because it was a title game, but that the Giants knew how to move the ball. However, the Bears knew how to shut down people that moved the ball. Doug Atkins, the tough defensive end of the Bears, was not concerned at all.

> To most of us, it seemed just like a regular game day. Playing in a championship game itself compared to a regular game, it's not so different. You're still playing a ball game, whether it's got a title attached to it or not. You just play the same way. You can't change anything that you've been doing all year, the rest of the year, with your offense and defense.

What the Bears did was settle down, translate what they had seen in films to what they were seeing on the field, and adapt. It became more and more challenging for the Giants to gain yards and make a dent in Chicago's D. King, who had eclipsed veteran Alex Webster in the New York backfield, ripped off some big yards in the second quarter. He gained 10 yards on a draw play and nine on his next carry. Then Webster took a turn and gained six yards. But immediately after that, Tittle hurt his knee for a second time. Morris did not sack him that time, or even tackle him, but fell on his knee. Tittle left the field for treatment with 6:35 to go in the half, and backup Glynn Griffing took over. The drive stalled and Chandler missed a 37-yard field goal attempt.

It looked as if the fate of the Giants' championship dream was in the hands of a twenty-three-year-old passer out of the University of Mississippi who had appeared sparingly in 13 games that season (and would never play again in the NFL) while attempting 40 passes and completing 16 of them. That placed enormous pressure on Griffing, and if Tittle could not come back, it would transform the Giants' offensive game plan. Sherman might have to insert himself at quarterback.

Tittle had never won a championship and desperately wanted to return to the game. The Giants were in their third straight title game after two losses and badly wanted to win this one. The sight of Tittle nursing his battered left knee had to be demoralizing for the Giants, and the rest of the second quarter basically fizzled out for them offensively. The Bears' most effective play was a 48-yard punt by Bobby Joe Green that pinned the Giants on their own two-yard-line. After Tittle was hurt and sat out the rest of the half, the entire offensive production of the Giants for the remainder of the quarter was a net gain of six yards.

At halftime, Tittle's situation was unsettled, but the score was New York 10, Chicago 7.

In the days leading up to the game Wade was quizzed about the role of the Bears' offense versus the role of the defense. Nobody wanted to give the offense any props at all.

> *Our defense can never get too much credit, but I hope the part that the offense is trying to play is not entirely overlooked. Our ball control theory paid off in beating Green Bay twice so there must be some good in it. Winning games is the main thing and that does not necessarily mean winning by high scores. The key to our success this season was, of*

course, the constant soundness of our defense. It helped us over rough spots when we sometimes couldn't get the offense clicking.

Which unit on which team that was clicking in the second half would determine the champion? Tittle was in pain. Never the most mobile quarterback in the business—certainly no football historians ever made comparisons between Tittle's nimbleness and Michael Vick's—Tittle soldiered on in the second half, dragging his wounded leg around like a ball and chain. Although the diagnosis wasn't official at the time, after the game was over Tittle was examined more thoroughly and it was learned he had been trying to beat the Bears' pass rush while playing on a torn ligament.

Everything was pretty frosty—the temperature was on its way down to six degrees as the Giants received the second-half kickoff. Hugh McElhenny, eventually a Hall of Famer, but now at the tail end of his career, caught the ball and dashed 47 yards to the Bears' 46-yard-line. It was great field position. Tittle reappeared on the field and Sherman kept McElhenny, who had once been a teammate of Tittle's with the San Francisco 49ers, in the backfield. The first two plays from scrimmage were handoffs to McElhenny. He gained two yards each time.

Then Tittle retreated to pass, testing how the knee would hold up. He fired a seven-yard pass to Joe Morrison for a first down. New York was already on the Chicago 35. The next play was a pass to Gifford, but it fell incomplete. On 2nd and 10, Tittle dropped back again and threw to Shofner, but he was off-target and Chicago's Dave Whitsell intercepted on the 26-yard-line to end the Giants' threat.

Chicago got its first chance to do something with the ball in the third quarter, starting at its own 26-yard-line. In a slight change of tactics, the Bears came out throwing. Wade hit Joe Marconi on a screen pass for 19 yards and a first down on the first play. He tried to find tight end Mike Ditka, but that toss went incomplete. Wade turned to Marconi again and he gained 34 yards to the New York 21. Marconi was not always the first look, but he had caught 28 passes during the regular season and his playing time had increased after Casares went out with his injury. The Bears were rolling.

Things were going so well that Wade kept passing. After a missed connection with Marconi, he tried for Angelo Coia in the end zone and then aimed a throw at Johnny Morris. Three straight incompletions left the Bears with a fourth down at the 21; stalled out. Roger LeClerc came in to try a 28-yard field goal to knot the score, but missed wide left and the Bears got nothing out of their parade downfield. It felt like an important missed opportunity in a close game which Chicago still trailed.

Whether the Giants got skittish or if Tittle was feeling too sore, but the next series they had—starting from their own 20—consisted of six straight runs, with one first down and possession ending with a 41-yard Chandler punt.

The booming punt set the Bears back to their own 19-yard-line. The way the defenses were taking charge on both sides made the end zone seem miles away. The Giants could afford to kill time for the rest of the day. The Bears could not.

Wade opened the series with a 15-yard pass to Ditka, and Barnes made a mistake that compounded the gain. He was whistled for unnecessary roughness, tacking 15 more yards on for the Bears. That put the Bears on their own 49 in one big gulp of a play. Wade completed two more passes quickly, one a loss by Bull and one a gain by Johnny Morris. Then Wade followed with incompletions and got sacked by Andy Robustelli. With another fourth down and the ball in no-man's-land, the Bears punted again. Chicago ran nine plays and didn't get very far before stalling out.

It was New York's turn again, and the Giants began from their own 35-yard-line. This time they tried passing and it was a disappointing failure. Defensive tackle Fred Williams honed in on Tittle, Tittle threw, and of all people, O'Bradovich intercepted. Defensive ends don't normally intercept passes, and in 10 years O'Bradovich never grabbed one during the regular season. This pass was intended for Morrison, but it never got there.

On the pass I intercepted I was coming in hard and Jack Stroud was blocking me. Stroud released much more quickly than he normally does and I looked for Tittle to see if he had backed off from where he usually throws and he had, so I left Stroud and went outside looking for the screen pass. He threw it and I lifted my right arm and hit the ball and it came down where I could catch it.

O'Bradovich took off and returned the interception 10 yards to the Giants' 14-yard-line. This was one too many mistakes for the Giants to hold off the Bears. Wade went for the end zone right away—throwing to Marconi—but the pass was incomplete. Bull took a handoff for a one-yard gain on the next play and then Wade returned to the sky, finding Ditka for a 12-yard gain. Ditka was dropped on the one-yard-line, which gave Chicago a 1st and goal three feet from pay dirt.

Wade attempted a quarterback sneak, but was stopped just shy of the goal line on first down. On second down, he did it again and this time the play worked. Touchdown Bears. Jencks kicked the extra point and the Bears had the lead, 14–10.

Now the Giants were playing from behind for the first time all day. McElhenny carried on first down and was dropped at the line of scrimmage by Fortunato. On second down, Morrison broke through the line and squirted free for 20 yards. Tittle hoped to catch Chicago off-guard and threw to Aaron Thomas, but Richie Petitbon broke up the play and nearly intercepted the ball. Two more passes in a row failed and New York had to punt. After Johnny Morris returned Chandler's kick two yards, the Bears started from their own 19-yard-line as play moved into the fourth quarter.

With 15 minutes remaining, neither team was really in control. One big play on either side could decide the championship. Although the Bears had scored on their last possession, they went nowhere on this one. It was three-and-out before Bobby Joe Green punted 40 yards and the Giants tried again from their own 39.

Morrison, who was a do-everything back for the Giants, took a handoff on first down and dashed for six yards. Tittle went right back to him for another run, but this time the ball bounced free and Petitbon recovered Morrison's fumble.

Petitbon was a 6' 3" 205-pound defensive back out of Tulane and during his pro career made four Pro Bowls. He had a long playing career, intercepting 48 passes, and in 1962 he returned an interception for the Bears 101 yards. Later, as an assistant coach with the Washington Redskins, Petitbon was part of three

Super Bowl teams and eventually became head coach of Washington for a season.

Petitbon was one of those players who were skilled in the art of getting his hands on the ball to break up offensive plays. After reviewing all of his experience, Petitbon said his favorite game was the one against the Giants. "You know there are so few championship games that you ever play in, if you're lucky. It was a good game. It sure was a close one."

Petitbon's fumble recovery gave the Bears a chance to pad their lead. They started to move the ball with Bull gaining seven yards off left tackle. Then Johnny Morris caught a pass for eight yards from Wade; Wade ran for a five-yard gain; Bull gained another four yards. Chicago had advanced to the New York 26-yard-line, setting up LeClerc for a 34-yard field-goal attempt. But frustratingly, the ball sailed wide right and no points went up on the board.

New York took over on its own 20-yard-line and after two running plays, Tittle started throwing on almost every play. An 18-yard completion came on a pass to Alex Webster. Some short throws fell incomplete and some short gains were made. On a third down on the Bears' 26, Tittle saw an open Gifford approaching the end zone. He threw long, but Gifford slipped and tumbled at the five-yard-line and Chicago's Bennie McRae picked off the toss for another interception.

When the Bears took possession of the ball on their own 20-yard-line, 4:28 remained in the game. Chicago did not have to score again. All the Bears had to do was run out the clock. At that point, Halas, Wade, and the Bears had no plans to throw another pass. They wanted the clock to tick. On first down, Bull gained one yard running up the middle. On second down, Bull rushed for 12 yards and a first down. The ball was on the 33 and the clock ticked below three minutes. The handoff again went to Bull and he gained five yards off right tackle. Chicago let the clock run down to the two-minute warning.

With the ball at the 40 after the officials' time out, Wade once more handed off to Bull, who gained two yards, but a measurement left the Bears about a foot shy of a first down with 1:52 remaining.

"I missed that first down by six inches," said Bull.

Green punted 41 yards and the ball was dead on the Giants' 16-yard-line with 1:38 left. Tittle began the bombs-away approach, throwing to Thomas for 10 yards and a first down at the 26. The clock read 1:24, though Bull recalled there being 1:23 left and him feeling twitchy about the Giants being on the move. "That last minute and twenty-three seconds was the longest of my life."

The next play was a Tittle pass to Hugh McElhenny for eight yards, and New York called a time out with 1:03 left. Tittle then passed to McElhenny for 12 yards and another first down. Thirty seconds to go. An incomplete pass was next and then Tittle threw to Gifford, but the ball was caught out of bounds. Incomplete. Tittle went right back to Gifford on a 15-yard completion and a first down on the Bears' 39. Another throw out of bounds counted the clock down to 10 seconds remaining.

New York was 39 yards away from the winning touchdown. Tittle dropped back and threw into the end zone; only the pass was intercepted by Petitbon. The last-gasp heave was Tittle's fifth interception of the game. It was a Hail Mary before such passes were referred to as Hail Mary's.

"It was really an easy play," said Petitbon. "We were in a zone and Tittle threw the ball to me. He overthrew his receivers." It was the finishing touch for the Bears and Petitbon simply handed the ball to the official instead of keeping it as a souvenir. "I didn't and I should have."

There were still two seconds on the clock when the Bears got the ball at the 20-yard-line. Wade kept the ball for a routine quarterback sneak that gained one yard and ended the game, 14–10, which was the same score that had been in place since the third quarter. The Chicago Bears NFL champions of '63. The Bears—and Halas—had won their first championship since 1946.

"It was fabulous," said Petitbon. "When you win your first one you don't realize it might be your last one. It was a great accomplishment."

Sherman said Tittle couldn't plant his left leg properly after the knee injury, which threw his form off. After his fifth interception, Tittle yanked his helmet off in frustration and slammed it to the ground. Petitbon said he may not have the game ball, but he has a photograph of Tittle throwing his helmet. Seated on the bench as the Bears ran off the final play, Tittle broke down and cried. Worn down and beaten up, his knee throbbing, Tittle limped to the Giants' visiting team locker room. No one took the disappointment of the loss more to heart than Tittle. He blamed himself for the defeat.

"They [the Bears' defense] did literally beat the hell out of him," said Bull.

Sherman said he was amazed that Tittle could even continue to play on the damaged knee and not a lot of other quarterbacks would have sucked it up to do so.

"He went out and played the second half in a condition, well, I couldn't find another quarterback in the league who would go out in that condition."

Tittle completed 11 out of 29 attempts for 147 yards and one touchdown, plus those glaring five interceptions. It was a good thing Erich Barnes' habit of giving fellow members of his defensive backfield cigars when they made interceptions did not extend to the other team, or he might have gone broke. Wade went 10 for 28 and 138 yards and Morrison was the game's leading rusher with 61 yards. There were no big offensive statistics in this confrontation.

"I think it was the greatest game ever played," said O'Bradovich. "It was the offensive team against the defensive team. It was the best pitcher against the best hitter. It was David versus Goliath. We weren't flashy. We were just tough and dogged."

As fans celebrated in the cold Wrigley stands, the players lived it up in their locker room. Fortunato shushed his teammates for a moment to give a speech, using his clout as a cocaptain to gain the floor. "I want to announce . . . that the game ball goes to the man who played such a great part in our fine defense—coach George Allen." Fortunato completed his only pass of the day by tossing the ball to Allen.

The Bears defense lived up to its reputation and ranking, and Fortunato, who called the defensive alignments on the field, gave credit to Allen for figuring out what the Giants were likely to do in most situations.

We had a pretty good tendency chart on the Giants. We followed that chart. They did just about what George Allen predicted they would do, based on their past tendencies. We just followed that all the way through the game.

It's doubtful that anyone in that giddy locker room was happier than George Halas.

> *It's like mountain climbing. The one who gets to the top of the mountain is the one with the persistence to keep climbing. Winning is great, but we've had a lot of disappointments in the past and we've stayed with it.*

Halas had the age and experience of a man with perspective. Some of his players, like defensive back Roosevelt Taylor, were young and savoring big-time victory for the first time in their careers. Taylor was very proud to be part of that Chicago defense.

"We did a thing on him [Tittle]. There were about four different times I stopped them with tackles when they were going for first downs."

Casares, who could only watch because of injury, was frustrated over being inactive, but drew pleasure from the team's avenging the '56 title game loss.

"It was the worst experience of my life because I missed the game. But it was a very satisfying day."

For the Giants, it was three straight championship game losses, and although they were confident they could come back and keep on representing the Eastern Division in the title game each year, several of them were older and coming to the end of the line in their playing days.

Frank Gifford, Andy Robustelli, and Y. A. Tittle all only played one more season. An outraged Sam Huff was traded to the Washington Redskins before the next season. The old gang was breaking up.

Reaching the championship game three straight seasons was an accomplishment, but losing three straight times was haunting.

Losing this game to the Bears was the worst of all, as it was the third consecutive time, injuries conspired against New York, and it was so close.

"We could have won it," said Sherman. "But we didn't. However, I'm proud of these Giants. They had to do a lot to get into the championship game. Remember, they are worthy. They proved themselves."

Huff was very down about the loss. He said he could understand losing to Green Bay, but the Bears were another thing.

> *The Bears were not in our class. There was a lot of talk in the papers about what went wrong, who was to blame, the usual kind of stuff when you lose. But anyone with half a brain had to know that if Y. A. Tittle hadn't hurt his knee there was no question about who the best team was and who would have been wearing those rings.*

In those days, the Most Valuable Player of the NFL championship game was given a flashy new Chevrolet Corvette sports car, sponsored by the now-defunct *Sport Magazine*. Before the game, Larry Morris, fellow linebacker Bill George, and defensive tackle Fred Williams huddled and made a pact that if any of them won the award, they would share it. The joke went around that Morris would get to keep the steering wheel and the brakes and Bill George might get the seats and Williams the tires. The way it actually worked was that Morris gave the others $1,000 each and kept the car. Ironically, earlier in the season, Morris' wife had drawn criticism for popping off and saying that it wasn't fair how offensive players always got all of the attention and honors.

It was intriguing, now that Chicago had won the championship, to look back on some Wade comments uttered the week before the game. It perfectly echoed Halas' thinking harkening back to Rensselaer training camp. "You could sense last summer the fellows thought we were capable of winning this year," said Wade. "I think everybody knew that the important thing was to beat Green Bay. We dedicated ourselves to that objective and we did it twice."

When the gun sounded and the sweat-stained, chilled men, uniforms streaked with dirt and grass tumbled into their locker room, it was almost like a fraternity party breaking out. Many had devoted years for the chance to experience this moment. Many knew that, as their careers were winding up, this was going to be their only chance to inhale the rarefied air. Stan Jones could only rave about the team and title.

> *I would say that was the highlight of my career. This was an outstanding defensive team. To be part of that defense was a real thrill and just a tremendous feeling of accomplishment. I remember the locker room cheer [on television]: 'Hurray for George, hurray at last, hurray for George, he's a horse's ass.' I don't know where that started, but the Bears had it ever since I was there. They would do it for everybody who does something great. They would do it after every game for someone who had the game ball, someone who had scored the winning touchdown.*

For Halas, the result was vindication of his vision and his season plan. He was seen at one point in the locker room leading cheers, letting his joy over at last claiming another title after such a long intermission seep deeper as each minute passed.

"We started the season with the No. 1 defense and we ended it with the No. 1 defense," said Halas.

When he tore himself away from celebrating with his guys, Halas explained to sportswriters just how much this triumph meant to him. Putting into perspective his long career and the long championship drought it made sense when he revealed the importance of this victory. "No game has meant as much to me as this one since we beat Washington 73–0 [in 1940]. I've waited a long time."

EPILOGUE

THE CHICAGO BEARS reported for training camp in July of 1964 fully expecting to repeat as champions of the National Football League. Coach George Halas believed it, too. The players who fought off the Green Bay Packers and New York Giants in '63 thought so as well. They were the best and they should be better, they figured. Those injured were healthy. Those young players who contributed were coming into their prime. Why shouldn't the Bears repeat?

Two players ready to take on more responsibility and play bigger roles in the offense were halfback Willie Galimore, a charming halfback out of Florida A&M who was probably the fastest man on the team and had gained nearly 3,000 yards rushing since 1957, while averaging 4.5 yards per carry. When fully healthy, the 6' 1" 190-pound Galimore, who had coped with knee injuries, threatened to be one of the best in the league at his position. Galimore was a Halas favorite, too, because he was a good guy who never made trouble and had a pleasing personality.

One of Galimore's pals on the team was wide receiver John "Bo" Farrington out of Prairie View A&M. The 6' 3" 215-pound Farrington caught 21 passes for the '63 champs and seemed on the verge of a big year when the gang gathered in Rensselaer, Indiana, to take another shot at winning a ring.

On July 26, a Sunday, Galimore and Farrington went out for some relaxation, but mindful of returning to training camp early enough in the evening so as not to miss their 11 p.m. curfew. The nearby country club was a regular stopover when the Bears had a little bit of time off from the harsh preseason conditioning regimen. Galimore and Farrington apparently played some golf early in the day there and then went out for pizza with several other teammates. They then returned to the club to hang around and watch a televised track meet. Teammate Bennie McRae said he almost rode with Galimore and Farrington that night, but didn't leave camp at the same time, even though they and several others visited with each other over the pizza.

Among other Bears at the club was defensive end Ed O'Bradovich, who saw Galimore and Farrington leave. "I guess I was the last one to see them alive. I said goodbye. Then four or five minutes later, it was all over."

All over. Only minutes after departing the club, Galimore and Farrington were dead. The two men were returning to St. Joseph's about 10:30 p.m. with Galimore at the wheel, when they encountered a sharp curve on a rural road.

The small car had a sun roof and it was open when the vehicle left the road and crashed into a ditch just two miles from the school in an area that normally had a warning sign posted reading CURVE. The sign was situated where cars approached an L-shaped turn, but it had recently been knocked down and not re-posted. The sign was actually leaning against a fence facing the opposite direction from where drivers approached.

Both men were hurled through the roof of the car. Although there were no witnesses to the accident, the investigating police said that the car rolled over at least once and that when the players flew through the open roof, they landed 60 feet apart. It was an empty stretch of road in the middle of farm countryside, but an individual who lived not too far away heard the noise of the crash and telephoned the Jasper County Sheriff's office for assistance. Farrington was killed at the scene and Galimore was pronounced dead at Jasper County Hospital.

Both victims suffered multiple skull fractures and Galimore's chest was crushed. The investigators determined that a rear wheel on the car collapsed when the vehicle slid off the edge of the pavement and that's what propelled it into the ditch.

At the team dormitory, quarterback Bill Wade glumly took on the role of packing Galimore's things into a cardboard box.

"This is a heart-breaking job," said Wade, "but it must be done. It's better I have everything packed instead of having Willie's relatives do it."

Bears players and coaches were shocked the night of the tragedy and their grief and horror completely transformed the mood of the team; the sense of optimism headed into the new season lost and never regained. Instead of forging into the '64 season as swaggering defending champs, the Bears were shattered and demoralized. They lost three of their first four games, never mounted a serious defense, and finished far down in the standings with a 5–9 record.

In a realistic sense, the Bears' '64 season ended on that lonely road in July, close to two months before the first real game was played.

"It was terrible," said defensive back Richie Petitbon five decades later. "That killed the whole year. That took a lot out of us. Because of that night I will never own a little car."

Halas spent decades running the Bears, and that night and really for the rest of his life, he thought of the automobile accident that killed Galimore and Farrington as "the saddest day" of all during his tenure. Halas saw both of his players deceased at the hospital as the doctors stopped trying to revive them. Both men were married—Galimore had three children and Farrington's wife was pregnant—and Halas was the one who picked up the phone and informed their widows what happened.

"The hardest thing I have ever had to do is to make those two calls to the wives," said Halas. "It's the first time I've ever had to do anything like that."

The numbness which afflicted the Bears almost instantly was like a disease that turned them into zombies in their daily actions and workouts.

"It is not like losing an employee in an office," said defensive end Bob Kilcullen. "These men were part of you. You work closely with them to make a thing called a team try to win. They become something like your right arm."

When the Bears returned to the practice field after the deaths of their teammates, they were listless. Halas gathered the players together at midfield, beyond earshot of any other spectators or reporters and said:

This was the saddest day in Bears' history. We all share the same sad feelings. Something like this reaches the heart and

*makes everything else seem petty. It's going to take a great
deal of will power to carry on, but I know you can do it. A
great honor can be bestowed on Willie and Bo if you will
dedicate the season to them.*

Wade also addressed the group asking players "each in your own
way" to utter a silent prayer.

The Bears did dedicate their season to Galimore and
Farrington, but although the sentiment was there, the gesture
turned out to be somewhat hollow with them not accom-
plishing much. They also suffered a huge rash of injuries; far
more than they had during the championship year. In the third
game of the season, the Bears lost to the Baltimore Colts, 52–0,
the worst defeat in team history. The once-admired defense gave
up 379 points that year.

"The tragedy haunted us all season," said tackle Bob Wetoska
when the year ended. "We kept looking at last year's game
movies and there would be Willie and Bo doing so well and that
gives you an awful feeling. But we were so bad most of the time
this fall that we couldn't come up with the big third down play
on offense or defense."

Bill George and Larry Morris both, two-thirds of the exem-
plary linebacker core, epitomized the season almost identically.
Both of them injured a knee and both of them said that the
deaths of Galimore and Farrington poisoned the atmosphere
at season's start. Things accelerated in the wrong direction after
that because of an epidemic of injuries.

"Then it seemed somebody got crippled every time we went
on the field," said Morris.

When J. C. Caroline, who was a close friend of both Galimore's
and Farrington's, assessed the '63 season, he said he felt "blessed"

to have played up to his capabilities and that he was thankful that the Lord allowed him and his teammates to play up to their potential that year.

"I had the good Lord's blessing that I was able to perform at that level."

In 1964, such blessings seemed in short supply for the Chicago Bears.

Any championship season by any team is to be savored, but it does not always signal the start of a dynasty. It is more often a rare achievement than signals the start of a dynasty. There are not more dynasties in sports because repeating a title run is surely one of the most challenging things to achieve. There is always someone else hungry to taste that champagne. There is always another team waiting in the wings, peaking at the right time, sitting there waiting to pick you off.

When the Bears faltered, it seemed logical to conclude that the Packers would step in, since they performed so admirably in '63, but they were shut out of the championship game. Paul Hornung returned to the Green Bay lineup, but although the Packers bested the Bears twice that season, it turned out to be one of Vince Lombardi's weakest years. Green Bay finished 8–5–1 and did not capture the Western Division.

The Colts, who so thoroughly manhandled the Bears in that early-season game, became division champs.

The Packers were far from finished, however. With many of the holdover All-Stars, Lombardi mixed in some new faces and the Packers became better than ever, winning NFL titles in '65, '66, and '67, capping their league championships with victories in the first two Super Bowls. In all, Green Bay won five titles in the 1960s.

Among the most prominent Packers of that era, it was Lombardi's early death from cancer in September of 1970 after he had left for the Washington Redskins that was the most shocking. The Lombardi era had just ended in Green Bay and he was only fifty-seven. He is well-remembered for his achievements with the Packers and the trophy for the Super Bowl winner is named "The Lombardi Trophy."

Bart Starr played the longest of the Packer stars with the team, from '56–71, and later returned to coach his old club from '75–83. Some of Starr's teams played well, but the old glory was not restored on his watch. Forrest Gregg, the guard who, like Starr, is in the Pro Football Hall of Fame, succeeded him as head coach and ran the team for four seasons, again without notable success.

Hornung, who lives in his original hometown of Louisville, and his backfield mate Jim Taylor, who is also back in Louisiana, were both chosen for the Hall of Fame. Some prominent stars of the Packers era, including Hall of Fame defenders Ray Nitschke and Henry Jordan have passed away, as has center Jim Ringo. Max McGee, the Green Bay star of the first Super Bowl, has also passed on. Hall of Famers from the Lombardi era who are still living and are in their seventies include Willie Davis, Willie Wood, Dave Robinson, and Herb Adderley.

Tackle Bob Skoronski still lives in Wisconsin and is one of the regulars at Packer functions in Green Bay, particularly ones held when the team conducts its annual alumni reunion weekend.

"We meet that way," said Skoronski. "I think there are twenty-seven of us left."

The New York Giants won three straight Eastern Division titles in the early sixties, but could not top the Green Bay Packers in two title games, nor beat the Chicago Bears in '63. Not only did the Cleveland Browns capture the division in '64, but they won the championship. In a startling reversal, the Giants fared worse than the Bears, dropping to last place with a 2–10–2 record. The New York run was over and a 1960s championship eluded them. New York did not have a winning record again until the 1970 season. One by one, the Giant greats began moving on or retiring. That was also a group of special players, but the oldest ones won a title in '56. New York saw its share of stars enshrined in the Hall of Fame, as well, but by 1964, their best days were behind them with few exceptions.

Owner Wellington Mara, Emlen Tunnell, who was a regular All-Star through the fifties, Y. A. Tittle, Frank Gifford, Andy Robustelli, Roosevelt Brown, and Sam Huff were all selected for the Hall of Fame. All except Huff among the players were retired by 1965, as he was playing for the Redskins, harboring a grudge for being traded away.

All I can say is that trade hurt me so badly, after all I'd given, after all I'd done. It never should have happened. I know it, the football fans of New York know it, Wellington Mara knows it, and surely Allie Sherman knows it. And that is why I'll never forget, nor will I ever forgive him.

By 2013, Mara, Robustelli, Brown, Tunnell, Alex Webster, Jimmy Patton, Jim Katcavage, Joe Morrison, Jack Stroud, Don Chandler, and Phil King were among the Giants that had passed away. Sherman was ninety, Tittle eighty-six, Gifford eighty-two, Huff seventy-eight, Del Shofner seventy-eight, Erich Barnes seventy-seven, and Darrell Dess seventy-seven.

In 1964, a television producer tried to convince Gifford to play Tarzan in an upcoming production. He declined, with laughter. "I think I'd make a poor Tarzan. I'd never do that." Instead he became a sportscaster basically equal in national prominence to the heights he reached as a football player.

The ravaged Boston Patriots had wounds to lick after being shredded by the San Diego Chargers, 51–10, in the '63 American Football League championship game. Boston was actually a better team in '64, going 10–3–1, but failed to reach a second straight title game because of the Buffalo Bills' success.

Boston slumped in '65, had another winning year in '66, and then did not post another above-.500 record for ten more years. By '76, of course, there had been wholesale roster turnover. Of all of the teams that played significant roles in the '63 season, death has been a far more hostile visitor to Boston than the others. A very high percentage of players from that squad have died, some of them at young ages.

Gino Cappelletti remained associated with the Patriots for almost the entire ensuing half century as a longtime broadcaster before retiring in 2012. He was seventy-eight in 2013. Quarterback Babe Parilli was eighty-two in 2013. Among those who passed away are receiver Jim Colclough, defensive end Bob Dee, safety Ross O'Hanley, running back Ron Burton, the team's first draft choice in history, and guard Billy Neighbors.

Receiver Art Graham, who was seventy-one in 2013 and living in Massachusetts, was a rookie in '63. "It was a very eventful year," he said of breaking into pro ball and reaching the AFL championship game. Graham played six seasons, all with Boston, and caught 199 passes.

He finds it hard to believe that a half century has passed since his pro debut and that Patriots–Chargers game.

"That's the amazing part," said Graham. "Fifty years. I feel good, but then you look in the mirror and you go, 'Who is that guy?'"

Tom Yewcic, the punter and backup quarterback, was eighty in 2013. He has maintained a close association with the Patriots over the years. Before New England Patriots home games at Gillette Stadium, the franchise hosts a group of players from different generations of team history to meet and greet fans and sign autographs, and Yewcic is a regular who enjoys the role.

Yewcic is proud that he got to play in the AFL during those early years, and said it was a different brand of ball, and not so easy to make a roster. "The linemen weren't as big as they are now, but we had a lot of great receivers and running backs. The league was good. The rosters weren't that big so you had better teams. You had more players and less teams so the competition was greater."

After claiming their championship in '63, the San Diego Chargers reached the title game again in '64 and '65, but lost both times to the Buffalo Bills. The '63 team was the San Diego showpiece club of the sixties and the Sid Gillman administration.

Gillman, who died in 2003, was selected for the Pro Football Hall of Fame and his flanker, Lance Alworth, who still resides in California, was the first American Football League player to be enshrined in Canton. Lineman Ron Mix, who is still a practicing attorney in California, joined him there.

Keith Lincoln, who retired in '68, was seventy-three in 2013, and living in Pullman, Washington, where he went to college. Lincoln said that the Chargers of '63 had so much size with guys like Ernie Ladd, Earl Faison, and Mix that they were like a team today. He also believed that the Chargers and the AFL clubs were just as good as the NFL teams that were supposed to be superior.

"I'm prejudiced on the thing," said Lincoln, "but I never felt we were overmatched."

Ladd died of cancer at sixty-eight and is a member of the halls of fame of the Chargers, Grambling, and World Wrestling Entertainment.

Defensive back Dick Westmoreland, who was still living in San Diego in 2013 at the age of seventy-two, works out daily to make sure he feels younger. He believes that between adding excitement to the sport, providing more jobs for players, and opening up new cities to pro football, "We [the AFL teams] were the best thing that happened to the NFL."

Westmoreland got sick of hearing the insults emanating from the NFL about how the older teams were better and that the AFL couldn't play defense and that new league didn't have any talent.

"Everyone said we had more exciting games. I thought we would have kicked the Bears' butts."

Interesting conjecture, but it was too soon in the NFL–AFL rivalry for any such game to be played. The '63 Bears went down in team lore as one of the most beloved in franchise history. That team gave Chicago a title for the first time in seventeen years and represented the last time the Bears won a title until '85. To this day, that squad holds a special place in the hearts of Chicago fans.

The '63 championship did not portend the beginning of anything special, but rather was a period at the end of an era for many stars who never again came close to winning a championship. That team also was George Halas' final title winner in his long career.

As the tragic deaths of Willie Galimore and Bo Farrington showed, for a variety of reasons teams do not remain together very long. Players are traded. Players retire. Players are cut. New players are acquired. Other teams become stronger.

However, each championship team possesses its own time capsule. For a period of months, for a season, it was the best and almost always a unique connection, and a bond is formed that links those players together forever.

Halas provided championship rings for his players on that '63 title team, and also championship bracelets for the players' wives. In professional sports, the ring is the best souvenir any athlete can have and keep.

Joe Fortunato, eighty-two in 2013 and living in Mississippi, was the cocaptain linebacker who called the defenses in the title game against New York. He was asked some fifty years later if he wears his Bears championship ring. You bet he does.

"I wear it all the time. Everybody asks me about it. I wear it with my wedding band."

Defensive back Richie Petitbon, seventy-four in 2013 and living in the Washington, D.C., area, won other championship rings while coaching and said he keeps them all in a bank safe deposit box.

Fullback Rick Casares, eighty-one in 2013 and living in Tampa, Florida, is another ex-player who wears his Bears championship ring all of the time.

"That's my most prized possession. It's always a stopper. It couldn't be any more imposing than if it was a 20-carat diamond."

Running back Ron Bull, seventy-three and living in a Chicago suburb, wore his Bears championship ring for forty-five years, and then about five years ago, gave it to his son Randy.

"I thought, *Why should he get it when I'm dead?* I can enjoy watching him wear it. If there's a convention or something he lends it back to me, but you can bet that two days later he's going, 'Where's the ring?'"

After fifty years, several of the Bears have passed away besides the two young men killed in that automobile accident in training camp in 1964. Hall of Famer Bill George was killed in a car accident as well when he was fifty-two. Larry Morris passed away in 2012 after a long illness, Stan Jones in 2010, Fred Williams in 2000, and Joe Marconi in 1992.

The most famous alum of the '63 team is Mike Ditka. Ditka was not only a Hall of Fame player, but the man nicknamed "Iron Mike" returned to coach the Bears' '85 team to the Super Bowl championship at the end of that season—the only one Chicago has won. Ditka, who was seventy-three in 2013, maintains a high profile in Chicago. He owns a popular restaurant and is a frequent presence on radio and TV shows during the football season.

To many in the blue collar city of big shoulders, Ditka embodies the Bears. To fans, he is the ultimate Bear and is closely associated with two of the Bears' greatest triumphs and their two most recent championships.

After the '63 season, George Halas was named the NFL coach of the year; an honor which he again won in '65. He finally walked away from the sidelines for the last time following the '67 season when he was seventy-two. Halas' career coaching record was 324–151–31, with his teams winning more than 68 percent of the time, and led them to eight NFL championships under his guidance.

Although he retired as head coach, Halas retained his role as president of the team he owned until his death at age eighty-eight in 1983. It was Halas who made the decision to install Ditka as coach in '82 to lift the Bears from the doldrums, but he did not live long enough to see the mission-accomplished Super Bowl glory of a few years later.

Halas was born on February 2, 1895, and died on October 31, 1983. He was at home when he passed away shortly before 10 p.m. on that night during the football season. Halas had been present at the creation of the National Football League and had been associated with the Decatur Staleys, the Bears' forerunner, and the Bears, for sixty-three years. The Bears remain owned by his family to this day. And Bears players display Halas' initials, GSH, on the left sleeve of their game jerseys.

A few days after Halas died, a funeral Mass was conducted at St. Ita's Church in Chicago, and 1,200 mourners attended. More people with a history in the NFL came than appear at Pro Football Hall of Fame gatherings. Commissioner Pete Rozelle, longtime Pittsburgh Steelers owner Art Rooney, Dallas Cowboys general manager Tex Schramm, AFL founder Lamar Hunt, and Oakland Raiders owner Al Davis were some of the league luminaries present. Ditka was there, as were former

Bears stars Gale Sayers, Sid Luckman, George Musso, George McAfee, George Connor, and the entire Bears' '83 team, which arrived by bus from the team's practice facility in suburban Lake Forest.

Following the service, Halas was buried in St. Adalbert's Cemetery in suburban Niles, Illinois. The football people gathered at a luncheon and swapped Halas stories. "He touched seven decades," said Rozelle, who himself served as commissioner for twenty-nine years. "He was to us what Dr. James Naismith was to basketball when he put up the peach baskets and invented a winter sport."

Rooney, who was then eighty-two, said of Halas: "He helped take the game to the people."

Earlier in 1983, there was an eighty-eighth birthday party for Halas, and someone asked him what it felt like to get old.

"I wouldn't know about old because I'm not old. I have only one rule: I don't date any women under forty-eight."

Those outside the franchise always said that the Chicago Bears were George Halas' family. It would probably be more accurate to say they were part of his extended family because he was married, had children and grandchildren, and they represented his real family. Halas knew how to draw that line.

The absolute true love of Halas' life was football; pro football as practiced by the National Football League. There was no one like him in NFL history, a player, a coach, a league founder, and owner. More than six decades of his life was invested in the game, growing the game, watching the game change and flourish. All of that was important to him, but so was winning. It mattered to him and he probably wished he had seized on a variation of the comment attributed to

Lombardi about winning being the only thing because that was how he felt.

Papa Bear George Halas won eight championships, but the last in '63 was very special to him. In its own way, winning that crown showed the world he wasn't really getting old. It also had been so long since a title was added to his resume. So many years had passed, yet in 1963, pushing seventy, the old man who would deny he was the old man became king of the football world one last time.

ACKNOWLEDGMENTS

THE AUTHOR WISHES to give special acknowledgment and thanks to all of the help provided by the Pro Football Hall of Fame in Canton, Ohio, the operators of the web site talesfromtheamericanfootballleague.com., the public relations staffs of the San Diego Chargers and Green Bay Packers, as well as all of the former pro football players who took the time to talk about the season of 1963.

SOURCES

—————

DUE TO THE passage of fifty years, a number of key individuals who played major roles in the 1963 football season have since passed away. In addition, a number of other players who were located or reached were found to be suffering from various infirmities that sadly made it impossible—according to relatives or spokesmen for the teams they were associated with—to grant interviews.

In the intervening years, some players who were previously interviewed by the author about games played in 1963 and the entire season have passed away or become unable to talk again since those original discussions, but they are quoted in their own words in this book.

The players reached to talk about that long-ago chapter in their lives were very helpful and generous with their time and offered enjoyable and informative insights about the season of '63.

PERSONAL INTERVIEWS

Doug Atkins defensive end, Cleveland Browns, Chicago Bears, New Orleans Saints; Pro Football Hall of Fame

Ronnie Bull running back, Chicago Bears, Philadelphia Eagles

J. C. Caroline defensive back/halfback, Chicago Bears; College Football Hall of Fame

Rick Casares fullback, Chicago Bears, Washington Redskins, Miami Dolphins

Mike Ditka tight end, Chicago Bears, Philadelphia Eagles, Dallas Cowboys; head coach, Chicago Bears, New Orleans Saints; Pro Football Hall of Fame

Joe Fortunato linebacker, Chicago Bears; NFL 1950s All-Decade Team

Art Graham split end/wide receiver, Boston Patriots

Paul Hornung halfback/fullback/quarterback/kicker, Green Bay Packers; NFL 1960s All-Decade Team, Pro Football Hall of Fame

Stan Jones guard/tackle, Chicago Bears, Washington Redskins; assistant coach, Denver Broncos, Buffalo Bills, Cleveland Browns, New England Patriots; College Football Hall of Fame, Pro Football Hall of Fame

Keith Lincoln fullback/halfback, San Diego Chargers, Buffalo Bills

Richie Petitbon defensive back, Chicago Bears, Los Angeles Rams, Washington Redskins

Bob Skoronski tackle/center, Green Bay Packers

Bart Starr quarterback, Green Bay Packers; head coach, Green Bay Packers; NFL 1960s All-Decade Team, Pro Football Hall of Fame

George Taliaferro halfback/tailback/quarterback/defensive back, Los Angeles Dons (AAFC), New York Yanks, Dallas Texans, Baltimore Colts, Philadelphia Eagles; College Football Hall of Fame

Roosevelt Taylor defensive back, Chicago Bears, San Francisco 49ers, Washington Redskins

Dick Westmoreland defensive back, San Diego Chargers, Miami Dolphins

Tom Yewcic quarterback/punter/halfback, Boston Patriots

BOOKS

Bishop, Jim, *The Day Kennedy Was Shot*, New York: Harper-Perennial, 1968.

Brown, Jim with Steve Delsohn, *Out Of Bounds*: Kensington Publishing, 1989.

Carlson, Chuck, *Game of My Life Green Bay Packers*, Champaign, Illinois: Sports Publishing, 2004.

Davis, Jeff, *Papa Bear: The Life and Legacy of George Halas*, New York: McGraw-Hill, 2005.

Davis, Jeff, *Rozelle: Czar of the NFL*, New York: McGraw-Hill, 2007.

Dunnavant, Keith, *America's Quarterback: Bart Starr and the Rise of the National Football League*, New York: Thomas Dunne Books, 2011.

Eisenberg, John, *Ten-Gallon War: The NFL's Cowboys, The AFL's Texans, and the Feud For Dallas's Pro Football Future*, New York: Houghton Mifflin Harcourt, 2012.

Freedman, Lew, *Game of My Life Chicago Bears*, Champaign, Illinois: Sports Publishing, 2006.

Freedman, Lew, *New York Giants: The Complete Illustrated History*, Minneapolis: MVP Books, 2009.

Freedman, Lew, *The 50 Greatest Plays In Chicago Bears Football History*, Chicago: Triumph Books, 2008.

Gregg, Forrest and O'Toole, Andrew, *Winning in the Trenches: A Lifetime of Football*, Cincinnati: Clerisy Press, 2009.

Halas, George with Gwen Morgan and Arthur Veysey, *Halas: An Autobiography*, Chicago: Bonus Books, 1986.

Hornung, Paul and William F. Reed, *Golden Boy*, New York: Simon & Schuster, 2004.

Horrigan, Jack and Mike Rathet, *The Other League: The Fabulous Story of the American Football League*, Chicago: Follet Publishing Company, 1970.

Huff, Sam with Leonard Shapiro, *Tough Stuff*, New York: St. Martin's Press, 1988.

Karras, Alex with Herb Gluck, *Even Big Guys Cry*, New York: Signet Books, 1977.

Katzowitz, Josh, *Sid Gillman: Father of the Passing Game*, Cincinnati: Clerisy Press, 2012.

Kramer, Jerry and Dick Schaap, *Instant Replay: The Green Bay Diary of Jerry Kramer*, New York: Signet Books, 1968.

Miller, Jeff, *Going Long: The Wild 10-Year Saga of the Renegade American Football League In the Words of Those Who Lived It*, Chicago: Contemporary Books, 2003.

Moore, Lenny with Jeffrey Jay Ellish, *All Things Being Equal: The Autobiography of Lenny Moore*, Champaign, Illinois: Sports Publishing, 2005.

Nitschke, Ray as told to Robert W. Wells, *Mean on Sunday: The Autobiography of Ray Nitschke*, Black Earth, Wisconsin: Prairie Oak Press, 1998.

Pluto, Terry, *When All The World Was Browns Town*, New York: Simon & Schuster, 1997.

Rappaport, Ken, *The Little League That Could*, Lanham, Maryland: Taylor Trade Publishing, 2010.

Shaughnessy, Dan and Stan Grossfeld, *Spring Training: Baseball's Early Season*, New York: Houghton Mifflin Harcourt, 2003.

Steidel, Dave, *Remember the AFL*, Cincinnati: Clerisy Press, 2008.

Tittle, Y. A. as told to Don Smith, *I Pass!* New York: Franklin Watts, Inc., 1964.

Youmans, Gary and Maury Youmans, *63: The Story of the 1963 World Champion Chicago Bears*, Syracuse, New York: Campbell Road Press, Inc., 2004.

Zimmerman, David, *Curly Lambeau: The Man Behind the Mystique*, Hales Corners, Wisconsin: Eagle Books, 2003.

MAGAZINES

College and Pro Football
  News Weekly
Pro Football Digest
Slam! Wrestling
Sport
Sports Illustrated

NEWSPAPERS

Atlanta Journal
Baltimore News-Post
Baltimore Sun
Buffalo Evening News
Canton Repository
Chicago American

Chicago Daily News

Chicago Tribune

Des Moines Register

Detroit Free Press

Detroit News

Fort Worth Star-Telegram

Green Bay Press-Gazette

Houston Chronicle

Los Angeles Herald-
   Examiner

Miami Herald

Milwaukee Journal

Milwaukee Sentinel

Minneapolis Tribune

Newark Star-Ledger

New Orleans States-Item

New York Evening Telegram

New York Herald-Tribune

New York Journal-American

New York Times

Palm Beach Post

Philadelphia Inquirer

Pittsburgh Press

San Diego Tribune

San Diego Union

USA Today

Washington Post

Washington Star

INTERNET SOURCES

JTA – Jewish & Israel News,
   blogs.jta.org/eulogizer.com

Packers History, packershis-
   tory.com

Pro-Football Reference,
   pro-football-reference.
   com

Tales from the American
   Football League, tales-
   fromtheamericanfoot-
   ballleague.com

WIRE SERVICES

Associated Press

Newspaper Enterprise
   Association

United Press International

OTHER

American Football League
   press releases

Buffalo Bills press releases

Pro Football Hall of Fame
   archival records

Pro Football Hall of Fame
program
Pro Football Hall of Fame
press releases
Chicago Bears media guide
Chicago Bears Newsletter
Chicago Bears press releases
Green Bay Packers media
guide
Houston Oilers Scrapbook
National Football League
game programs
New York Giants press
releases
San Diego Chargers press
releases
WGSO 1290 Radio written
report

INDEX